GW01191157

GUIDING THE BEHAVIOUR
OF CHILDREN AND YOUNG PEOPLE

GUIDING THE BEHAVIOUR OF CHILDREN AND YOUNG PEOPLE

Jennie Lindon

HODDER
EDUCATION
AN HACHETTE UK COMPANY

Dedication

To the heads, staff teams and children from Sun Hill Infants School and Thongsley Fields Nursery and Primary School – a heartfelt thanks for making me so welcome in summer 2008 and for sharing your excellent practice.

Picture credits

The author and publishers would like to thank the following for permission to reproduce material in this book:

page 2 © Bubbles / John Powell; page 4 © Bubbles / Jennie Woodcock; page 9 © Bubbles / Loisjoy Thurstun; page 13 © Steve Skjold / Alamy; page 40 © Sally and Richard Greenhill / Alamy; page 47 © Bubbles / Jennie Woodcock; page 57 © Photofusion Picture Library / Alamy; page 60 © Bubbles / John Powell; page 66 © Bubbles; page 83 © JUPITERIMAGES/ BananaStock / Alamy; page 92 © Bubbles; page 97 © Bubbles / Jennie Woodcock; page 102 © Jennie Lindon; page 104 © Bubbles / Jennie Woodcock; page 126 © Photofusion; page 128 © Jennie Lindon; page 130 © Terese Loeb Kreuzer / Alamy; page 156 © Big Cheese Photo LLC / Alamy; page 173 © Bubbles / Pauline Cutler; page 176 © Bubbles / Loisjoy Thurstun; page 189 © Bubbles / Loisjoy Thurstun; page 206 © Bubbles / Lucy Tizard; page 223 © Bubbles / John Powell; page 229 © Richard Mittleman / Alamy; page 229 © Photofusion; page 238 © Bubbles / Loisjoy Thurstun; page 242 © Sally and Richard Greenhill / Alamy

Every effort has been made to obtain necessary permission with reference to copyright material. The publishers apologise if inadvertently any sources remain unacknowledged and will be glad to make the necessary arrangements at the earliest opportunity.

Orders: please contact Bookpoint Ltd, 130 Milton Park, Abingdon, Oxon OX14 4SB. Telephone: (44) 01235 827720. Fax: (44) 01235 400454. Lines are open from 9.00–5.00, Monday to Saturday, with a 24 hour message answering service. You can also order through our website www.hoddereducation.co.uk.

British Library Cataloguing in Publication Data
A catalogue record for this title is available from the British Library

ISBN: 978 0 340 98398 0

First Published 2009
Impression number   10 9 8 7 6 5 4 3 2 1
Year   2012 2011 2010 2009

Copyright © Jennie Lindon, 2009

All rights reserved. No part of this publication may be reproduced or transmitted in any form or by any means, electronic or mechanical, including photocopy, recording, or any information storage and retrieval system, without permission in writing from the publisher or under license from the Copyright Licensing Agency Limited. Further details of such licenses (for reprographic reproduction) may be obtained from the Copyright Licensing Agency Limited, Saffron House, 6–10 Kirby Street, London EC1N 8TS.

Hachette UK's policy is to use papers that are natural, renewable and recyclable products and made from wood grown in sustainable forests. The logging and manufacturing processes are expected to conform to the environmental regulations of the country of origin.

Cover photo © Imagesource/Photolibrary Group
Illustrations by Barking Dog Art

Typeset by Phoenix Photosetting, Chatham, Kent

Printed in Great Britain for Hodder Education, an Hachette UK Company, 338 Euston Road, London NW1 3BH by Martins the Printer, Berwick-Upon-Tweed

CONTENTS

CONTENTS

Acknowledgements and thanks

In the writing of this book, I realised how much I have learned from other people since I first approached the issues of guiding children's behaviour in the second half of the 1970s and early 1980s. From that era I still want to thank Bill Mitchell, Tim Smithells and the day nursery teams with whom I worked at that time, especially Joyce Heywood (from my time in Tower Hamlets) and Carol (whose surname I cannot recall, from Red Gables in Haringey).

I am grateful for many conversations over the decades with fellow adults, from the full range of professional roles and services for children, young people and families. I have also benefited from so many conversations with children and young people, both as individuals and in small group discussion.

From more recent times, my appreciation (expressed in alphabetical order) goes to teams at: Balham Community Centre and After-School Club, Balham Nursery School (both in South London), Buckinghams Nursery School and After School Club (Staffordshire), Crabtree Infants School (Hertfordshire), Kids City (London playschemes), RAF Marham Rainbow Centre (Norfolk), Southlands Kindergarten and Crèche (Staffordshire) and a considerable number of Essex residential and foster carers. I want to thank these individuals: Paul Bonel (SkillsActive), Peter Elfer (University of Surrey at Roehampton), Tim Gill (Rethinking Childhood), Laura Henry (Childcare Consultancy Ltd), Jessica Johnson (Kingston Friends Workshop Group), Kevin Kelman (Primary Head), Diane Rich and the What Matters to Children team, Wendy Russell (University of Gloucester), Val Stothard (Special Needs Teacher) and Penny Tassoni (early years consultant). Thanks to Lance Lindon (partner) for his professional advice on concepts from organisational psychology.

My thanks for specific visits linked with this book go to:

- Rachel Myer, her team and the children of Thongsley Fields Primary and Nursery School, Cambridgeshire.
- Kim Owen Jones (head), Rosie Waring Green (deputy), their team and the children of Sun Hill Infant School, Hampshire.

I am grateful that a range of actual settings gave me permission to describe their practice. I have not therefore created a series of fictional places to form scenarios in this book. Also that option would have muddled real and imagined settings.

The Ladders to Inclusion (page 218) and Happy Surgery form (page 128) are reproduced with the permission of Thongsley Fields. Marian Hayley of South Lanarkshire Council gave permission for the Sticks and Stones poem on page 140. Please continue to acknowledge the source of these items if you find them useful.

Using this book

In any book about childhood and adolescence an author has to make some decisions about words and phrases. These are my choices for general terms.

- **Parent**: anyone who takes the main family responsibility for children. Please assume the word always includes '**and other family carers**'.
- **Practitioner**: anyone whose work brings them into face to face contact with children and young people on a regular basis.
- **Pupil** or **student**: I prefer to call children in primary school 'pupils' and reserve 'students' for adolescents in secondary and further education.
- **Setting**: any group provision, attended by children or young people, when I am talking in general.

Opinions vary on how to refer to the blurred age boundaries on the way to adulthood. I have made the following decisions.

- **Early childhood**: the period from birth to 5 years.
- **Middle childhood**: the period from 5 to 12 years.
- **Adolescence**: the period from 13–19 years. In some services **adolescents** are called **young people** and I have used both terms.

I take the usual responsibility for the content and approach of this book. If you disagree with my perspective, I hope that will stimulate reflection and discussion – for you as an individual practitioner and in your team, if you have colleagues. The information on resources was correct at the time of writing (early 2009) but organisations move and websites are changed. Readers have the responsibility to follow up information, especially on those issues where I have touched the edge of a complex area of practice. If I have made actual errors, please contact the publisher and mistakes will be corrected as soon as possible.

1

Guiding behaviour – the big picture

Adults responsible for children and adolescents need to be actively involved day by day, but they also need to be able and willing to reflect on what they do. This chapter explores the general themes that form the backdrop – the big picture – that surrounds how adults approach the practicalities of guiding the behaviour of the younger generation.

> **The main sections of this chapter are:**
>
> ✳ **Raising the next generation**
>
> ✳ **Key issues about guiding behaviour**

RAISING THE NEXT GENERATION

In my professional role I have focused on issues around guiding behaviour since the mid-1970s. Planning this book was a real opportunity to reflect on what has changed over those decades and what has not.

What is the main plot?

Part of an adult's responsibility when raising the next generation is to focus on socialisation. Children and adolescents learn from adults, in all their many different roles. Adults need to think, at least sometimes, about the main plot: using the first two decades of life to raise young people whom you will welcome alongside you as they reach adulthood. The aim should be that children and adolescents are enabled to emerge as confident and competent grown-ups.

WHAT DOES IT MEAN?

Socialisation: the process by which children learn the values, priorities and shared knowledge of their cultural and social group.

During early childhood, young girls and boys learn ways of behaving shaped by their experiences. They are unique individuals and it soon becomes clear that they have their own temperament, which in turn influences how they react to circumstances. It is impossible to treat every child in the same way, because each child will react differently to very

The main plot is that children grow into confident and competent young people

similar experiences and treatment by adults. The grown-ups have a responsibility to treat children with fairness and in an even-handed way.

The term 'socialisation' is often used with the positive overtones of supporting children to learn the habits of prosocial behaviour and the values that will support this pattern of choices. However, the process of socialisation is non-specific; in a social or cultural group that values aggression and disrespect children will learn what might, by a different group, be seen as antisocial patterns.

- Socialisation can be an active process in which adults consciously guide and model particular values and choices.
- Alternatively adults may be less aware, or blithely assume that learning only evolves when they have set out deliberately to teach, tell or show.

A key point is that children, and adolescents, are active within their own socialisation. Learning does not switch off and on according to adult attention or deliberate actions: children are always learning from what happens to them. They are sharp observers and they draw conclusions from what happens in their daily life – sometimes with, from the adult perspective, unexpected consequences.

Growing up in early twenty-first century UK

Babies, children and adolescents today are no different from those of previous younger generations, but their social world has changed over the last quarter of the twentieth century. One visible change has been the huge growth of technology in everyday life, such that responsible adults need to address ground rules around 'screen time' and use of mobile phones.

Members of the younger generation are given contradictory messages about when and how they are 'grown up'. Young children are regarded as legitimate targets for marketing commercial products. Yet individuals well into adolescence are called 'children' and treated as needing high levels of adult protection and direction on other matters. Boys and girls not yet in adolescence can be held legally responsible for their criminal actions. Yet, at the same age they may not be trusted to judge that a tree is safe to climb, nor to sort out interpersonal problems without a hovering adult.

A considerable number of adults within society are not directly involved with the younger generation, so are not mentioned in the rest of the book. So now is the time to emphasise that these people matter too. It is sometimes said that, 'It takes a village to raise a child'. This phrase is confidently quoted as being 'an African proverb'. Apparently, there are a number of folk sayings from the African continent that promote the message that children are the responsibility of the community and not exclusively of their birth parents (see http://en.wikipedia.org/wiki/It_Takes _a_Village.) Regardless of the exact origin of the phrase, the message of community involvement is valuable. The younger generation is everybody's business at some level. Everyone has the social responsibility to value fellow adults directly involved with children and adolescents. Everyone needs to make some space for children, accepting that they need places to play and time to enjoy being children and adolescents.

Griping about the younger generation appears to have as long a history as written accounts of societies around the world. Complaints have been found from ancient Rome and Carl Honore (2008) describes the discovery of an Assyrian clay tablet, dated around 2800 BCE, which apparently moaned that children no longer obeyed their parents and the end of the world was definitely nigh. Any society should be judged by how the younger generation are treated. It is unacceptable adult behaviour to tolerate, even encourage, an atmosphere of social hostility towards older children and adolescents. In the UK it has become common to make discriminatory, public denouncements of an entire age group, using offensive terms like 'yob' and 'feral'. The behaviour of a minority of the younger generation is antisocial, but no other group – ethnic, cultural or older age – is routinely demonised in this way. There is now a real danger of being criticised for wilfully lurking within the years of adolescence and perpetrating the crime of standing in one place, talking with your friends and looking young.

Children like to play and adolescents continue to want and enjoy playful activities. However, for at least a decade the political justification for much play funding has been to show that providing services will reduce antisocial behaviour. Do you know of any example when adult leisure facilities have been required to prove a causal link to crime reduction? Generous play provision should be easily available as part of a happy childhood and visual evidence that the younger generation are welcome members of their local community (see reviews like Fowler and Taylor, 2006 or Lester and Russell, 2008).

KEY ISSUES ABOUT GUIDING BEHAVIOUR

A large number of adults are directly involved with children and adolescents, either in a professional role or as parents and other family carers. All the principles of how you guide behaviour in a positive way apply to family as well as professional life.

Children learn within their relationship with a familiar adult

Be clear what you believe – your values

Values are beliefs that are seen as worthy of esteem for their own sake. Values have intrinsic worth to the individual or group who expresses them. In terms of how you aim to guide the behaviour of children and adolescents, these values are expressed as moral principles. They are a statement about the basis of your ethical judgements and how you weigh up priorities when your line of action is not immediately clear.

Whether you use the actual phrase or not, an expressed value statement can always start with the words, 'I believe it is right to…' or 'I believe it is wrong to…' Fully-considered values also have a sense of 'because…' and what follows may be a series of logical reasons. But the explanation is not always highly rational, nor is the logic necessarily acceptable to other adults who hold very different values.

For example, one statement in the behaviour policy of a nursery may be, 'We talk with children; we do not shout. The only justification for shouting is if a raised voice is the only way to ensure a child's safety.' The value underpinning the statement is, 'We believe it is wrong to shout at children as a regular form of communication.' The follow-on reasoning is that such behaviour sets a bad example to children, especially if they are likely to be told not to shout. A related value may be that this team believes strongly that they should guide children through positive role modelling; they never expect of children behaviour that the adults do not show themselves day by day. A related practical point is that if practitioners, during an exhausting 'bad' day, shout at children for no good reason, then they apologise.

MAKE THE CONNECTION WITH…
WHAT IS EXPECTED OF CHILDREN

Maybe some readers are thinking that this section is rather abstract and are tempted to speed-read onwards. Please remind yourself that adults (probably including you) often take a high moral tone with children and adolescents.

In the Early Years Foundation Stage framework (for England), one of the early learning goals for the Personal, Social and Emotional Development is that most 5-year-olds (at the end of this 0–5 stage) will 'Understand what is right, what is wrong and why'. This goal was established in the previous Foundation Stage and was rather a show-stopper then. Practitioners who tune into the social world of young children can find an interpretation that makes developmental sense. However, adults working with children can fairly be expected to have done some serious thinking themselves on 'what is right, what is wrong and why'.

Self regulation is the goal

It is vital to recall the main plot of childhood and adolescence: that children and adolescents emerge as confident and competent young people, able to take their adult role in their immediate social and cultural group and within broader society. That priority requires that they learn to guide their own behaviour: that they have been enabled, steadily, to learn self-regulation or self-discipline.

Children need to be guided in their behaviour rather than 'managed'. The emotional tone of the phrase 'behaviour management' risks setting the scene for impersonal approaches and a focus on techniques rather than sustained relationships with children and adolescents. Furthermore, the adults will not always be there to intervene; children need to learn habits of prosocial behaviour that will last. If adults try to micro-manage behaviour then they are likely to create dependence on adult direction or specific reward for this behaviour.

Behaviour arises for a reason

It is sometimes hard to fathom the why behind the what. But friendly and effective guiding of young behaviour depends on adult willingness to acknowledge that there always is a reason. It may not make sense to you, it may not seem like a 'good enough reason', the reason may rest upon a misunderstanding or highlight other problems that need to be resolved.

Reasons are explanations, a possible light on the way out of the current impasse. They are not excuses or justifications for behaviour that hurts, disrupts or deeply troubles other people. Some children and adolescents really do not know why they behave as they do, or they struggle to put thoughts into spoken words. Sometimes they have never considered their own behaviour as something they could reflect on, talk about and then change. Sometimes they have learned there is no point in giving reasons because familiar adults so far have responded with yet more yelling.

LOOK, LISTEN, NOTE, LEARN

Asking 'Why did you do that?' is rarely a wise question – especially in the heat of the moment – and adults often do not have a coherent response to that question. But reflecting on different kinds of 'why's can be useful. Chapter 2 offers different theoretical approaches to cause-and-effect for human behaviour. Here is an opportunity to speculate about the different ways in which people – adults and older children – might reflect on 'I wonder why I do (or don't do) that…'

Look at the following list of possibilities, think them over, add any you like. Discuss with colleagues or fellow students what different kinds of explanations are raised by the choice of words.

- ◆ It was the obvious way to behave – doesn't everyone?
- ◆ It felt like the right thing to do… *or* It would have felt wrong if I had…
- ◆ When I was a child I was told 'Courtesy costs nothing' (or other sayings)
- ◆ I don't want to get into trouble… *plus* I'd be found out…
- ◆ I know I shouldn't… But I couldn't help myself…
- ◆ Everybody else was… *or* Lots of people do that…
- ◆ Girls/boys don't do that… *or* I'm not allowed to…
- ◆ I don't know what else to do when…
- ◆ I had no choice… *or* S/he made me…
- ◆ I feel better when… *or* I'd feel guilty if I…

Look at yourself

An acceptance that children learn from their earliest experiences leads, almost inevitably, to a focus on adult behaviour. What the grown-ups do matters; it is definitely one of the ingredients in the whole situation. Little progress will be made if most discussion about behaviour focuses on what children or adolescents are doing or should not be doing. Adults are the older ones in an interaction and are supposed to be more mature. It is not acceptable for practitioners or parents to be reluctant to consider that how they react could be making a situation worse and maybe could have created an impasse in the first place.

MAKE THE CONNECTION WITH... YOUR OWN MEMORIES

You will find it useful to remember your own childhood and adolescence – without inaccurate reworking. Your insights into what happened to you, and how it felt to experience different kinds of treatment by adults, can be valuable now that you are one of the grown-ups.

- Recall how much it mattered, even when you knew you were in the wrong, that adults gave you the chance to save face or to make some kind of restitution.
- Possibly you can recall how much you appreciated that space to manoeuvre. Now you can give that back through your adult behaviour.
- If you recall being nagged over your behaviour, and criticised into a corner, then make a real effort not to do the same in your turn now.

Your perspective is different now that you have adult responsibilities. You may feel sure that you have good reasons for what you do – maybe also that it is unacceptable for children or adolescents to question your behaviour now that you have joined the grown-ups. Recall how it feels when adults refuse to listen to your side, are manifestly unfair or blatantly disobey their own ground rules.

Lead through positive relationships

Any sensible material for parents recognises that their role with their own children is, and should be, different from that of practitioners. It is a different kind of committed, emotional relationship. However, the key principles are consistent across professional involvement and the long-term relationship between parent and children. In an emotionally warm atmosphere, created by adults, children would rather have us pleased with them than annoyed.

Genuine support for guiding behaviour is respectful of individual children and adolescents.

- It is important that they feel sure they are liked (or loved in family relationships) however they have behaved today.
- Adults need to keep the child or adolescent separate from their behaviour – positive as well as negative as far as adults view the situation.

Behaviour 'management' policies frequently focus on behaviour in a disconnected way. The related practice can become impersonal, with a strong emphasis on sanctions. Such an approach disrupts the possibility of a relationship between adult and child – and this development is important

*Children need to feel
emotionally secure
throughout childhood*

in nurseries, schools, clubs and other settings. Belinda Hopkins (2008), writing about residential care but with total relevance to other kinds of provision, emphasises the shift of emphasis 'from managing behaviour to focusing on building, nurturing and repairing relationships' (page 2). She promotes the model of a 'relationship management policy', which regards any setting as a community in which all members have personal needs and responsibilities towards each other.

Be clear about what you want and be realistic

Children and adolescents find it hard to work out what behaviour is expected of them when adults only, or mainly, pay attention when they observe children making the wrong choice. Adults themselves complain bitterly if they are expected to learn a new job or role by being criticised every time they make a mistake. A strong focus on wanted behaviour shows what you value and why you are guiding children in one direction rather than another.

Children's ability to learn from experience is shaped by their age. It is up to adults to link what they want closely to realistic expectations of what very young children can understand. Adults also need to allow for the extent to which older children can guide their own behaviour, especially when emotions are running high. Adolescents have greater understanding and potential ability to guide themselves but they are somewhere in the process of changing from childhood to young adulthood.

Focus on learning – not labelling

A key theme throughout much of what is written to advise adults is that children learn ways of behaving. Another way of expressing this approach is that they develop habits of behaviour. Habits that have been learned can be unlearned – more easily if there is an alternative to put in their place. Good ideas and tips on guiding behaviour are most likely to take time to work – learning is rarely a matter of the quick fix.

Children are born with their own individual temperament, but that does not imply patterns of behaviour that are determined from the outset and cannot be changed. Children have a great capacity to learn positive ways of handling everyday life if adults actively help them. The unrealistic alternative to this view is that everyone is fixed in terms of temperament or personality and nobody can do anything about it.

Language matters because choice of words (spoken and written) gives a message about adult attitudes and priorities. I resist phrases like 'aggressive children' because that implies that aggression is an integral part of them as an individual. More accurately, adults are dealing with a child who reacts with aggression to specific situations or kinds of events. 'Difficult children' are struggling with relationships and events that are beyond their current ability to cope and their dilemma is sometimes worsened by 'difficult adults'.

Some children or adolescents have significant or chronic difficulties in handling social situations, like the playground, that their peers manage with much more ease. Some children react in an unkind or self-centred way to the ups and downs of daily life. But they will be disinclined to change their ways if the adult response is to label them as 'an unkind child' or an adolescent who is 'always so inconsiderate'. Approaches to guidance of behaviour need to be compatible with the main plot of raising a younger generation who are able to regulate their own actions. They will be unable to manage that task if they feel trapped in a label rather than confident to make choices.

Theoretical explanations of behaviour

This chapter describes the main theoretical approaches that aim to explain human development. You will find a description of the key concepts, with a particular emphasis on what can be relevant to understanding and guiding behaviour. Each section suggests the potential benefits of each approach and possible drawbacks.

The main sections of this chapter are:

  * ⭐ **Biological processes and maturation**

  * ⭐ **Emotional development and behaviour**

  * ⭐ **Behaviour as learned habits**

  * ⭐ **Cognitive and moral development**

  * ⭐ **Behaviour in social and cultural context**

BIOLOGICAL PROCESSES AND MATURATION

Theorists who ground their ideas in biology argue that genetic programming and the internal workings of the brain are a powerful influence and should not be underestimated. They do not dismiss the impact of experience: of nurture as well as nature.

A focus on physical maturation

Arnold Gesell and his colleagues, working during the 1920s and 30s, documented the fine details of changes during childhood. They believed that the sequence of development for babies and children was controlled by a common process of maturation, governed by the information in the genes. Gesell believed that the environment had a supportive role within child development, but that internal biological forces provided the more significant push towards change. A related idea was that certain kinds of behaviour, like 2-year-olds who collapsed into a tantrum, were usual events for that age group and so were phases that would pass. The maturational approach offered relief to parents, that they were not personally responsible for every troublesome aspect of their child's behaviour This stance was a contrast with the psychoanalytical approach (see page 15), prominent over the same decades, which focused more on what could go wrong.

WHAT DOES IT MEAN?

Maturational theory: focus on a developmental sequence of changes, controlled by instructions in the genetic code shared by all children.

Developmental norms: statements about what a child is likely to be able to do or understand within a given age range.

Biological maturation theories of development and behaviour went out of favour by the mid-twentieth century. One problem was that the maturational approach to 'normal' child development evolved within a western and Eurocentric context.

The idea of a 'universal child' has been roundly criticised since the 1980s, led by social constructivist approaches (see page 32). The original, rigid approach to developmental norms failed to allow for much variety within a given culture, let alone cultural variations in child rearing. More flexible approaches have focused on the need for realistic expectations based on a sound knowledge of the understanding and likely abilities of children at different ages.

Potential benefits of this approach

- Information about the normal range of behaviour has continued to offer potential reassurance to parents. Other people's children also make a six-act drama about bedtime. Their reactions are not evidence of disordered development and a future of antisocial behaviour.
- Practitioners need to have realistic expectations: what is within ordinary developmental range and what is out-of-the-ordinary. Without this basis, it is too easy to talk, or write, about 'difficult' or 'challenging' behaviour, when the actions of these children or adolescents are unremarkable for their age.

Possible disadvantages

- Saying 'it's just a phase' does not offer practical advice about how to intervene positively over this time. Adults need to do more than grit their teeth through normal behaviour like adolescent mood swings.
- There is also a risk of inappropriate developmental labelling, like 'the terrible twos' or 'uncommunicative teenagers'. Practitioners and parents may believe that such problems are inevitable. They may also refuse to accept that their behaviour is worsening the situation.

Understanding brain development

The human brain is biologically designed to adapt to experience. Compared with other mammals, a considerably larger proportion of our brain is not wholly committed to certain experiences or skills. This flexible capacity enables us to develop complex psychological and thinking functions such as voluntary remembering, reasoning and language. These connections enable older children and adolescents to reflect on their choices in behaviour and to talk about options and strategies, along with problem solving, with supportive adults.

Young people are able to resolve more complex interpersonal problems

The years of early childhood are a crucial time for laying down neural networks – especially for emotional security, an enthusiasm for language and secure physical skills. However, the human brain is far from mature by 4-5 years of age. Children at the edge of middle childhood should not be expected to anticipate the consequences of their behaviour in a detailed way. Young children, especially very young children, have real limits to how much they can regulate their own behaviour. Nor is it realistic to expect them to talk much about their reasons for what they have done, or not done. Young children have some ability to understand the feelings and perspectives of other people, but only when linked meaningfully with actual experiences.

At around 4 years of age a spurt in brain development is associated with a new level of fluency for children in spoken language. Over middle childhood, with appropriate adult support, children become more able to talk about and think around choices in behaviour. At around 10-12 years of age the frontal lobes of the cerebral cortex take a leap in maturity. The results can be seen as these older children become more adept at planning ahead, working logically and organising their memory skills. From early to mid-adolescence, there is a sustained burst of energy in areas of the brain that deal with abstract thinking. Adolescents are increasingly more able to analyse possibilities and bring together separate experiences and sources of information. Their cognitive skills are brought to bear on adults whose pronouncements are inconsistent or whose behaviour is unjust.

During adolescence the human brain is working hard to integrate those areas that deal primarily with emotions and those which are more concerned with the thinking skills. Adolescent brains are working hard to connect different functions concerned with self-control, emotional judgement, skills of organisation and planning. Bursts of brain activity, bringing more integration between feeling and reasoning, seem to be one explanation for sudden mood swings and apparently irrational choices. Some adolescents manage to be 'sensible' for a lot of the time but the logical-emotional seesaw is still a real struggle.

Development of the human brain is not fully complete within adolescence. The refining of the frontal lobes of the cerebral cortex in the brain continues from around 17 years of age until about the mid-20s. This part of the brain, which controls the ability to use logical thinking and build that skill into planning ahead, is not usually fully mature until early adulthood. Mature adult brains continue to react to experience and create neural linkages. Otherwise, it would be impossible to learn in adulthood and continued professional development (which this book aims to support) would be a hopeless cause.

Potential benefits of this approach
- An understanding of research into the brain highlights a balanced approach between nature and nurture. Experience makes a difference, but adults need realistic expectations for how children and adolescents can guide their own behaviour and reflect on choices.
- There is significant support for the importance of early childhood, including experiences that affect emotional development. An understanding of the further burst of brain activity during adolescence can help adults to pick up the pieces with young people who agree that what they did was 'really stupid'.

Possible disadvantages

- There is still a great deal we do not know or fully understand about how the human brain works. Some applications of the research are inappropriately confident about 'what we know', 'left brain–right brain' and the behaviour of 'most' boys and girls.

- Commercial interests are keen to exploit the possibilities of 'the brain research says…' in order to sell products and services. It is possible to challenge these misrepresentations and false claims without abandoning valuable insights from the research.

EMOTIONAL DEVELOPMENT AND BEHAVIOUR

Psychoanalytic theory

Sigmund Freud shared common ground with theorists rooted in biology because he believed that basic biological drives underpinned human behaviour. However, Freud changed direction once he became convinced that energy from the libido, an unconscious sexual drive, was the key force behind most human behaviour. He developed a stage theory of early development which depends on his assertion that the libido exerts impact in the part of a child's body that is most sensitive at a given age.

Freudian theory places great significance on the early years of childhood, since the basics of adult personality are determined by 5 years of age. Negative events within those crucial years will leave unresolved emotional conflict with which adults continue to struggle. A related aspect of Freudian theory views a great deal of behaviour (from adults as well as children) as driven by unresolved conflicts and anxieties. The details of actions are determined by the relative balance between the id (raw emotional demands and needs), the ego (conscious self) and the superego (the demands of society, which operate as a conscience).

WHAT DOES IT MEAN?

Psychoanalytic theory: a school of thought focusing on the impact of early childhood and unconscious thoughts. The movement started with the ideas of Sigmund Freud, so theorists are sometimes called Freudian, or more recently neo-Freudian.

Stage theory: an approach to explaining child development (not exclusive to the psychoanalytic approach) proposing that all children, and possibly also adolescents, pass in order through the same basic stages.

15

Anna Freud developed her father's theoretical concept that people cope with anxiety through a range of psychological defence mechanisms. This self-protection operates at different levels from conscious choice, through much reduced mental awareness to a well-buried unconscious process. In broad terms the defence mechanisms operate in the following ways.

- An unhappy experience or uncomfortable dilemma is pushed to the back of your mind.
  This process may be largely conscious (suppression) and you are aware that feelings have been put on hold, the problem will need to be faced later. However, very strong emotions or the memory of distressing events may be swept into a remote corner of the mind (repression). The feeling may scarcely rise to conscious awareness but can nevertheless influence the person's behaviour. Problems and the related anxiety may also be handled by refusal to accept that a distressing event happened or that it affected you in this way (denial).

- Strong feelings are redirected away from the original source.
  Frustrations are directed at a less threatening or more accessible target, even someone not involved in the actual event (displacement). Anxiety about your own impulses is resolved by attributing the feeling to the other person (projection). Perhaps you convince yourself that someone you dislike (but feel you should not) actually dislikes you, so deserves your reaction. Strong impulses are released in an acceptable way (sublimation): anger may be released through physical activity. You take up the opposite impulse from that which is genuinely felt (reaction formation): you behave in a very friendly way to someone you actually dislike or fear.

- Anxiety is reduced by stepping aside from the emotional content of the current problem.
  You focus on the intellectual issues of a distressing situation and ignore the emotional dimension (intellectualisation). A logical explanation reduces the emotional discomfort (rationalisation): you claim you did not really want this success, or that failure is from circumstances outside your control.

- Problems are made more bearable by behaving at a less mature level. Individuals go back to an earlier developmental stage (regression): behaving like a younger child, a child rather than an adolescent, or an adolescent rather than a mature adult.

The psychoanalytic approach is that defence mechanisms can be adaptive, enabling older children, adolescents and adults to reduce anxiety to a manageable level. A great deal depends on individual awareness of what they are doing and willingness to use conscious strategies as a short-term coping tactic. Problems arise for the individuals, and those around them, when the original problem or hard-to-manage emotion is not addressed in any constructive way. Other problems may follow as a direct consequence of the coping strategy, such that other people's emotional well-being is under threat. (See the example about attachment in day care on page 43.) Serious problems, including mental health issues, arise when the coping defence mechanisms depend on a significant distortion of reality through interpretation of events, other people's behaviour and their alleged feelings and motivations.

The Adlerian approach

Alfred Adler broke professional ranks with the Freudians to develop a theoretical framework of individual psychology that emphasised the struggle against feelings of inferiority and increasingly explored children's life within their family and the impact of birth order. The Adlerian approach proposes that children's behaviour is shaped by their interpretations of social interactions. Their beliefs about themselves affect a sense of self-worth, which in turn influences their ability to relate to others. His theoretical concepts have much in common with systems theory (page 28).

Rudolf Dreikurs developed Adler's ideas to bring together emotions and behaviour, the importance of encouragement and using consequences rather than punishment (page 198). His practical approach to guiding children's behaviour has provided the underpinning concepts for some parenting programmes. A key idea has been that adults can guide children's outlook and behaviour in a more positive manner once they recognise the purpose behind the child's behaviour. Dreikurs also developed these ideas for application in schools: the adult role as teacher and the specific situation of classroom behaviour (page 173).

Potential benefits of this kind of approach

- The striking contribution of psychoanalytic theory was to highlight unconscious feelings and thoughts; everything is not described by what we observe on the surface. Adlerian concepts explore feelings and purposes in behaviour, so that encouragement of active choices is more feasible.
- A focus on the importance of early childhood directs practitioners and parents to ensure that children's experiences are positive during those years and embedded in strong relationships.

Possible disadvantages

- The Freudian view can imply a depressing view of family life as a minefield of inevitable problems. The concept of infantile sexuality sets a regrettable precedent that children's need for physical intimacy has sexual overtones.

- There is a risk of over-analysing feelings and behaviour. Defence mechanisms must not be treated as closed conceptual systems. Denial is not always a protective device, sometimes 'that didn't happen' is a statement of fact.

BEHAVIOUR AS LEARNED HABITS

Behaviourism, or learning theory, developed in the first quarter of the twentieth century and was the alternative to Freudian theory. The behaviourists focused on what children, or adults, learned through the details of experience and the consequences of specific ways of behaving. Like the psychoanalytical tradition, behaviourism has evolved over the decades into different theoretical strands.

WHAT DOES IT MEAN?

Behaviourism or learning theory: an approach to explaining human actions that focuses on visible behaviour and the circumstances that can be deliberately altered in order to change that behaviour.

Learning through conditioning

Behaviourism started with research into animal behaviour. Ivan Pavlov studied the digestion of animals and found that he could train them to salivate at the sound of a bell, when that event preceded the appearance of food. He called the process 'classical conditioning' and extended the ideas to explain human psychiatric problems. Classical conditioning occurs when a new signal or stimulus reliably evokes an existing behavioural response. John Watson applied the ideas to children's behaviour and, with Rosalie Rayner, used the techniques of classical conditioning to make 9-month-old Little Albert scared of a white rat. (I accept Christian Jarrett's 2008 overview of confusing reports and apologise for saying it was a rabbit in Lindon, 2005.)

Albert was happy to play with a series of animals until the researchers hit a steel bar with a hammer right behind him (unconditioned stimulus) just as he reached for the rat (conditioned stimulus). Albert was immediately distressed by the loud noise (unconditioned response). It took no more than a few repeats of this noise associated with the sight of the rat and the baby began to panic as soon as the rat appeared (conditioned response). Later his fear spread to other white fuzzy objects. Watson and Rayner were challenged at the time because of inconsistencies in their written reports and they provided no evidence of their claims that learned habits of fear could be unlearned. The ethics of the study did not seem to worry their contemporaries in the 1920s. John Watson continued to promote emotion-free childcare and no-nonsense behavioural training in advice books for parents.

Supporters of learning theory struggled to explain human behaviour exclusively through classical conditioning. B.F. Skinner developed his ideas from the 1930s, drawing from both Pavlov and Watson. Starting with animal studies, Skinner extended the behaviourist approach to encompass a process that was known as either 'instrumental' or 'operant conditioning'. Edward Thorndike had proposed a theory around 'instrumental learning', dependent on the effect of different behavioural options. The term operant became the more usual word and flags up that the specific learned response enables individuals to operate more effectively on their environment to bring about wanted changes.

Operant conditioning is a process that links a new response to an existing stimulus; whereas classical conditioning links an existing response to a new stimulus. In contrast with classical conditioning, operant conditioning involves a deliberate action as response to direct experience. Skinner managed to train birds and animals to perform complex actions, including getting pigeons to play a kind of table tennis. He applied the ideas to human behaviour and emphasised a carefully planned approach to reinforcement. Skinner developed programmed learning by teaching machines, which supported children or adults to learn at their own pace and rewarded correct responses.

The basic principles of behaviourism became:

- Human behaviour is strengthened by reinforcement. Positive reinforcement is the direct experience of something pleasant and might be tangible rewards but could also be verbal praise. Negative reinforcement is the removal of something unpleasant or unwanted from the situation.
- Behaviour that is reinforced on a partial schedule is stronger, more resistant to stopping altogether, than behaviour that has been reinforced every time.
- Punishment is the removal of something pleasant from the situation or the addition of something unpleasant. Apart from ethical issues

about some punitive options, punishment is generally an unreliable way to shape human behaviour and can have unpredictable effects, even with rats.

■ Extinction is the permanent removal of a pattern of behaviour. Specific actions no longer occur because the behaviour is never reinforced, positively or negatively. The fade-away takes longer with a pattern of partial reinforcement.

Social learning theory

By the 1960s behaviourists interested in children's behaviour wished to get beyond the limitations of classical and operant conditioning. Albert Bandura found the theory inadequate to explain aggressive behaviour patterns in the adolescents he was studying. Bandura believed that human learning did not always require the kind of direct and visible reinforcement described in operant conditioning. In a nutshell, the approach was a direct challenge to a view that humans were rats or pigeons who just happened to talk.

Bandura noted that a powerful predictor of children's behaviour was what they could directly observe of other children's or adults' behaviour. Bandura added the significance of personal feelings of reinforcement and the link between thinking and observational learning. Bandura's approach of social learning theory used the foundations of behaviourist understanding of reinforcement. However, the theory acknowledged the greater complexity of human thought and behaviour. The actions of children and adolescents were explained through a continued interaction between the messages of their environment, existing patterns of behaviour and psychological processes.

Bandura built on the basic propositions from behaviourist theory to add the social learning dimension and a more sophisticated view of cause and effect. He described that children and adolescents:

■ are influenced by patterns of reward and punishment that they observe happening to other children

■ learn new behaviours through the process of modelling: adults showing through their behaviour what is wanted

■ do not only learn actual behaviours, they also learn ideas, expectations and develop internal standards

■ can learn to make active choices and self-regulate their behaviour.

Bandura proposed that learning through observation is an active process and affected by cognitive and emotional development. The end result depends on:

- the exact focus of children's attention and what they are able to remember
- what children can physically copy, given their skills at the time
- what they are motivated to imitate: children are far less likely to copy an adult whom they dislike, unless it is in mockery
- how children develop abstract ideas from observational learning: working out what is admired or disliked behaviour, developing attitudes and a sense of their own worth.

By the 1980s Bandura referred to his approach as social cognitive theory. Bandura's ideas are a reminder that theories of practical relevance to guiding children's behaviour are often a blend of different approaches. Albert Bandura's fully developed theory has much more in common with the cognitive-developmental theories than with behaviourism.

WHAT DOES IT MEAN?

Social learning theory: a development of behaviourism recognising that human actions are shaped by feelings, direct observation and thinking about experiences.

Modelling: learning through imitation of someone else - another child or an adult - whose actions are then copied. This term is also used to mean deliberate actions to provide a model for someone else to imitate.

Potential benefits of this kind of approach

- Attention is focused on what is actually happening, not guesses about feelings and possible intentions. Practitioners and parents observe visible actions and are able to see when behaviour changes.
- The social learning approach addresses many of the problems of earlier behaviourism. The focus on observational learning and imitation highlights that adults should set a good example through their own behaviour.

Possible disadvantages

- A focus on basic tenets of behaviourism, without social learning theory, runs the risk of a mechanistic, impersonal system. Adults may overlook the importance of a warm relationship or how children actually experience what is believed to operate as a reward or sanction.

▪ Efficiency should not exist without principles and adult responsibility. Just because an approach works to change unwanted behaviour, it does not mean that it is ethically right to follow that line of action.

COGNITIVE AND MORAL DEVELOPMENT

Theories about children's cognitive development often have only limited application to how they behave in a more general way.

▪ Thinking and communication have an impact on behaviour and Albert Bandura brought them together, approaching from the behaviour side.

▪ Judy Dunn (1993) brought together the emotional and cognitive aspects by focusing on the behaviour of young children within their ordinary family life. She focused on how much even young children understood of the ground rules at home and the subtle dynamics at work in play between siblings.

▪ The ability to talk, listen, express thoughts and to reason is the foundation of helping children learn social and problem solving skills linked with behaviour (page 220).

▪ However, the most direct link into behaviour from theories of cognitive development is the work of Lawrence Kohlberg who studied the moral reasoning of children and adolescents.

WHAT DOES IT MEAN?

Cognitive theories of development: approaches that focus on the intellectual aspects of child and adolescent development – thinking but also often language.

Moral reasoning: using the skills of thinking and talking to explain or justify taking a given action, or making one choice over another.

Moral reasoning for behaviour

Lawrence Kohlberg built on Jean Piaget's stage theory approach to cognitive development in order to reach a theoretical model for moral development. Kohlberg undertook research into how children of different ages resolved a series of hypothetical problem situations. Story dilemmas provided a narrative which laid out 'What if…' problems from tough choices arising when the person in the story was pulled between two views of what was right. Kohlberg's stages depended not so much on the choice that children or adolescents made, but the reasoning that underpinned their choice. Children and adolescents had to give their view on and explanation of the right choice when, for instance, a husband (Heinz) had tried every way he could think to obtain a drug for his terminally ill wife and finally in desperation breaks into the pharmacy and steals the medicine.

Lawrence Kohlberg proposed three levels of moral development, with two stages in each. He undertook a range of studies, followed by other researchers interested in this approach to moral reasoning and behaviour.

Level One: preconventional morality

- Stage 1: punishment and obedience orientation. Children decide something is wrong if it is punished. They value obedience but follow adult rules because the adults have power. At this stage children have difficulty in recognising that the perspective of other people can be very different from their own.
  Children need communication skills that enable them to voice their views on the story dilemmas, so the levels cannot be explored with young children. From about 5 years of age through to 7–8 years, children's thinking operates within the first stage of this level. Children tend to say that Heinz should not steal the medicine because he will be put in jail.

- Stage 2: instrumental morality. Children follow rules when it is in their immediate interest. Other people are recognised to have interests too and fairness is a matter of equal exchange. There is a growing awareness that different interests may come into conflict – so maybe the right thing to do will be relative to the situation. Over the second half of middle childhood, up to about 10–11 years of age, children reasoned less on the basis that an action was wrong and you would get into serious trouble. Now children were more likely to argue that Heinz should steal the medicine, because some day he might be seriously ill and he would want somebody to take this action for him.

Level Two: conventional morality

- Stage 3: mutual expectations within relationships. Children view 'being good' as worthwhile for its own sake, because it pleases other people who matter. They stress the importance of living up to the expectations of significant relationships such as family or friends. Kohlberg found that older children moved into this way of reasoning, based on valuing the loyalty of friendships and the importance of mutual trust in relationships. Children sometimes based their reasons on an overarching rule such as treating other people how you would like to be treated. In the story, Heinz's love of his sick wife overrules the social prohibition against theft.

- Stage 4: social system and conscience. This way of moral reasoning is sometimes called the 'law and order' stage because it moves on from relationships between familiar people and the known social group. The source of morality stretches into a broader social context, including the laws of a given society and the goal of maintaining a harmonious social order for everyone.
  This kind of reasoning emerges over the years of adolescence. However, stage 3 reasoning continues to be important and can still dominate arguments around moral questions into early adulthood. Kohlberg and others using similar research methods, found that many adults did not go beyond stage 4.

Level Three: principled or post-conventional morality

- Stage 5: the social contract. This way of reasoning argues that people hold different values and opinions. However, there is a sense of obligation to the law, because it forms a social contract that overall works for the general good. Rules may not be seen as absolute, but moral behaviour takes account of the good of the many and not only individual wants.
- Stage 6: universal ethical principles. Individuals have developed a personal system of moral principles that guide their actions. Kohlberg and others concluded that this level was not reached until adulthood, if at all for many individuals. Moral reasoning that enters level three takes another step shift over how dilemmas are argued through and resolved. Respect for the law is seasoned with recognition that sometimes legal requirements clash with moral principles, and perhaps laws need to be changed. Stage 6 is reached if moral judgements are made on the basis of ethical principles that the individual truly believes are more important than the rules of any society.

Some writers have disagreed with Lawrence Kohlberg's system and the implicit values that underlie the hierarchy of stages. Carol Gilligan (1982) challenged the claim that justice and fairness were key features of mature moral reasoning. Gilligan argued that an equally valid basis emerged from an orientation of caring or of connectedness. She predicted that girls were more likely to be socialised towards a care orientation and boys towards the justice perspective. Some research found small sex differences in the direction that Gilligan proposed, but only for adults' moral reasoning. Other studies found that some males were as strong on care-oriented reasoning as females.

At first sight, Kohlberg's approach seems to contradict the observation that young children can behave in a prosocial way that allows for the feelings and needs of others. This apparent contradiction is a useful reminder that the story dilemma method asks children to think and explain in a hypothetical 'what if' model. The research was also, appropriately, with children from middle childhood, not within early childhood. Nancy Eisenberg (1992) looked at how children explained considerate behaviour by giving them hypothetical dilemmas in which there was a clash between self-interest and helping someone else. Younger children (under-fives) might choose the prosocial (helping) option, as did the older children but their reasoning was different. The younger ones were more likely to help – or choose not to help – for reasons of self-interest, summed up as, 'If I help her now, she might help me another time'. This orientation shifted to a focus on the other person's needs, that, 'He'll feel better if I helped'. Adolescents, not children, were the ones who might reason on the basis of general principles, 'It's a good idea to help' or 'Society is better if people help each other'.

Potential benefits of this kind of approach

- The approach reminds adults to focus on guiding the behaviour of younger children, without demanding a mature level of understanding about why they should act this way. Children cannot move towards moral reasoning based on social rules, unless they have positive experiences of how ground rules work.

- Adults need to grasp how children's cognitive skills may appear to be set against your adult authority. By middle childhood, their choices in actual dilemmas may not be the preferred adult option. Loyalty to friends may be a more important rule than being truthful to adults. Thoughtful and articulate adolescents may argue you into a moral corner.

Possible disadvantages

- Everyone has to remember that what children or adolescents (and adults) say they would do, or not do, in a hypothetical situation is not a reliable prediction of how they actually behave if faced with this dilemma in real life.

- Lawrence Kohlberg claimed that his stages were universal and research has supported this claim to an extent. There is disagreement over whether the final level is an 'advanced' or socially welcome way of moral reasoning.

BEHAVIOUR IN SOCIAL AND CULTURAL CONTEXT

Another broad group of theorists have approached development and behaviour from the perspective of trying to place the key issues within a social context.

An ecological approach

Urie Bronfenbrenner (1979) studied the relevance of children's social environment through his approach of the ecology of human development. Instead of treating the social environment as a single whole, Bronfenbrenner described the different aspects that influenced children in more and less direct ways. He developed a model which is presented visually as a series of layers, or a pattern of concentric circles. The innermost circle is that part of the environment that creates the daily life of children and adults, determining their direct, personal interactions. Then, the series of circles moves further away from the individual experience and towards broader social factors. Some people prefer the visual image of a set of nesting dolls. Urie Bronfenbrenner was interested in development as a whole; I have applied the theory here to behaviour.

The innermost circle is the microsystem, which encompasses children's immediate personal environment. This includes their family, peers and friends. It also includes settings of which children have personal experience like their early years setting, school or after school club.

- Children's direct social learning about what is expected occurs within this system. In terms of behaviour, young children's experiences build up from time in their own home or the hours they spend in nursery.
- They find consistency or inconsistency in the expectations from one or more familiar adults within the family or out-of-home care. There may be a match, or mismatch, of expectations for behaviour between children's family and their nursery, school or club.
- Older children and adolescents may have to weigh up the different pressures from family and from their friendship group, both of which are equally important over the same time period.

The exosystem is the next layer, including the social system that may not initially appear to exert a direct impact on children and adolescents.

- However, their life is affected because events elsewhere make a difference to the immediate environment. For instance, the pressures within a parent's job may be brought home and change the family atmosphere for the worse.
- Unhappiness and confusion at home in turn affects a child's behaviour, which is noticed, but not immediately understood at his school.

- Parents' friends may exert strong influences on how they discipline their children or adjust their expectations for behaviour and general achievement.

The outer layer is called the macrosystem. Bronfenbrenner includes the local neighbourhood in the macrosystem and the immediate surroundings in which a child or adolescent lives can make a difference to behaviour.

- Are facilities for young children welcomed by local people, or are nurseries or drop-ins regarded as a source of noise? Are local youth clubs seen as welcomed centres for adolescents or magnets for troublesome hoodies?

- Are there places to play or is there great temptation to get up to minor or more serious mischief? Is the local area dangerous, so that law-abiding adolescents feel obligated to carry a weapon, which puts them at risk of trouble with the law? Is there funding for detached youth workers to go out to young people?

- Cultural and social background affects children directly by its impact on their parents' beliefs and priorities. However, cultural values affect broad social structures, such as education, economic systems, national policies and cultural values.

What may sound like remote social ideas nevertheless affect children and adolescents, because these broader systems influence daily life.

- Families, and other adults responsible for children and adolescents, do not operate in a social vacuum. They are affected by the ways in which the surrounding community judges their actions. Cultural traditions establish expectations, which may be a strong source of support or a source of conflict.

- Adults in their professional capacity are affected by their training and current expectations about what they should or should not do. National law and policy trickle down into guidance that influences how familiar adults approach the behaviour of children in nursery, school or club.

- A toxic atmosphere around young people can mean that what they regard as reasonable actions are judged as antisocial behaviour. Initiatives of control may be aimed disproportionately at children and adolescents, for example the Mosquito device which transmits noise at a level which only younger people are likely to be able to hear (search by this term on the Internet).

Urie Bronfenbrenner originally set the whole ecological model in the chronosystem, describing broad social changes over time that affect the experience of childhood and adolescence. The concept helps reflection about behaviour with the focus that key perspectives and firm advice can

27

change over time and back again. Research to study the subtle effects of environment can be complex and the most likely influences are of interactions rather than linear patterns of cause and effect.

WHAT DOES IT MEAN?

Sociocultural theory: emphasises the context for development, including behaviour, and argues against universal stages or norms of development.

Systems theory: focuses on the interaction between the whole and the parts of any social system or group.

Social constructivism: emphasises the sense that people, including children, make of their situation; they construct meaning. This approach values subjective methods and the power of a personal narrative.

Systems theory

Bronfenbrenner's model is an example of a systems theory, which aims to describe social environment as a whole. Systems theory in general rests on the proposal that all biological, economic or psychological systems are holistic entities. They have a wholeness that cannot be explained only by their separate elements. You need to understand the interrelationship between parts and that change in one part of the system will affect other parts. Systems theory has been applied to understand the group dynamics of family life: that it is created by the relationships between parents, children and any other close family members. It is also possible to look at group settings like schools as a social system: an approach that Dennis Lines (2008) uses to discuss bullying (page 137).

Families as social systems

Up to the 1970s most approaches to making sense of 'difficult' behaviour focused almost entirely on what individual children were doing, and the nature of the problem they were judged to pose. Experiences mattered but were mainly seen either as a source of trauma (the psychoanalytic approach) or as methodical ways to shape children's behaviour (behaviourism before social learning theory). The Adlerian approach focus on social interaction was an exception. As systems theory came to the fore, there was an equivalent rethink about psychological and therapeutic approaches to the behaviour of children. Awareness grew that children did not develop patterns of behaviour in a social vacuum.

Systems theory led to the development of family oriented therapy: an alternative to therapeutic intervention focused only on the individual child or adolescent. Informal support and effective parenting courses recognise that helping parents, or other key family carers, to change their behaviour can be the most important first step. If parents will change their approach, then it can be more possible for children or adolescents to take a different line in their own behaviour. However, parents may resist help with the misbehaviour of their son or daughter because they need the child or adolescent to be the problem. Tanya Byron (2005) has provided case studies from her parenting television programmes that illustrate this family dynamic. Some couples had to address their own relationship once their young child was no longer the centre of attention and a constant drain on their energy.

Family relationships

Researchers made sense of the diversity in families by identifying four descriptive dimensions along which families varied:

- the emotional tone of the family: the relative balance of warmth versus hostility in the home
- the responsiveness of parents to their child(ren)
- the way in which control was exercised over children by the parents
- the quality and amount of communication.

Very young children raised with warmth are likely to be emotionally closer to their parents, more securely attached (page 38). Children experience a higher level of self-esteem and this base enables them to be emotionally generous to others and responsive to their distress. Children flourish in terms of their language development in a communicative family atmosphere, where parents listen and respond sensitively to young and older children. But this responsiveness seems in turn to strengthen emotional attachment and provide children with social as well as language skills that help them in interactions outside the family.

Warmth and responsiveness within the family creates a situation in which children are generally more responsive to guidance over their behaviour. Their parents show an unfaltering commitment to their children and so what the parents say, and their values, exert an influence over their sons and daughters. Despite the apparent blasé attitude of many adolescents, their core values are often very close to those held by their parents. Children who have been welcome to form a strong attachment to loving parents are also less likely – although nothing is certain – to become older children or adolescents who treat others in a very aggressive way or get into trouble with the police. Affectionate and responsive commitment by parents to their children exerts a protective effect in neighbourhoods where many factors are stacked against children's physical and emotional well-being. Disadvantaged neighbourhoods do not inevitably produce disaffected and dangerous adolescents, although the parenting task is made much more difficult (Bailey, 2005; Batmanghelidjh, 2006; Seaman et al., 2006).

Emotional commitment works alongside parents' approach to the inevitable choices around exercising control over children and adolescents. Like most areas of research, the study of possible cause-and-effect in family life has a high quotient of 'ifs', 'buts' and 'maybes' (Bee and Boyd, 2004). However, the main themes to emerge are that children are less likely to be defiant, non-compliant or to get into serious trouble when parents have clear and consistent rules, and monitor their children's behaviour. Children rise positively to high expectations of their behaviour and role as a family member, but not so high that the standard is unrealistic given the child's age.

Carole Sutton et al. (2006) describe the pattern that is established by middle childhood when children have experienced emotionally, and possibly also physically, harsh parenting. The harshness is often combined with random patterns when there is next to no parental supervision and inconsistent discipline. Children have no idea what each day will bring, nobody appears to care about them – so why should they care about the feelings or possessions of other people. Children are seriously adrift from any helpful adult anchor and can easily be attracted to the peer support and structure that comes from joining a gang. Such treatment by parents, or any other responsible adult, would be described as neglect or abuse and be a legitimate child protection concern (see Lindon, 2008a).

Parenting style
From the mid-1960s onwards Diana Baumrind observed family life and categorised parents' style of child rearing by how they approached:

- warmth or nurturance
- level of parental expectations, which she called 'maturity demands'
- the clarity and consistency of rules, which she referred to as 'control'
- communication between parent and child.

She then described three particular combinations of how parents dealt with the possible options within these four dimensions: an authoritarian, a permissive or an authoritative parenting style (see resources section under 'Baumrind'.) These ideas can be applied to how any responsible adults behave and are applied to practitioners' choices from page 155.

The typical behaviour of adults sets the emotional atmosphere of daily life and significantly affects children's reactions.

- Parents who behave in an authoritarian way are high in attempts to control children and hold high expectations for their behaviour. However, these adults are low on nurturance and communication. This style is similar to the 'autocratic' pattern identified by Rudolf Dreikurs and Vicki Soltz (1995) and Don Dinkmeyer et al. (1997).

- Permissive adults behave in ways that are high in nurturance but low in expectations of their children. They are reluctant to exert control and tend to be low on communication, because the adult does not discuss options for behaviour. This parenting style has sometimes been described as 'indulgent' or 'laissez-faire' by other writers on family dynamics.

- Authoritative adults accept an active role in guiding children, showing emotional warmth. They set boundaries, yet are willing to share control on some issues. Adults follow through when a child misbehaves or contravenes ground rules. This style is similar to the democratic approach described by Rudolf Dreikurs and Don Dinkmeyer.

Some writers have suggested a necessary division in the permissive style into permissive-indulgent and permissive-neglectful. Rudolf Dreikurs described the problems arising from indulgence or pampering in the context of family but also the impact on children's behaviour in the classroom (Dreikurs et al., 1998). Maggie Mamen (2006) acknowledged a debt to Alfred Adler in her description of the 'pampered child syndrome'. She explored reasons why some parents were reluctant to guide their children's behaviour. Some had followed the strand of parenting advice that claimed placing limits would permanently damage children's self-esteem. Others appeared to opt for the path of least resistance. Whatever the reason, parents who choose not to behave as grown-ups create behaviour in their children that, Maggie Mamen argues, can mimic conditions like Attention Deficit Disorder and minor levels of emotional and learning disabilities. When children face the demands of the classroom environment, they are unable to inhibit their impulses or to regulate their own behaviour.

Diana Baumrind intended to describe the variety across families where parents were making a genuine effort to raise their children. Eleanor Maccoby and John Martin (1983) proposed a clear-cut fourth style to cover the reality that some parents were uninvolved and neglectful of their children, sometimes actively rejecting them. This parenting style is low on all four dimensions of relationships. Children meet with limited or no warmth, few if any expectations, minimal attempts to control their behaviour (sometimes with the view that somebody else should take on this task) and restricted communication of any kind.

The uninvolved and neglectful style is not restricted to specific social classes in society. Sylvia Hewlett (1993) described the problems of child neglect in well-off families, when the demands of a career become a far higher priority than spending time with the children. This category, in its extreme version, covers the family situation when parents effectively resign from the task of parenting their children, either out of choice to pursue their own adult concerns, or as the consequence of desperate and unresolved problems of the parents themselves. Children effectively raise themselves, and sometimes also their siblings. Some parents with this style treat their children as unwelcome interruptions or with undisguised and unrelenting hostility.

A sociocultural perspective

The sociocultural model has drawn from theorists in developmental psychology, like Lev Vygotsky, but there are also strands from sociology, cross-cultural studies and also philosophy. The theoretical stance is sometimes called social constructivism, and over the last decade of the twentieth century became the dominant theory within early childhood studies in the UK. Key concepts are:

- Childhood is seen as a social construction: a period that only makes sense when observed within the context of time and place.

- In any society, social circumstances and prevailing values shape the experience of childhood and adolescence. In some countries around the world the years of dependent childhood may be far shorter than in others.

- Within one neighbourhood, expectations of the behaviour of children and adolescents may be significantly different between families, whose outlook is shaped by a different cultural background, with or without the additional factor of religious faith.

A key part of the sociocultural approach is that social structures and dominant social values influence how childhood is viewed and the daily experiences of children. Berry Mayall (1994) considered the avowed value in many settings for children that practice was 'child-centred'. From her observations she concluded that adult priorities tended to dominate how the time was organised. However, the repeated mantra that 'we are child-centred' could block practitioner awareness of the impact of their behaviour choices. It was then tempting to label children's behaviour as the problem. The adult reasoning, not necessarily explicit, was that it must be the individual children being 'difficult', since the setting was allegedly centred on their needs.

Berry Mayall (2002) has also explored how school and this specific set of educational expectations have come to dominate family life – a process she called 'the scholarization of childhood'. Mayall has applied this idea to the years when children are required to have an education and the ways in which parents are often expected to organise family life around the requirements of school goals. I think the concept can usefully be applied from early childhood, given the expectations that are often laid upon children in the name of 'getting them ready for school'. There has been an acceptance, even an enthusiasm within parts of early years practice, to use the terminology of 'pre-school'. This framework sets up a social construction of early childhood as being in the service of the expectations and demands of primary school. The consequences for behaviour are that young children are burdened with unrealistic expectations from adults (page 239). Approaches to guiding behaviour are imported down the age range, with the unspoken assumption that what appears to work well in school must therefore be appropriate to 'pre-school' (page 46).

WHAT DOES IT MEAN?

Social construction of childhood: the idea that there is no universal image of a child and childhood. The reality is created by social attitudes grounded in time and place.

Ways of talking about children can themselves be a window on to how childhood is viewed in this given group. Additionally, the choice of language in turn places boundaries or offers directions for development including patterns of behaviour.

Discourse is a key concept for the social constructivist approach (Lindon, 2005). The prevailing pattern of discourse determines what is regarded as natural, normal or obviously the right choice. Discourse is made visible through verbal and non-verbal behaviour. The choice of words shapes thought and the details of how people talk about an issue or area of practice communicate a great deal about attitudes, priorities and values. When you become aware of the choices of language, it is possible to understand much better the power relations that exist in this situation, for example:

- Provision for younger children is called pre-school, but later provision is never called post-nursery – why?
- It sets a very different tone when practitioners have learned to talk about 'behaviour management' rather than a phrase like 'guiding children's behaviour' – my preference, obviously.

▓ It sets a different professional agenda when practitioners are at ease talking of 'problem children' or 'difficult parents'. It is not simply a different form of words to discuss 'children who struggle to cope when…' or 'parents whose approach I experience as difficult'.

Potential benefits of this kind of approach

▓ A focus on social context and systems makes it less likely that adults will view problems as starting and finishing with the children or adolescents. There is a dance of interaction between adults-as-practitioners and children.

▓ Greater sensitivity to choice of words around behaviour can avoid a sense of blaming children and adolescents – some of whom are reacting in a reasonable way to unreasonable circumstances.

▓ The stance that children and adolescents are active makers of meaning within their social world focuses on interpretation of events from a non-adult perspective. Even young children can be brought into simple conversation that genuinely helps them to guide their own behaviour.

Possible disadvantages of this kind of approach

▓ Hostility to the concept of a 'universal child' can lead to rejection of any kind of developmental information. Practical approaches to behaviour need sound knowledge to inform realistic expectations.

▓ The high value placed on subjective views and personal narratives can get stuck with firm adult views about appropriate interpretations.

▓ Some social constructivists criticise behaviourism from a simplistic and inaccurate understanding. Others have dismissed insights from the brain research because they arise from a non-valued objective, scientific approach.

3

Experiences within early childhood

This chapter covers the significance of brain development, highlighting the links with observable behaviour. Young children need to form close attachments and the ability to develop affectionate relationships. In turn, adults caring for young children need to hold realistic expectations of their behaviour and take very good care of them. Experiences during early childhood create a template for how children behave towards other people and how they expect to be treated.

> **The main sections of this chapter are:**
> * **Learning within secure relationships**
> * **Childcare outside the family home**
> * **Taking good care of young children**

LEARNING WITHIN SECURE RELATIONSHIPS

During the first five to six years of their life, children build up their first image of themselves as individuals. Their early significant attachments create the broad framework, a template if you like, for personal relationships. Young children develop expectations about how adults in general will behave and they base their working theory on family and other grown-ups who have become familiar to them.

Early childhood exerts a strong influence on later events and most theorists (see Chapter 2) agree with that stance. The disagreements arise from views about:

- How the impact of early experiences is laid down in the young mind and the process by which the ripples from early childhood continue to influence middle childhood, adolescence and adulthood.
- The most significant aspects of early experience for positive or negative outcomes into middle childhood and beyond.
- The extent to which it is possible to reduce, or even effectively erase, the impact of very negative early experiences.

Most theories share the view that the consequences of significant disruption in early childhood take time and serious energy to rectify over middle childhood, let alone the years of adolescence.

Early experiences develop young brains

Detailed research into early brain development has confirmed the perspective that early childhood really matters. Writers like Rima Shore (1997), Jane Healy (2004), Sue Gerhardt (2004) and Collette Tayler (2007) offer reviews to help practitioners through the complexity, as well as recognising that there is a great deal we do not know about how young brains work.

Human brains operate basically on a combination of electrical impulses and chemicals. Groups of cells become wired together and operate as a neural pathway, seen as a learned pattern of behaviour that operates as a sequence. Neural pathways are established for many patterns of behaviour. Once the connections are secure then the actions and reactions look automatic, because the child no longer needs to stop, think and start again. From infancy, and even before birth, new brain connections are made through the experiences of babies, toddlers and young children. So, it matters a great deal how their primary carers – at home and in out-of-home care – behave towards them. Complex research about the minute details of early communication can now be understood through good quality visual material (see The Children's Project, 2000 and Siren Films, 2008).

MAKE THE CONNECTION WITH...
PATTERNS OF REINFORCEMENT

Neuroscientists study brain development and have used the possibilities of computer imaging, along with other complex techniques, to map what happens in the brain during particular experiences. They tend not to use the language of behaviourist theory, as they describe the insights of neuroscience for development. However, it is a legitimate link to remind you of the basic idea of behaviourism: actions which are rewarded tend to be repeated.

- Happy early experiences tell some babies that a smile and tuneful babble usually gets a warm response from this familiar adult – whether a parent, childminder or key person in the nursery. The friendly attention does not have to be every time, but it has to be on a regular basis and with a very short delay. These babies and then toddlers will be far more likely to show socially communicative ways of trying to get attention, at least some of the time.

- The early experiences of other babies or toddlers have shown them that smiling and babbling do not bring attention, whereas serious screaming is generally effective in bringing an adult. That adult is tetchy but is at least present.

■ Some babies learn that life is uncertain – coos and babbles sometimes bring a smile and yet another time, with the same person, the response is blankness or irritation. Adult reactions are hard to predict and life for these children is therefore stressful.

These different kinds of early experience are laid down in the complex pathways of the young brain, weaving in those areas that deal with communication, early thinking and the body chemistry that underpins human emotions. Neural pathways are established and different patterns of behaviour already look typical for this toddler, in contrast with his or her peers.

Happy or unhappy experiences?

Body chemistry is closely linked with direct experiences. Sue Gerhardt (2004) describes the importance of cortisol: a steroid hormone that is important in the biochemistry of the brain. Human brains need cortisol but too great a level caused by stress blocks children's ability to learn in emotionally secure ways. But, equally important, their brains make other connections that show through their behaviour, including uncertain, anxious or aggressive actions.

Babies and young children, who have experienced warm and consistent nurturing, have lower average levels of cortisol than those babies and toddlers whose daily lives have been highly stressful or traumatic. The other significant difference is that, when the nurtured infants experience stress, the natural elevation of cortisol reduces more rapidly. The brain connections of secure infants are telling them that this is a minor disruption to an otherwise happy existence. The insecure infants experience further proof that daily life is unpredictable, unpleasant and adult carers are not to be trusted. Young children become what is described as 'hard-wired for trouble' and are swift to interpret the actions of others, including their peers, as a potential threat.

Levels of cortisol are raised when young children have to deal with a significant change in their familiar care arrangements, such as starting at day nursery or primary school. Studies, that have measured cortisol over time, have found that the level tends to drop as young children feel more at ease. There is also some uncertainty about distinguishing between children's own emotional stress and how much they pick up of their parent's emotional tension about starting a toddler at day care or a child at school. This kind of research, whatever the exact pattern of cause and effect, supports what attentive adults can see and hear in terms of the distressed or very quiet behaviour of children.

There are very good reasons for adults not to force the pace of development through pushing babies and young children into an intellectual rat race, whether technologically enhanced or not. Trying to make young children learn something earlier and quicker can disrupt their confidence and well-being. Positive emotions for learning are facilitated by chemical secretions in the brain that help the messages to cross the synapses. These substances, called neurotransmitters, seem to help positive learning when children feel emotionally secure and able to make their own choices, taking their time.

On the contrary, feelings of exhaustion, anxiety or pressure can make it impossible for the neurons in the child's brain to send or receive the necessary signals. Children always learn something, but in this case those connections will be more like 'adults nag you' or 'I always make mistakes, and that is a bad thing'. You will be able to observe children whose play is highly directed by adults coping by being overly cooperative - 'good' children who play as required. Others will be the creative objectors, who may be labelled as 'non-compliant' and 'unable to concentrate'. Or they are children who are 'always complaining': about having to do boring, adult-dominated activities. Jacqui Cousins (2003) described the behaviour of children whose play choices were regularly interrupted or redirected by practitioners anxious about their agenda of targets for today.

Collette Tayler (2007) sums up practical issues from research into brain development. Young children need a harmonious atmosphere, without frequent negative adult behaviour targeting them. They need continuity in their early years and a personal approach to their care. They also need give-and-take, a reciprocal feel, to their experience of conversation and play. Collette Tayler sums up the situation for early childhood: that it is the erosion of relationships that brings negative consequences for children. Children learn patterns of behaviour that enable them to cope with circumstances that are far less than ideal and such behaviour habits tend to bring further troubles.

The importance of attachment

Babies' first, strongest and most enduring bond needs to be within their own family, with their own parent(s). However, older babies and toddlers also form strong bonds of attachment with their siblings and other close family members, with whom they spend significant amounts of time. Judy Dunn (1993) and her team made extensive observations in the setting of children's own homes. She showed the strong, if sometimes lively, emotional relationships between siblings.

John Bowlby and maternal deprivation

John Bowlby was influenced by the work of zoologist, Konrad Lorenz, and applied the research about young birds and mammals to the early attachment behaviour of human infants. Working in the 1940s, Bowlby argued that the development of attachment between baby and mother was an innately driven set of behaviours and that secure bonding operated to protect infants at this vulnerable time. He followed the tenets of psychoanalytic theory that the most important early attachment was between mother and child. Bowlby made a causal link between insecure early attachment and later antisocial behaviour from his study of juvenile delinquents and the problems experienced by children evacuated from the cities without their parents during the Second World War.

The 'maternal deprivation hypothesis' was offered as a powerful argument that the young children of working mothers would be irreparably damaged and so would society from the older children's delinquent activities. This stance was thoroughly challenged for several decades, see for instance Michael Rutter's reassessment (1972) However, it is important to note that by the mid-1950s, John Bowlby had modified his stance, judging that he had overstated the negative consequences if mothers were not continuously with their young children (Clarke and Clarke, 1998). By the 1980s Barbara Tizard (1986) had made a strong case that fair objections to specifically maternal deprivation theory had obscured the fact that John Bowlby was right about the pressing emotional needs of very young children. The wheel has steadily turned and the importance of early attachment has come back to centre stage: within the family and the implications for good quality out-of-home care.

WHAT DOES IT MEAN?

Attachment: strong feelings of emotional closeness and commitment between children and significant people in their daily life.

Maternal deprivation theory: specific focus on the bond between mothers and their children and the negative consequences of disruption of this attachment.

CHILDCARE OUTSIDE THE FAMILY HOME

The emotional attachment between a baby or toddler and their parent(s) needs to grow during early childhood as the consequence of generous time spent together in play, communication and through the routines of physical care. There is good reason to be concerned if young children do not form a secure emotional bond, or if parents actively reject emotional commitment with their children. When young children are not with their own family, they need to build a strong and affectionate relationship with their non-family carer. So, there is also good reason to be concerned if children's emotional commitment in out-of-home day care is disrupted or they are actively dissuaded from becoming attached to their childminder or practitioners in their nursery.

Feeling 'at home' in out-of-home care

Life in day care

Until the 1970s it was mainly assumed that children would be harmed by time spent in group day care, arising from inevitable problems of disrupting their emotional attachment. It was equally assumed that time spent in nursery class or nursery school would be beneficial, largely because children did not attend this kind of provision, often part-time, until they were at least 3 years of age. By the late 1970s several research reviews (for example, Belsky and Steinberg, 1978) had challenged the stance that day care for young children was inevitably negative. Such reviews did not take a blithe positive view and raised specific practice issues around the quality of children's experiences, staff training and sufficient personal attention.

By the mid 1980s some day care researchers were revising their earlier positive conclusions about the impact of day care and raising some concerns. Jay Belsky talks of a 'slow steady trickle of disconcerting evidence' (2001, page 847) that 20 or more hours of non-family day care, started in the first year of life, increased the risk of insecure attachment between infants and mothers. There were also possible consequences of children later behaving in more aggressive and less cooperative ways. Early and more extensive day care was associated with less sensitive mothering, as babies grew into toddlers, and less engagement with their very young children. The expressed concerns, on the basis of research data, are not presented as absolute; they identify a risk level.

The possible dynamic may be that parents – and the primary carer is still often the mother – need to spend enough time with their children. Babies and toddlers learn habits of behaviour from the affectionate guiding of familiar, caring adults. The problem of longer hours of day care, especially when started in very early childhood, is that young children may struggle to build detailed knowledge of their parent's ways. In turn, the time that is spent with a baby or young toddler may seem to the parent like unrelieved hard grind after a day of paid work. Guidance for early years practitioners emphasises, very properly, the crucial importance of building personal relationships with individual children and spending time with them. The same argument applies to family life.

It matters a great deal how non-family carers behave and how they organise the day for very young children. Practitioners need to be highly responsive to babies and toddlers and young children. But the supported argument of long-term day care researchers like Jay Belsky is that quality is not the only issue – timing and the total hours of non-family care also matter.

TAKE ANOTHER PERSPECTIVE

Times have changed and in an academic review Jay Belsky (2001) comments on the invective that is unleashed from some quarters when doubts are expressed about day care. Steve Biddulph's (2005) more conversational book about under-threes and group care was criticised as an 'attack' on day nurseries, working mothers and early years practitioners. I have read the book and can see no evidence of attack. Read these two sources and then decide for yourself.

For the sake of children, it is important to step aside from 'day care is definitely good for children' just as much as the previous stance of 'non-family childcare must be bad'.

Worrying behaviour from children

Concerns about young children's behaviour within day care were raised in observational studies within the early 1980s by researchers looking at day nurseries and to an extent at the childminding service. The main concern was that young children in groups could fail to be offered sufficient personal attention. Two observable consequences followed in terms of children's behaviour, neither of which were (or are) emotionally healthy for early childhood.

- Some young children gave up trying to get physically and emotionally close to practitioners. They were then seen as 'good' children, who were 'no trouble' and judged to have settled well into the provision, because they did not cry and make a fuss.

- Other children developed strategies to ensure that they would get attention, through being physically aggressive towards their peers or tactics which secured attention because of refusal to follow adult instructions. These children were successful in gaining attention, but were often labelled as behaviour problems and as 'attention-seeking' (meant as a criticism).

I raised methodological problems with some of the 1980s studies in a literature review at the time (Laishley, 1984 – I was then working under that surname). One reservation arose from the tendency to make negative generalisations about day care as a whole from observation (sometimes very informal) of one or two nurseries. I also challenged an unproven assumption in comparative studies that nursery educational facilities and the behaviour of teacher-trained staff were inevitably more beneficial to young children. Writing now 25 years later, I stand by those criticisms, but my continued experience of a wide range of provision leads me to agree with the broad conclusions about possible risks.

I have been privileged to observe very high quality day nursery practice with young children. These teams, and their leadership, have resolved the issues discussed in this section with the emotional well-being of babies and children as the top priority. They run key person systems that are truly personal and care routines follow children's, not adults', convenience. Equally important, children are welcome to be emotionally and physically close; these settings do not have any problem with cuddling (page 59).

However, in some settings young children continue to be faced with the two unacceptable alternatives given earlier. There needs to be careful reflection, and some tough decisions by adults, if children's developmentally predictable reactions are not to be categorised as behaviour problems. Young children must not be labelled as 'clingy' or 'demanding' when they are desperate for personal attention and nurture from familiar adults.

Young children need the same quality of experience wherever they spend their days. It is unacceptable to tolerate standards in any out-of-home care, including a high level of emotional detachment, which would raise concerns in a young child's own home.

Resolving adult problems over attachment

Since the 1980s there has been far greater recognition of what good practice looks like in day care and a reduction in the unhelpful, artificial division between provision called 'care' and 'education'. Some of the earlier studies were undertaken at the Tavistock Institute in London (Bain and Barnett, 1986). That approach has been developed by Peter Elfer (2006, 2007) and by Julia Manning-Morton (2006) who have highlighted what can undermine children's opportunities to become emotionally close to their non-family carers in day nurseries.

Peter Elfer describes the difference between the avowed aim of some day nurseries to welcome close relationships between individual children and their key person and the day-by-day reality. Adult choices over how to organise routines are sometimes made in ways that do not allow sustained personal interaction. In some settings practitioners are uncertain that emotional commitment to other people's children is compatible with a professional outlook. Peter Elfer applies the psychoanalytic concept of defensive reactions (page 17) to explain how some practitioners opt for emotional distance to protect themselves against the personal distress of caring deeply about babies and young children who will leave them, sooner or later.

Peter Elfer's observational research is supportive of day nurseries and uncertain practitioners, some of whom are still in the early years of their own adulthood. His interpretation avoids assigning blame for the dilemmas, while being clear that any perceived problems have to be resolved in ways that do not put young children at emotional risk. One practical conclusion is that early years practitioners should have easy access in their nursery team to support in order to talk about feelings. I would add the emphasis that team leaders, advisors and trainers have to discuss the issues in an open way. They certainly must not worsen matters by suggesting that it is acceptable to keep other people's young children at a distance, let alone that limiting physical contact is part of professional safeguarding practice (Lindon, 2008a).

Early years practitioners are often concerned, or feel that parents are anxious, about young children becoming 'too attached' to their childminder or key person in a nursery. Early years professionalism is compatible with closeness; it has to be, otherwise social systems are established that are emotionally dangerous for young children. If children are emotionally adrift, then they behave in ways that are attempts to reconnect and which can give rise to different kinds of problems for the adults. Without the emotional bond, you cannot guide behaviour through personal communication and the fact that children would rather please than displease you. If practitioners choose, or are told, to step aside from an affectionate, personal relationship with young children, then adults are far more likely to embrace systems of mechanical reward and sanctions, rather than encouraging self-regulation based on the power of the relationship.

LOOK, LISTEN, NOTE, LEARN

Over their first five years young children stockpile a considerable amount of experience that builds their image of how the adult world behaves towards them.

By 5–6 years of age, children will have some views on the following and their attitudes will show in their daily behaviour.

◆ Do adults usually like me? Am I a likeable child? Or do many adults seem to think I am an irritating nuisance and bring nothing but trouble? Or am I only a 'nice child' when I behave 'nicely'?

◆ If adults tell me I should not do something, do they really mean it? Or if I keep moaning or throw a tantrum, do they usually give in and let me do it?

◆ Can I work out pretty much how my familiar adults will react or do they change from day to day? Are the adults within one place consistent? Do my parents stick by the same rules? Or can I play one of them off against the other – is this a good thing?

◆ How do my familiar adults let me know they are pleased? Do they mainly tell me, smile or hug me? Am I given rewards like sweets or stickers? If I don't get a reward, have I failed to be 'good enough'?

◆ Are they rarely, if ever, pleased with me, so far as I can tell? Do I assume they are pleased, if they are not nagging me or shouting?

◆ Can I work out what to do next time, so I do not get into trouble again? Do I get any warning, so I can put myself back on track? Am I forgiven, can I start again or do I never hear the end of it?

◆ Do you get treated differently because of who or what you are? Do boys get treated differently from girls?

Reflect on what could cause problems for children. Add some more thoughts, expressed from the perspective of a young child.

Quality in work with babies and young children can only be delivered through a caring, personal relationship between baby or child and practitioner. In nurseries, a key person system needs to link an individual practitioner with individual key children and with their parent(s). Shared or partner key person working deals with the shift system that applies in full day childcare, in contrast with sessional provision. Communication with parents fills in some of the early gaps of knowledge. However, it should become possible that the key person is able to guide the behaviour of individual children on the basis of intimate knowledge of their ways and reactions. It is an emotionally healthy reaction if a young child, who is now familiar with nursery, still wants their key person if the child is distressed, tired or unwell. In the same way it is a normal reaction for young children to hang tight to their childminder under similar circumstances. These issues are further discussed within the context of partnership from page 244.

When do children start school?

In England, reception class is the final year of children's early childhood stage and not the first year of primary school. This situation is not a recommendation: it is a legal requirement from the Childcare Act 2006. In Scotland and Wales the age for statutory education (school or otherwise) is defined as the term after a child's fifth birthday, but the age is a year younger in Northern Ireland. Problems arise because reception classes, and sometimes also nursery or playgroup provision, are located on school grounds. Children and families therefore walk through the school gates each day. Children in reception may be required to wear the uniform or meet the informal dress code worn by the older children. All this visual information gives a message, 'They have started school'. See also the discussion about 'pre-school' on page 33.

TAKE ANOTHER PERSPECTIVE

Working with some nursery teams, I have had the explanation of, 'Well they'll have to do that when they get to school' to justify unrealistic expectations of young children such as:

- Forming pointless queues for the toilet, when children are capable of deciding when they want to go and dealing with their own care in the toilet.

- Hanging around while everyone gets their coat or hat on, in order to go outside, when an early years setting is perfectly well organised for free flow.

- Organising an overstructured day in which young children have to 'do their work before they can go to play'.

- Requiring children to tolerate long (and rather boring) mat sessions or large, very adult-directed circle group time.

- Insisting on a formal PE session with young children rather than welcoming lively physical activity and games as part of the playful flow of the whole day.

Some 'trouble times and spaces' (page 235) arise from the imposition of a formal classroom model on early childhood. The children are not showing 'behaviour problems'; the problem lies in the situation created by adults.

Questions

- Reflective practitioners recognise that you never help a child genuinely to get ready for future situations by simply importing those precise requirements down the age range. Have you been in a working situation with young children where that approach was the dominant style?

- What is the likely impact of any of the above ways of organising a day with under-fives? How might young children behave, faced with these requirements?

- Look at the ideas on page 173 about how children need to be able to cope in the classroom environment. What might be some realistic steps along the way? What is likely to be genuinely helpful in 'getting children ready for school'?

If the local reception class is run inappropriately, then the nursery team has even greater responsibility to ensure that young children do not lose their playful early childhood. Of course, some reception teams organise in an appropriately flexible way. I have listened to reception teams who, even under pressure from colleagues in the rest of school, have taken steps to ease young children into the community of their primary school. Examples include that:

- 4- and 5-year-olds spend much of the year within their own indoor and outdoor spaces. They eat their lunch in their own room and only start to visit the large lunch hall slowly over the summer term. Timings are organised so that the youngest children experience this larger space, and possibly different routines for the meal, over the quietest period of lunchtime.

- The reception class is not taken into whole school assembly until practitioners judge the children are confident to deal with the large space and number of bodies. Again, that slow familarisation process usually happens over the summer term, with a careful choice of which assembly will interest the group and care over the entry and exit of this young group.

- Children have plenty of physically active play throughout the year. They are given steady practice without time pressure to become used to the routine for PE, with all the undressing and dressing that is involved.

Children learn from opportunities within ordinary daily life

Changes and transitions over early childhood

A realistic focus on the need for out-of-home childcare, plus a high value placed on flexibility that suits adults, has sometimes lost sight of the nature of this experience for the children involved. The broad consequences of this social change are that during their early childhood, some young children encounter a series of different people and places.

The importance of routines

Babies and young children like a shape to their day; even the more come-what-may individuals get uneasy if there is no predictability to what happens, where, when and with whom. Children – just like adults – need some time and friendly support to become familiar with 'how it all works here' when they start somewhere new and unfamiliar. When time and guidance is easily available, babies and young children become at ease in a situation that was strange at the outset. In a warm emotional atmosphere, children who are now at ease, often offer support and explanation to peers who look puzzled or close to upset.

Some young children are fortunate to experience continuity with the same childminder or nursery up to their entry into reception class or the beginning of formal school. Babies and young children need their family and key person to develop a friendly working relationship (page 241). Under the most positive circumstances, family and non-family adults have to put time and effort into ensuring young children do not have to negotiate inconsistencies over expectations for their behaviour. In most family life, raising children is a joint enterprise involving more than one adult. However, many families now need to bring together their own commitment with the involvement of early years practitioners.

Too much change?

The emotional resilience of some young children is tested to fracture point by regular changes of individual carer and/or familiar place, sometimes with limited prior warning. Problems arise for children who experience a patchwork for their days and weeks, or a sequence of many changes over their early years. Even the most resilient of young children struggle with the energy to find out all over again what this bunch of adults want and expect. Their invisible, internal emotional distress shows itself in visible patterns of behaviour. For example:

- Some young children cope with weekly attendance at several different group settings by organising their own play experiences. If they are fortunate enough to attend on the same days as some other children, they develop a friendship that creates their familiarity here.

The other children will be their safe base and they are likely to be adrift or actually distressed if those peers are absent.

- Sometimes the peer friendship route is not possible, or children have been overwhelmed with too many change. Then a child may make a beeline for a specific item of play equipment or a play area like the home corner. These resources and this space have become their familiar benchmark for this destination within their week. They will be distressed, or show flat refusal, if adults try to persuade them to change this emotionally secure pattern.

- Alternatively, young children may take the strategy of sticking like a little limpet to an adult in each of the different places within their week. They do not let go, they do not 'settle' – or they take ages to appear to be at ease – because too much regular change is being asked of them.

TAKING GOOD CARE OF YOUNG CHILDREN

Good quality early years provision does not draw a firm line between care (or nurture) and early education (I prefer 'early learning'). The artificial care–education divide was a significant issue in the early 80s (Laishley, 1984), although isolated parts of the workforce had already started to try to overcome the problems. There is greater recognition 25 years later that early years practitioners, of any professional background, have to create a nurturing environment, respecting children's needs for physical care, and an individual approach to learning and behaviour.

Respect individuality

Inevitably you cannot treat young children exactly the same because they are unique individuals. A responsible aim for adults is to treat children fairly and in an even-handed way, yet adjusted for your knowledge of individual children – another reason for a proper key person system in group provision. The available research (Lindon, 2005) suggests that babies are born with some basic differences in temperament which show in their behaviour from the earliest weeks. There is, however, a significant impact of early experiences, not least the possibility of a match or mismatch between baby or child and familiar adult(s).

Theorists and researchers who have explored temperament in childhood have proposed different categories. But the broad differences come down to these kinds of areas, which are described with some thoughts about possible adult perceptions and reactions. Please use this section to reflect for yourself and ideally also discuss with colleagues or fellow students.

How active are children?

Children vary in their personal comfort level around activity. Some children are physically very mobile and react in a vigorous way to the possibilities in their environment. Some are considerably less active and may prefer sedentary play activities. Some may react passively, waiting for experiences to come to them.

- Some adults welcome an active toddler as 'lively' or a child as 'keen to explore' and see the more passive child as one who would benefit from some encouragement (which may be true).

- Other adults see the less active child as 'good' or 'no trouble'. They may complain that the naturally more active children are 'into everything' or 'won't ever sit still'. Maybe these adults are by temperament less active or possibly want an easy life, avoiding physically active play with children.

- Adults who think children should be passive and compliant may already be thinking that a very active 3- or 4-year-old, who is nevertheless within normal range for behaviour, has a problem like attention deficit disorder.

- If young children attend early years provision where they are expected to cope with only short bursts of energetic activity, then some children will tolerate this regime more easily than others. It is not a sign of 'good' behaviour that some children are willing to sit around, uncomplaining, while nothing of interest happens.

How sociable are they?

Some individuals appear more sociable from the outset. These differences show between toddlers or young children in how they relate to less familiar people, but also to new experiences or resources.

- Some children are keen to make contact or explore and they may be swiftly at ease in a new situation. They are not born more socially skilled then their peers, but their willingness to make contact may ease the social learning.

- Some babies and children are less socially outgoing, maybe they take time to warm up. They are not necessarily 'shy', often an unhelpful label, and they welcome support, but not pressure to 'make friends' before they are ready.

- Bear in mind that most, probably all, children like some time on their own. Children are not necessarily showing unsociable behaviour if they sometimes retreat to a cosy corner for a bit of peace and quiet.

How do they react to the unfamiliar?

Some babies are 'jumpy' from the earliest weeks, whereas some appear to be remarkably unfazed by similar events.

- Very wary babies and toddlers may withdraw from new experiences and people, especially if they cannot cling to their safe base and familiar adults fail to manage the situation so it is not overwhelming.
- These children are often called 'shy', 'sensitive' or even 'over-anxious' (not useful labels) and the wariness is not only about people. It helps to recognise a child's outlook and encourage him or her to take new experiences one small step at a time.
- Adults who are also wary about the unknown may feel attuned to a child like this but need to avoid being overly protective of a child who would benefit from support to stretch out from the familiar.

How do they cope with strong emotions?

Toddlers and young children differ in how they handle strong emotions and the extent to which they react to experiences with anger and irritability. All children feel annoyed at some point, but some children are more easily provoked by minor frustrations from a very young age.

- Some young children seem to 'go over the top' more easily than their peers. They may need more active adult support in order to regulate and deal with 'negative affect': feelings of anger, resentment or upset at perceived unfairness.
- Even babies who cry a considerable amount compared with their peers do not necessarily develop into irritable, easily upset toddlers. The difference seems to arise from whether their primary carer has been highly responsive to the cries. Sensitivity and patience with a crying baby is more possible when the parent is supported by family and friends.
- Babies whose crying has been met by irritation and anger are more likely to develop into defiant toddlers. They now have more options for fierce expression of emotions, including the model demonstrated by the adult carer.

How hard do they try – how soon do they give up?

All young children struggle to an extent with effort and persistence, especially on something that is hard or confusing and when there are distractions.

- Attention control is partly developmental, yet some children struggle to concentrate as well as their peers. Helpful adults hold realistic expectations in terms of a child's age but they also find strategies that fit children who are temperamentally inclined to give up at the first hurdle.

- The flip side to this behavioural style is that young children who are very persistent may be experienced as 'awkward' or 'stubborn' by adults who want them to move on to another activity. Young children who really want to keep trying until they fix something object strongly when told to 'leave it now'.

WHAT DOES IT MEAN?

Temperament: inborn tendencies that shape how a baby or young child reacts to daily experiences.

Behavioural style: the individual pattern of behaviour that a child shows from a very young age, reflecting inborn temperament.

TAKE ANOTHER PERSPECTIVE

Adults choose words to describe children's behaviour and that choice often says a great deal about adult assumptions and beliefs. Reflective practitioners avoid labelling children by their behaviour, but even thoughtful adults benefit from stepping back sometimes from the words that they use.

Look at these possibilities and ideally discuss them with your colleagues or fellow students.

- What does 'shy' mean? Is it applied to behaviour that would be better described as 'quiet', 'reserved', 'thoughtful', 'watchful', 'private' or other words?

- Why does a child get called 'stubborn' and when is the word 'persevering'?

- What is 'sensitive' and is this word more of a criticism if applied to a boy?

- When does 'lively' or 'full of energy' become 'overactive' or 'unable to concentrate'?

Behaviour – fixed or fluid?

If you still have contact with the same children some years later, you will almost certainly notice that the child who looked confident and was central in the nursery play is a social leader in the primary school. Children who clung to an adult in nursery or preferred the sidelines until they felt at ease, may not actually hang on tight now. But they probably seek friendly reassurance, especially in a new or anxiety-provoking situation. Avshalom Caspi et al. (2003) suggest that there are continuities between temperament in early childhood and behavioural style as adults. They followed a large sample of children in New Zealand and found that temperament in childhood was reasonably predictive of adult behaviour. The basics of childhood temperament seem to evolve into an adult personality; you will not change the core of what makes you an individual.

TAKE ANOTHER PERSPECTIVE

Young children are not fixed in their behaviour from the earliest age, yet there can also be continuity over behaviour that adults regard as a problem. At least some of this continuity seems to arise because of a vicious circle.

Children whom adults describe as having a 'difficult temperament' are far more likely to show what those same adults judge to be behaviour problems. These are children who tend to get upset very easily, find it hard to settle and require a lot of adult attention. The problem worsens when the children are labelled as 'demanding' and the adult feels the child should stop behaving in this way. Or in a group setting the adult is criticised by colleagues for 'spoiling' a distraught child. A 'difficult' temperament will not inevitably lead to later problems, if positive approaches to guiding behavioural reactions can be taken at the early stages.

Hold realistic expectations

Avshalom Caspi et al. use their results to challenge developmentally appropriate practice (DAP) that dissuades practitioners from setting out their expectations or trying to encourage children towards more mature behaviour. Caspi et al. may be correct in their assertion about how DAP is interpreted. I would argue that a firm base of developmentally appropriate expectations does not exclude active help for children over social and problem solving skills. The research on continuities in temperament confirms an approach in which support from adults needs to be based on the behavioural style of the child. Helpful adult behaviour has to be a personalised approach and not a one-size-fits-all system.

A positive tone will not be set if the ordinary ups and downs of daily life with under-fives are labelled as 'behaviour problems' that have to be 'managed'. It is very usual that young children behave in the following ways, at least some of the time.

- Prefer to do what they want rather than what you want, when these two are in conflict, and to argue in words and body language. They like to have their own way as much as possible.
- Fail to follow requests or instructions the first time around, especially if these instructions were given to a whole group of young children. Sometimes they nod in agreement and head off and do it. Sometimes they nod in agreement and proceed to do the exact opposite.
- Be unimpressed with requests to share – especially if they have just got hold of this resource and the adult does not help with even-handed turn taking.
- Want your attention and close physical contact – it is not 'demanding' for young children to wish to be physically close to familiar adults, nor to want personal comfort if they are uneasy or distressed.
- Have a limited ability to control their own strong emotions. Young children get frustrated easily and when they run out of options and words it is very normal behaviour for them to fling themselves around and possibly go into a full scale emotional meltdown (tantrum).
- May hurt other children or adults physically – not necessarily intending hurt or realising that this action will hurt. They have a limited understanding of the consequences of their actions and a limited ability to use their words and stop themselves when the emotional temperature starts to soar.
- Be perplexed by being asked 'why did you..?' or to step back mentally and talk about what they did, especially some time after the actual event.
- Say things that at one level they 'know' to be untrue, but at another level they really want to be accurate, like they are going on an exciting trip this weekend. Truth, lies and fantasy have some blurry boundaries over childhood. This uncertainty is not exactly helped when adults are economical with the facts or tell deliberate untruths, for example about the existence of Father Christmas.

Unless the pattern is unrelieved and highly confrontational, these kinds of actions are not 'challenging behaviour' in any sensible use of that phrase.

They are simply the result of toddlers being toddlers and sometimes being tired young children who are now beyond their ability to guide themselves.

Trouble ahead?

Susan Campbell (2006) describes her professional perspective from clinical practice that it is less usual now that problems arising from the behaviour of young children are simply brushed to one side. However, she identifies a new, concerning tendency to regard age-appropriate behaviour as pathological and to predict serious and long-term negative consequences from normal, age-related struggles. Young children who occasionally deal with frustrations by hitting out, or who throw a serious emotional wobbler as an extended non-compliant 'No!', are not on the road to a life of antisocial behaviour. Susan Campbell is based in the United States, but her informed views ring warning bells for the UK.

TAKE ANOTHER PERSPECTIVE

Richard Tremblay's presentation to the Royal Society in October 2007 explored how young children can learn to regulate their use of physically aggressive tactics during early childhood. A great deal depends on the actions of the adults who care for children – whether they actively guide girls and boys to alternatives and the model they provide for children to imitate. This kind of conscious adult intervention is part of the responsibility to socialise children.

It is very usual that young children use physical means to express their feelings, to get what they want or hold tight to what they have. Pushing or pinching can be the preferred option when they run out of words, which happens swiftly for toddlers and very young children. However, this presentation, and the research behind it, was discussed in the media along the lines of children being more aggressive or violent than adults (Google 'Richard Tremblay'). The tone of discussion was set by the Society's own press release entitled, 'Terror tots born that way but not destiny says research'
http://royalsociety.org/news.asp?year=&id=7206

Researchers who look for continuities from childhood into adulthood all emphasise that there is no neat cause-and-effect. It is sometimes possible to look back and see negative patterns of behaviour in early childhood for individuals who are now well into adolescence or young adulthood. However, some young people who pose serious problems to their local neighbourhood have supportive families and trouble-free early childhoods.

There are also considerable numbers of that age group who were a serious handful in their earlier years and are not showing antisocial patterns now.

A great deal depends on nurture: whether children and young adolescents experience active support from caring adults with regulating strong emotions and making choices about how feelings are expressed. In contrast, children are likely to continue in developmentally immature ways of dealing with problems and relationships when familiar adults are unavailable, insensitive or unresponsive, or possibly so absorbed in their own problems that they have minimal time or energy to guide.

Basic nurture and behaviour

Taking good care of young children, and older ones, requires adults to know when to worry and when the answer really is, 'Don't panic'. The basics of good physical care are also part of this adult responsibility.

Good nutrition

Human bodies benefit from a subtle mix of nutrients and the details of body chemistry are complicated to understand and explain. However, the basics for good nutrition are relatively straightforward:

- Enough to eat to meet feelings of hunger, to support physical activity and for children and adolescents to fuel essential growth.
- A variety of meals or snacks, balanced across the different food groups and as much as possible freshly prepared, non-processed and without additives.
- Enough to drink to assuage thirst and avoid dehydration – led by ordinary tap water, milk and small amounts of fruit juice, avoiding (or keeping to an absolute minimum) fizzy and other processed drinks.

Children who are fed an unbalanced diet – in content and/or quantity – are more likely to be cranky, tired or lethargic. The case linking additives to hyperactive behaviour in childhood has sometimes been overstated. However, there is sound evidence of a connection (Whiting, 2005 and Benton, 2008) and that some children are especially sensitive to specific food additives.

Children need to start the day with a meal. Many primary schools have introduced breakfast club to deal with this issue, as well as offering an extended day for parents who need to get to work before the official beginning of school. Descriptive reports frequently highlight a positive impact on children's behaviour within the classroom environment and their general concentration. Part of the change seems to be explained by not having to wait until lunchtime for food. However, an enjoyable, social breakfast club experience also gives children an easier transition into the school day. Thongsley Fields Primary School offered a breakfast and play start to the day to a significant number of pupils as part of their 'Fit to Learn' initiative.

Primary school children need a good start to their day

Rest and sleep

Children also need enough rest and sleep. Babies vary as to how much they sleep in total hours, the patterns in which they sleep and how long they take to take to sleep through the night. Young children still vary over how much night sleep they need and whether they benefit from one or more daytime naps. However, all young children need sufficient rest and there is growing anecdotal evidence that too many young children nowadays do not have enough sleep. This deficiency can show itself through behaviour when young children are easily irritated, disinclined to be cooperative and given to a great deal of whingeing for no good reason – from the adult perspective.

Tanya Byron (2005, 2007) describes her supportive work with families experiencing problems with their young child's behaviours. She offers case studies from her television parenting programmes and clinical practice, starting with helping parents move their child into a predictable bedtime routine and therefore a decent night's sleep. Tanya Bryon's advice, and I agree with this approach, is to address the sleep issues first and then deal with any remaining problems around behaviour. Young children often cannot recognise that they are tired. In the same way, they are unlikely to recognise that their cranky feelings arise from being hungry or thirsty. Young children are certainly not going to tell you, 'I'd probably behave better if you put me to bed now.'

- If you offer advice to parents, you need to get across that young children will usually resist the introduction of a regular bedtime. They will persist in waking up and/or getting up in the night, until they realise their parents are serious about the new sleep routine.
- If you take responsibility for young children, especially for whole days, you have to allow time and comfortable space for their nap or peaceful times to snuggle up in a cosy corner with a book or other restful activity.
- In partnership with parents, you need to reach a workable joint routine, which does not involve forcing exhausted children to stay awake through long days.
- Of course, responsible practitioners do not assume that every fractious toddler or irritated 3-year-old needs to take a nap. Sometimes they just want your help to resolve the social problem that has made them cross.

Physical contact and cuddles

Young children will not believe that you care about them if you are reluctant to snuggle up, have cuddles or be happy for a child to lean against your shoulder. Children need contact and affectionate communication and this physical closeness helps them to feel safe and cherished (Lindon, 2006a and 2006c). Heather Piper and Ian Stronach (2008) describe the distortion to human relationships when touch is viewed as a problematic area to be managed and ordinary human contact is seen as a necessary but calculated risk. Wariness over physical contact has become entangled with a highly anxious approach to safeguarding children and young people (Lindon, 2008a). Reluctance or refusal to make ordinary human contact with children is a child protection issue, because under those circumstances the adults have lost the word 'child' in 'child protection' and 'adult protection' has taken its place. Safe practice with children means that we have to detox the whole issue of physical contact.

I have been struck that schools, let alone nurseries, with an appropriate nurturing atmosphere have practitioners, and therefore children, who are comfortable with touch. During my visit to Thongsley Fields Primary I noticed countless instances of children comfortable to be close to practitioners, to lean in against them and be happy to show, 'I'm pleased to see you' or 'Haven't we done well?' with a hug. Older children were at ease taking younger ones by the hand, to guide, keep safe or help on their way. In contrast, I have heard of schools where any kind of touch between peers is labelled as 'inappropriate behaviour'. You cannot create supportive relationships with such alienating rules and you cannot guide children's other choices for behaviour once you have set the bar for interaction at such an impersonal level.

Physical activity and general behaviour

Avoidable troubles arise when adults judge that young children are posing behaviour problems because they want free movement and physically lively play. As Sally Goddard Blythe has pointed out (2004, 2008), staying still is actually the hardest movement of all and adults need to respect the physical ABC of attention, balance and coordination. Restriction of children's movement has a negative effect on their whole development and is an unhealthy regime for childhood. However, injecting some activity back into a sedentary day regularly leads to the disappearance of problems caused by unrealistic expectations. A better balanced day or session then shows which children have out of the ordinary problems in regulating their own behaviour.

In early years provision an appropriately flexible routine gives children plenty of opportunities for lively and outdoor play. Helen Bilton (2000) noted the operation of a self-fulfilling prophecy when young children were allowed very limited outdoor time. She observed the changes when a scant quarter hour of timetabled outdoor play was altered to free flow between indoors and the garden. Children's play outside became less manic and more sustained when they were no longer trying to pack all their favourites into such a short time. The organisation Jabadao (www.jabadao.org) focuses on the importance of plenty of physical movement for young children, games and the growth of skills by developmental movement play (DMP). In their work with early years settings the Jabadao team have observed reduction in problems around behaviour when children are able to move more and stay still less. Adults need to share control of choices over play activities and worry less about accidents that might, but never actually, happen.

*Wise teachers know the
importance of physical breaks*

Specialists like Sally Goddard Blythe and Jabadao offer balanced
programmes for physical movement and these ideas are valuable for getting
practitioners back on track. The experience supports adult reflection about
the links between physical activity and the pattern of children's behaviour.
However, it will be less effective if early years teams see physical movement
as a specialist session. Generous time for freely chosen play and being
outdoors will enable children to be suitably active. The importance of
activity is just as relevant in primary school, where children need proper
breaks and lunchtimes. Wise school teams also make regular physical
interludes part of classroom life. In Sun Hill I watched the Activate set of
lively physical movements that started the morning and afternoon class
work. In Thongsley Fields I watched Take Ten, another whole class plus
teacher chance to move about with music. These physical breaks are for
everyone and not only for children who are judged to find it very hard to
stay still.

4

Feeling, thinking and behaving

Children and adolescents do not only behave; they experience feelings and have thoughts about possible actions or what they have done. Supportive adults are aware of the ways in which feeling and thinking relate to behaviour, and they also acknowledge their own feelings. This chapter explores moral reasoning and judgement, but also the crucial emotional underpinning to more and less conscious choices over actions.

> **The main sections of this chapter are:**
>
> ⁕ **Moral values and beliefs**
>
> ⁕ **The emotional underpinning to behaviour**
>
> ⁕ **Supporting emotional literacy**

MORAL VALUES AND BELIEFS

A sensible, and fair adult approach to children's behaviour has to be grounded in reasonable expectations of their ability to grasp moral issues within their own social world. Children's understanding develops steadily and they can be much more observant and intellectually sophisticated than adults assume. However, through early and middle childhood, girls and boys do not see daily life through adult eyes. Adolescents, despite their more mature grasp of social relations and what other people may be feeling, still find themselves perplexed by the grown-ups, as well as profoundly irritated on occasion.

From thoughts to actions via feelings

The studies of moral reasoning by Lawrence Kohlberg (see page 23) are thought-provoking. But studies, and a wealth of anecdotal evidence, show that adults frequently do not always behave in line with their expressed principles. So it would hardly be realistic to expect a neat connection between what children or adolescents say would be the right choice and how they actually behave in the given situation, along with all the associated emotions and sometimes stresses.

The role of a genuinely helpful adult is often to understand what is getting in the way of the wise or considerate choice for children or young people.

- Young children succumb to the pressures of the moment or strong desires – 'I know I shouldn't but I just want to' is often the message, in actual words or expressed through their body language.

- Through middle childhood, girls and boys become increasingly vulnerable to group pressures from their peers. It feels more important to do what your friends urge. It is an uncomfortable prospect to be labelled as someone who is pathetic and far too worried about what the grown-ups think.

- Children who are willing to try non-aggressive ways of handling conflict are put in an impossible position if adults do not create safe space and the expectation that 'we use our words here'. Talking out your problems is a strategy that requires cooperation from peers. Children whose family values (or experiences in a previous setting) support talking rather than fighting can feel emotionally fragmented. It is impossible to do what feels right and still feel safe in this provision.

- Sometimes, adolescents are embarrassed or distressed, because they genuinely did not know that their action was not allowed here. Some children are caught between significant differences in practitioner style when they move on from a setting in which they are trusted and are welcome to get out materials and make active choices. In the second setting they find themselves told off for going into 'my cupboard' and not waiting until they are told what to do today.

- Children, just like adults, sometimes rethink a 'wrong' action as acceptable, for instance, hitting their brother is excusable because of his unforgivable action earlier in the day.

TAKE ANOTHER PERSPECTIVE

Some years ago I encountered, and was impressed by, a key phrase in the behaviour policy of Balham Nursery School, close to me in South London. The team had highlighted the point that everyone should recognise that for children, 'It can be very hard sometimes to do the right thing'. Our aim has to be that, in the end, children guide themselves (self-regulation) but we should never expect standards that we would be hard pressed to meet ourselves, all the time.

Practitioners responsible for school playtimes or club activities realise that children who have to be pulled up regularly for their actions often know they have crossed the boundary into unacceptable behaviour. The problem is not confusion over ground rules. These children know what they should and should not do; their difficulty lies in controlling their own behaviour.

Helpful adults who watch and listen do not waste their breath in repeating the rules yet again. They talk with the children about what is getting in the way, what are the temptations that divert them from making the right choice. Adult input is often needed to help children to resist an impulse or to learn alternative ways of dealing with explosive situations.

Understanding moral development

Babies are born morally neutral but inherently social, because humans are a social species. Moral development has little, if any, meaning unless the different aspects are embedded in a social context of relationships. Moral values are relevant to how we treat other people, or how we expect to be treated in our turn. So a consideration of children's moral development is intertwined with their social and emotional, just as much as their intellectual development.

There are three main aspects of moral development, all of which are relevant to understanding and guiding children's choices over actions.

- Behaviour – the ways in which children behave or what they learn not to do. Children may behave in line with ways that gain adult approval, for instance, taking turns in the playgroup, without fully understanding the idea of 'sharing' that the adult is trying to explain.
- Understanding – grasping the different concepts that underpin choices in behaviour. Children need skills of observation and language to decipher what adults mean by words like 'cooperative' or 'spiteful', or systems of ideas around 'right' and 'wrong'.
- Judgement – coming to conclusions about their own and other people's behaviour on the basis of moral concepts, values and priorities. Children learn about moral judgements from familiar adults, but also increasingly from daily experience with their peers. They become able to voice judgements: that one should or should not do certain things or that particular behaviour is wrong, but perhaps excusable under given circumstances.

**MAKE THE CONNECTION WITH...
CHILDREN'S AGE**

As you read this section, bear in mind individual children you know – how old are they?

Young children are at a different point in their understanding of moral issues from older children or adolescents, let alone adults. Often, adults responsible for young children need to be satisfied that the children will follow the adults' guidance and will, for instance, behave in a kindly way or show basic awareness of the needs of a peer. It is unrealistic, and unnecessary, to expect young children to be able to voice abstract concepts underlying what adults ask and model. It is quite enough that young children feel and say, 'It's nicer to take turns' or 'It's unkind to call somebody a horrid name like...'

What is right, what is wrong and why

During early childhood, girls and boys develop a network of social relationships with other people: adults within the family and outside, children of their own age and those older or younger. Children come to recognise the varied expectations and constraints of settings and grown-ups. It is not unusual for children to behave differently in response to different expectations and different people.

WHAT DOES IT MEAN?

Moral development: the process of learning to distinguish between right and wrong, in line with the values of a given social and cultural group.

Social cognition: thinking about relationships and behaviour in a social context.

Children apply their growing powers of thinking and reasoning to what they observe of other people in a social setting. This area of development is sometimes called social cognition. Children try to 'read' other people, to anticipate what they may do or could want. Children and adolescents seek some level of predictability in their lives and can be concerned when friends or adults behave out of character.

Children's moral reasoning develops along the following lines:

- Babies and young children discover the 'don'ts' in their environment. Curiosity drives them to things they should not touch and to consequences that either they cannot foresee or overlook in the heat of the moment.

- Young children do not understand adult moral judgements like 'destructive', but they grasp adult disapproval. Older children start to understand guidelines to behaviour, rules and interpretations of the behaviour of others.

- Children move from direct observation to making some inferences. Younger children focus on what has just happened to them. Whereas older children begin to look for more general principles or causes beneath the surface.

- By 6 or 7 years, children are potentially able to think in a more sophisticated way around what and why. Their ideas about intentions and consequences include considerations of 'I didn't mean to…' or 'She didn't know that…'.

- Children's judgements move from very definite to more qualified. The rules expressed and followed by younger children tend to be more fixed. Further experience, thinking and talking leads to more 'ifs' and 'buts' and 'it depends'.

- Young children tend to believe that their familiar rules are universal: everyone follows them. Even adults retain some elements of this kind of thinking. Experiences within the family, as well as in their childminder's home, nursery, school or club show children that everyone does not commit to the same rules.

THE EMOTIONAL UNDERPINNING TO BEHAVIOUR

Feelings and thinking combine with actions to create visible patterns of behaviour. A consistent theme in this book is that supportive adults resist a tunnel vision focused only on observable behaviour. You have to deal with the 'what', but adult actions and reactions must also be informed by a sense of 'why'.

TAKE ANOTHER PERSPECTIVE

Adults are often baffled about the reasons for children's behaviour especially when that behaviour poses problems for the adult. Think about it – do you and your colleagues have long conversations trying to fathom why this child or adolescent is so cooperative or thoughtful.

In the search for reasons for unwanted behaviour, adults are usually looking for something that will make sense from their own point of view. Louisa Leaman (2005) offers an insightful phrase when she talks about the need to 'make sense of senseless behaviour'. Leaman focuses on highly challenging behaviour in schools, but her point is general: helpful adults need to go beyond what seems obvious and rational to them.

If adults listen, they will hear the perspective of children and young people

Brain development and emotions

The human brain is driven by chemicals and electrical impulses. Strong emotional states provoke chemical changes in the brain. By middle childhood, the experiences of early childhood have already set up expectations and patterns. The impact of cortisol, a steroid hormone, is discussed on page 37.

Disruptive early experiences leave their traces on children and practitioners who work with boys and girls in middle childhood observe the difference between individuals. Some children bring experiences that make it easier for them to guide their own behaviour. Some of their peers visibly find it much harder to stop and redirect themselves. These children are at a disadvantage, especially in a school classroom that requires a high standard of cooperation and compliance (see page 173). The children who struggle and need some specific guidance may also be swift to interpret the actions of others as a potential threat. They have learned to protect themselves – attack is the best form of defence.

Body chemistry and adolescence

Whatever the nature of earlier experiences, all children experience the inevitable shift that is part of further brain development over adolescence. Karen Evans (2007) offers a readable explanation of these complex events in the brain. There are significant changes in the human brain over this period, as it reorganises the connections between processes of higher order thinking, the ability to reason and a sophisticated awareness of emotions. As the physical changes of puberty take hold there is another surge of chemicals within the adolescent brain. These sex hormones are crucial for the changes that turn boys and girls into young men and women. In the meantime, the changing body chemistry makes for intense emotions and mood swings. For some individuals this process is well underway before they reach adolescence in terms of years.

- The sex hormones directly influence serotonin and other neurochemicals that are a normal part of body chemistry and which regulate mood. Adolescents experience surges of these chemicals which contribute to risky behaviour and a desire for excitement without much reflection on the consequences.

- The problem is that the heightened sensation-seeking coexists with relatively immature judgement about weighing up consequences and risk assessment. Karen Evans offers the image of driving to sum up the reality of adolescence: high horsepower in terms of impressive cognitive skills, aligned with poor steering, in terms of emotional immaturity and shaky links between rational thinking and the feelings of the moment.

- The struggle not to behave 'like a complete idiot' is that much harder when adolescents are together. A group of friends of either sex tend to encourage the sensation-seeking and risk-taking and jointly ignore the awareness of consequences. Regular use of alcohol and drugs creates a volatile, often dangerous combination.

- Even the most 'sensible' of adolescents will show a pattern of emotional highs and lows for no obvious reason – even to them. The 'best behaved' of adolescents will sometimes realise they have done something they know to be foolish or wrong and could not seem to stop themselves.

Hormones do not directly change behaviour, but they do influence how individuals express themselves by action in a social situation. It is unhelpful if adolescents are simply excused on the grounds of body chemistry. Supportive adults – professionals and parents – need to be clear about the consequences of the wrong choice, but then help young people with the aftermath. Part of the help is about 'how are you going to stop yourself next time?' It seems very likely that adolescents who better manage the tightrope have positive experiences to draw on from earlier years. Adults have helped them to understand, recognise and regulate their emotions. However, all young people need strategies for handling peer pressure towards actions they will regret tomorrow or genuinely dangerous behaviour.

Basic drives and needs

Abraham Maslow (1943) developed a hierarchy of needs model to explain human behaviour and his ideas have been applied in many contexts, frequently for adult behaviour at work. Maslow worked in the United States from the 1940s and at that time his approach offered an alternative to Freudian or behaviourist theories (see Chapter 2). Maslow came to be seen as the founder of humanistic psychology, with a powerful focus on well-being and peak experiences, rather than abnormal and problematic behaviour. Maslow was influenced by contemporary thinkers, including Alfred Adler, whose practical ideas are discussed later in this chapter.

The main idea of the pyramid model is that needs in the lower levels take precedence over higher levels and that people cannot move into the top level of self actualisation unless they are reasonably satisfied within the other four levels. At the base of the pyramid, the human biological and physiological needs are dominant. If these needs are met, at least to a reasonable level, then human behaviour is influenced by a drive to be safe and feel protected. In a safe enough environment humans have spare energy to acknowledge and strive towards affectionate relationships and a sense of belonging. When people feel secure in this way, they have a firm basis on which to build the sense of competence that supports secure self-esteem. Finally, this emotional security enables people to strive to fulfil their personal potential in individual ways.

Although the model has been often applied to adults, Abraham Maslow discussed children in the key 1943 paper. He claimed that the model was applicable in a universal way to human behaviour. Critics argue that the

```
                        ▲
                       ╱ ╲
                      ╱   ╲
            ┌────────────────────────┐
            │ Need for self-actualization │
            │ personal growth, self-expression and creativity, │
            │ individual fulfilment, aiming for an ideal │
            └────────────────────────┘
         ┌──────────────────────────────┐
         │        Esteem needs           │
         │ sense of achievement, personal reputation, status, │
         │      self-respect and respect of others │
         └──────────────────────────────┘
      ┌────────────────────────────────────┐
      │ Love, affection and belongingness needs │
      │ family and close relationships, intimacy, giving and receiving │
      │ affection, feeling part of a community or group │
      └────────────────────────────────────┘
   ┌──────────────────────────────────────────┐
   │              Safety needs                  │
   │ Being protected and secure, sense of order and limits, stability, │
   │              safety of routine │
   └──────────────────────────────────────────┘
┌────────────────────────────────────────────────┐
│              Physiological needs                  │
│ food and drink, clean air and shelter, rest and sleep, sex │
└────────────────────────────────────────────────┘
```

Abraham Maslow's pyramid model of the hierarchy of needs

ideas are more attuned to the Western, middle class sociocultural group within which Maslow undertook his work. I think you can allow for that possible restriction and still seize the insights that aid reflection about children and adolescents.

Biological needs and behaviour

The basic need states at the base of the pyramid dominate and will exert an observable impact on behaviour when they are not satisfied. If children are hungry, thirsty or sleep-deprived, their behaviour will be different from when they are not cranky from hunger or lack of sleep or feeling dehydrated. These issues were raised with regard to young children on page 56, but they also apply to older children and adolescents, who may increasingly recognise why they feel tetchy and it is that much harder to make the right behaviour choice.

Maslow includes sex as a basic physiological need. Practitioners involved with adolescents need to acknowledge that the hormonal changes of puberty will be an issue at this time, whether the sexes are together in a co-educational environment or not. Behaviour will sometimes, maybe often, be motivated by the wish to attract and uncertainties about one's own attractiveness. There is a great deal for young people to learn about boundaries to acceptable behaviour, in the quest to satisfy this physiological need (page 150).

Safety and behaviour

The development of prosocial behaviour requires that children and adolescents feel safe. It is right that school teams should take bullying seriously (page 136). Unrestrained ill treatment between peers, or different age groups, creates an atmosphere in which the drive to be and feel safe will overrule any ideal about following prosocial codes of behaviour. Some children and adolescents live in genuinely unsafe neighbourhoods and see no option but to carry weapons in order to protect themselves. Moral values about not using physical attack, or logical arguments of getting into serious trouble for carrying a weapon, will fail to overrule the more crucial human drive for safety.

Camila Batmanghelidjh (2006) explains the long-term impact on children and adolescents when they have had no choice but to look after themselves at the most basic level, and often attempt to keep younger siblings safe as well. Camila Batmanghelidjh describes in powerful detail the work that is required to redirect children whose antisocial behaviour has been created because, in Maslow's terms, they are strangers to the level of belonging and love – never mind the next two levels of the model.

A sense of belonging

So long as children are not distracted by basic needs of nurture and of safety, they will have energy spare for satisfying the need to be part of a social group. Children need to receive affection and to experience positive relationships within which they are pleased to give in return. Children and adolescents flourish with this sense of social and personal identity and it becomes feasible to establish ground rules around 'what matters here' or 'how we behave and deal with problems'. When children have a secure sense of belonging then their sense of self-esteem need not be at the cost of undermining other people.

On the other hand, if experiences work to disrupt this secure base, then the behaviour of children and adolescents may be driven by attempts to be accepted by a group. Perhaps they will behave in whatever ways will secure them group membership, even if this requires behaviour that gets them into trouble. Isolated children and adolescents are likely to doubt their self-worth.

Emotional needs and behaviour

Rudolf Dreikurs described how strong feelings could be expressed by children in ways that get their behaviour labelled as a problem in their family (Dreikurs and Soltz, 1995) or school (Dreikurs et al., 1998). Dreikurs explained the behaviour of some children through their emotional commitment to gain attention, show superiority or power, get even or seek revenge and avoid a sense of defeat or failure. Dreikurs and his colleagues wrote about these four mistaken goals of behaviour that develop when children's legitimate emotional needs have become blocked or diverted through unhappy experiences. Dreikurs and his colleagues also raised the significant issue of adult feelings: that children and adolescents were not the only ones who felt strong emotions in tense situations. Reflective adults can gain a sense of children's mistaken goals by the feelings the child successfully arouses in that grown-up.

MAKE THE CONNECTION WITH... ACCEPTABLE EMOTION – UNACCEPTABLE FORM OF EXPRESSION

The ideas of Alfred Adler, developed by Rudolf Dreikurs, are a primary source of the useful concept of acceptable emotions yet unacceptable form of expression. Considerate adults try to recognise the likely goals or purposes behind children's behaviour. Practitioners, and parents can help a child seek and gain attention through non-disruptive means. Adults can address a young child's fear of failure, creating a situation in which he or she no longer needs to cope by appearing inadequate. Caring adults are sensitive to children's feelings and help children to redirect them into acceptable and constructive ways of behaving.

Children want to feel recognised, to gain adult attention

It is reasonable for children to want recognition as an individual, to seek attention. It is only because some strategies they use are irritating to adults that the phrase 'attention-seeking' is used as a criticism. It is appropriate to be worried about a child who does not want the attention of a familiar adult. It is emotionally healthy for children to ask, verbally and non-verbally, for their parents, and familiar non-family adults, to show an interest, to play, communicate and cuddle them.

Just like other habits of behaviour, children learn strategies from very early childhood that will get them the full, or nearly full, attention of familiar adults. Some 3-year-olds have already learned to use strategies of fairly gentle touch (or tug), calling, showing and even getting up close and waiting a bit. These strategies have been welcomed by key adults, sometimes actively guided and so have been successful. However, some children have learned that quiet or patient approaches rarely bring success. Their familiar adults – at home or in poor quality out-of-home provision – do not react unless the child makes noisy, persistent and dramatic bids for attention.

The problem then is that these strategies which successfully gain a child recognition also bring adult disapproval and irritation. Some adults in the past (or present) will be part of the problem; it is their behaviour that has set off these habits. Children tend to carry their successful strategies with them to other people and places. The difficulties come with learned behaviours that adults experience as 'being a nuisance', even if it is low-level talking out of turn, bothering other children, 'showing off' or simply never sitting still.

Your own feelings, once you acknowledge them, are a useful clue to a child's underlying motivation. Perhaps you feel annoyed, unable to resist telling a child to stop fidgeting, fiddling with his pen, poking the child next to her and so on.

- Recognise your feelings and put them on the side, so that your actions work better to redirect the child.

- It will not help at all if you take the route of trying to make the child feel overlooked. She or he will only redouble the effort to get your attention with the same or similar strategy.

- Work hard to give limited attention for the behaviour you want to discourage. Give friendly attention to this child for the behaviour you would like to encourage and when there have been no explicit demands. It is too easy to heave a sigh of relief and ignore the child when she is not 'being irritating'.

Children want a sense of importance, to feel powerful in their own world

It is reasonable for children to want to feel special, to be of some significance. They want a sense of power in their own lives. Some children feel this particularly strongly and some have learned ways of satisfying this need that draw adults into win-lose power battles. Some children gain their sense of being special by performing in front of a group, having their work on display or by adults' taking trouble to ask their opinions. Unfortunately, other children take every opportunity to behave in a stubborn or uncooperative way. They may appear deliberately contrary, disobeying you for the sake of it. They go up the emotional gears swiftly and throw temper tantrums whenever their wishes are not met. You may be needed regularly as a negotiator and diplomat because children with a strong motivation for power try to boss around their peers.

Again, your feelings are a very useful clue here. If children are seeking a sense of power and importance, you are likely to feel angry or irritated, perhaps frustrated, probably embarrassed over public tantrums. In addition a major clue is that you will probably be thinking angrily, 'Who does he think he is!' or 'She's not going to get away with this!'. These feelings all boil down to 'I must win!' and you have become a fellow child or young adolescent.

- You are unlikely to change children's behaviour by making them feel insignificant. Also, trying to redirect children by harping on their youth or weak points is an underhand strategy.
- Try to avoid power struggles where possible; decide the ground rules on which it is essential to stand firm. Refuse to engage in power struggles that do not matter. Cut back seriously on what has probably become a long list of 'don'ts', and build in some realistic 'do's'.
- Look for any opportunities to give responsibility and decision making power to children in a constructive way. However, like any other approach, giving a child a responsible role is not a one-off magical trick. It may take time.
- Home in on what this child's behaviour is telling you – is it, 'I want to feel important and I know no other way to be centre stage in the youth club.'

Children want to feel accepted and trusted

It is reasonable that children should want evidence that adults like or love them, that they are trusted and accepted. If this need is frustrated, some children want to get back at people: they feel hurt, so set out to hurt others, gaining the satisfaction of revenge. Can you see the links here with Abraham Maslow's hierarchy of need (page 69) and how he was influenced by Adlerian theory?

Children who doubt that they are accepted, or feel they are unlikeable may react by saying or doing hurtful things to others. They may hurt by verbal or physical means, without apparent provocation. They may behave in ways that they almost certainly know will distress or embarrass adults, whose affection they would actually appreciate. Children who feel they cannot be trusted may react by looking sullen and unfriendly or by refusing to cooperate in enterprises where they could actually show you that they are trustworthy.

Once again your feelings are a vital clue in this interpersonal detective job. Children or adolescents are probably successful in protecting themselves by turning emotional pain towards you. You probably feel hurt, with a sense of, 'How could she do this to me?', even when you have knowledge of the background that has derailed this girl or boy.

■ It would be unacceptable adult behaviour to retaliate in words or body language that rejects the child. If you judge it is appropriate to show your hurt, take care about what you say, avoiding the 'How could you ?' accusation.

MAKE THE CONNECTION WITH... SUPPORT FOR YOURSELF

Adults really need support from colleagues, or other family members when this pattern occurs at home. It is emotionally draining to deal with children and young people whose expression of needs and feelings has been redirected in these ways. You need to talk sometimes with a fellow-adult: to release some of your feelings and to be strengthened in a sensible approach, that will work in time.

■ A child who shouts, 'I'm not your friend!' should not be answered with, 'I'm not your friend either!' Go for an alternative like, 'I'm sad you don't feel friendly towards me at the moment'. The attack of, 'I hate you, you're horrible!' can be met with, 'You hate it that I've...' (your action that preceded the child's outburst).

■ Use the consequences (page 201) of the child's unacceptable behaviour and be consistent on usual limits. However, communicate to the child that you still care for her as an individual. The message needs to be 'I like you (or love you, if appropriate), I don't like it when you ...'

■ Is this adolescent's behaviour 'shouting' at you, 'I want to feel loved but I'm so sure now that I'm not lovable'?

When the emotional damage is significant, a vicious cycle is established. Children's habits of behaviour make it less likely that adults will feel or show affection towards them. It becomes harder to believe that this defiant, hurtful child is desperate for affection. Camila Batmanghelidjh (2006) describes the emotionally exhausting work of insisting on caring about children or young people who are scared of believing they are worthy of care.

Children need to feel competent

It is reasonable that children should want to feel successful in their own world and to view mistakes as a sign they need some help, not proof of their incompetence. Some children seek withdrawal as their chosen strategy if they have not developed this confidence. Their ability to cope may have been undermined by the very adults who should have boosted their realistic sense of can-do.

Some children then solve their anxiety by a pattern of 'learned helplessness'. They cannot fail because they rarely, if ever, try to succeed. You will notice patterns of behaviour that look 'helpless and hopeless'. Children give up very easily or behave very passively, so that adults end up not expecting much of them. Children may withdraw in a more general way, even from mixing with other children. In a busy setting, especially with an unreflective team, helpless-hopeless children may fail to be noticed. They do not demand attention like some of their peers and may even be regarded with relief as the 'good' children of the group – as the one who is 'no trouble'.

Adults who work with children are usually adept at bringing out a quiet child, or one who needs a boost in confidence. However, a child who is seriously withdrawn does not respond to the usual overtures. The adult can feel helpless, inadequate or even annoyed with the child.

- Do not say or do anything that will make the child feel even more inadequate. You need to encourage every effort that the child makes – but in a low-key way. Public praise may be overwhelming.

- Make no criticisms at all and encourage any small steps away from passivity. Give the child time and plan activities that are set up to enable the child to 'succeed'.

- Realise that children in this state may reject compliments because they genuinely do not believe them. Their message in actual words or body language is, 'I'm really stupid. So you must be saying that just to make me feel better'. Continued reassurance will be necessary to deal with the message of, 'It's beyond scary to do well. It only means I have to do even better next time'.

Sharing insights with older children

No way of approaching children or young people is a magical formula. However, reflection on what needs could underpin a child's behaviour offers a new perspective and ideas for action to a perplexed and frustrated adult. Rudolf Dreikurs et al. (1998) applied the ideas to the school classroom. Part of that application to older children and adolescents was the possibility of raising with them the dynamics of feelings and their actions. Bill Rogers (2004, 2006) further developed this approach within the school environment, but the approach is applicable in after school clubs or youth settings.

- The conversation is a one-to-one dialogue between the adult and child or adolescent. The exchange happens at a calm time and without an audience. In some cases, the older child or adolescent will have persistent problems with regulating his or her behaviour. Bill Rogers describes the approach as part of an individual behaviour recovery programme in school.

- The adult may use his/her own actions to show the child or adolescent what typically happens (a process that Bill Rogers calls 'mirroring') and then asks, 'Maxine, I've just shown you what I see you doing a lot in class. Do you know why you do that?'

- The 'why?' question is to invite the older child or adolescent to express what Rudolf Dreikurs calls their 'private logic': their hidden reasons for actions and way of solving their problems.

- The answer is often a shrug or 'Dunno'. The adult carries on with, 'Maxine, I'd like to tell you what I think. I think that you want me to stop asking you questions in class, because you don't want to risk a wrong answer.'

- Another way of expressing the idea is to use the 'Could it be…?' starter suggested by Rudolf Dreikurs and his colleagues. Examples might be, 'When you clown around in club meetings, could it be that you want the rest of the group to notice you?' or '… could it be that you want me to feel embarrassed in front of the class?'

- Children or adolescents may not agree but may give what Dreikurs calls 'the recognition reflex': a nod, half-smile or wry grin, a brief look and then away. Bill Rogers suggests that the adult response is then a quiet 'I thought so' and the conversation continues.

- A firm 'no' from the child or adolescent can be answered by, 'If that's not the reason, do you know why you…?' or 'how come you…?' (brief reference to the behaviour again).

The effectiveness of this approach depends utterly on how adults make the comments, body language as well as the words used. The tone has to be supportive, an attempt to get further with this intractable problem and within the time for a proper conversation. The tone must never be smug or snide – no sense of 'I can read your mind' or 'I've got your measure, so watch out!'

SUPPORTING EMOTIONAL LITERACY

Adults, who are helpful in guiding behaviour, recognise the importance of emotions – their own feelings as well as the feelings of children and adolescents. Children become more able to recognise and react to their own feelings when familiar adults have focused on the development of emotional literacy. An essential part of that process is that the adults are themselves acting in an emotionally literate way.

Emotional intelligence

Daniel Goleman (1996) focussed on adult behaviour when he developed the idea of emotional intelligence, as a counter-balance to definitions of intelligence weighted towards cognitive skills and knowledge. Goleman's stance was that emotional intelligence in adults was shown through five broad strands:

- Knowing your own emotions – the self-awareness of recognising a feeling as it happens to you, being honest with yourself about how you feel.
- Managing emotions – handling feelings so that they are appropriate for the situation. This ability to self-regulate has to build upon self awareness.
- Motivating yourself – dealing with emotions to be able to concentrate; the ability to direct and focus your feelings in a productive way.
- Recognising emotions in others – empathy includes being able to notice the social signals and tune into the emotions of other people.
- Handling relationships – social relationships depend on using empathy to support other people and respond to the emotional content.

Daniel Goleman's description of the emotionally intelligent adult provides a good description of what would also be regarded as emotionally literate behaviour. Certainly adults will not get very far in encouraging children towards emotional literacy, unless they – the grown-ups – understand and model such behaviour as a normal part of daily interactions. The other important strand is to understand realistic expectations in terms of child development – emotional literacy is a learning journey for children and adolescents.

> ## WHAT DOES IT MEAN?
>
> **Emotional intelligence**: awareness of your own and others' emotions, the ability to harness feelings to motivate yourself and to develop positive relationships.
>
> **Emotional literacy**: ability to express your own feelings and to recognise and understand the emotions of other people.
>
> **Empathy**: sensitivity to the feelings of other people and ability to tune in to their emotions – the sense of 'feeling with' and not pity or 'feeling sorry for'.
>
> **Emotional vocabulary**: the range of words to describe different emotions and phrases that can invite an expression of feelings from others.

Adult emotional honesty

Adults bring their own childhood to their emotional reactions within adulthood. Some experiences will help you to be an emotionally literate grown-up. However, some experiences will get in the way, unless you deal with them. The objective of the language of choice approach (page 153) is that children take ownership of their own behaviour and learn to make an active choice. Some of the phrases that pop out of adults' mouths are troublesome because they blur the boundaries between behaviour and feelings. They also disrupt a clear understanding of ownership of actions and emotions. For instance:

■ Some adults are keen to play the guilt card, maybe without thinking of that strategy as a choice: the pattern was typical of their own childhood. This unhelpful approach emerges with comments like, 'Don't you think that was a rude thing to say?' The focus is then on the child or young person, who 'should have known better' and is now faced with a non-question, which has no answer that will satisfy this adult.

■ An emotionally honest comment has 'I' somewhere in the sentence. It might be, 'I feel that comment came out in rude way. Can you find a better (or more courteous) way to tell me that?'

■ Adults have a clear responsibility to sort out who is feeling what. Practitioners are sometimes concerned about boisterous play and this situation needs a problem solving approach. It is not emotionally literate behaviour if anxious practitioners resolve that feeling by behaving as if the children (often boys) are being deliberately aggressive, so must stop. This approach tries to make children responsible for adults' discomfort and doubts.

Potential development over childhood

Children and adolescents learn to recognise that they have an emotional, as well as an intellectual and physical, life.

- Young children make sense of the puzzling world of emotions by watching what familiar adults are doing. This process is called social and emotional referencing. In an uncertain or unfamiliar situation, older babies and toddlers look into the face of their parent, or non-family carer. They take reassurance from a smile or a cuddle and follow at least to an extent how the adult is dealing with this situation.

- Caring adults help children as they learn about controlling their impulses and dealing with strong feelings. Very young children cannot inhibit their impulses and need adults who will help them deal safely with strong emotions. Learning impulse control and emotional regulation is not about denial or suppression of feelings. The aim is that children become aware of their feelings and make active choices about how and to what extent the feeling is expressed.

- During early childhood, young boys and girls can learn to recognise their own feelings and name them. By 5 and 6 years of age children can have built a good working emotional vocabulary: words and phrases to tell other people how they feel and to ask someone else how they are feeling. Even these young children can be adept in talking about feelings in a straightforward way and so long as the situation has not become emotionally overheated.

There is a great deal of potential in terms of what boys and girls on the brink of middle childhood can manage but that potential depends on their experiences.

- Is it safe to express feelings or are they seized by peers, or by harsh adults, as a sign of weakness to be exploited?

- Have children already learned that some emotions are more welcome to familiar adults than others? Is there a different package that is acceptable, depending on whether you are male or female?

- Are the adults in the children's social world reasonably consistent or do they have to navigate different expectations, depending on who is in charge?

> **WHAT DOES IT MEAN?**
>
> **Emotional and social referencing**: when young children make sense of what to feel or a puzzling social situation by looking at the reaction of a familiar adult.
>
> **Impulse control**: ability to hold back on inclinations or expression of feelings.
>
> **Emotional regulation**: ability to direct or redirect how feelings are expressed.

Immediacy or later reflection

It is important not to underestimate the ability of some over-threes to identify key emotions that they actually feel right now. They are also able to communicate some basic ideas about how this feeling has been provoked. Susan Campbell (2006) distinguishes between the capacity of under-fives to express themselves within direct social interaction and their limited ability to reflect in the abstract on their behaviour and what it means. I agree with this observation and have listened to many 3- to 5-year-olds who have been able to tell a peer, 'I'm cross with you, because you bashed into my castle' or to confide in a familiar adult, 'I'm a bit worried about...' Young children understand what they are saying under these circumstances and they have chosen to start this short conversation.

On the other hand, it is important not to overestimate the ability of young children to step back mentally and to talk about feelings without any meaningful context. I have observed communicative 3- and 4-year-olds look very perplexed when they have been expected to manage a disconnected circle time discussion about emotions in general. They look puzzled when the adult wants to discuss what someone was probably feeling in an incident that happened earlier in the day. If children regard the event as definitely in the past, young faces start to show irritation as well as puzzlement. It is a different matter if children want to talk about an incident; as far as they are concerned it is still current, because the event is in their thoughts. (More about small group time from page 112.)

An emotional vocabulary

Study of emotional literacy reminds us that some emotions are not at all easy to identify from someone's face and body language. It seems that human beings are able to read up to six emotions with a fair degree of accuracy and this set appears to be universal across cultures.

- The four main emotions that are usually read correctly by non-verbal communication are fear, anger, happiness and sadness.

- Another two emotions – surprise and disgust - are fairly straightforward to read.

Other emotions are simply not that easy to deduce from facial expression, backed up by all the subtle signals of body language. One person's puzzled face is a sign of anxiety from someone else. Strong emotions like jealousy or embarrassment are shown in very different ways by individuals. Uncertainty is increased if you do not know the other person and even people who know each other well still misread emotional expression.

- This is the reason that we need to talk with each other, and we help children to be able to put feelings into words. This section places a strong emphasis on ordinary, spontaneous communication between adults and children, and increasingly between children themselves.

- Some step back approaches through group discussion and story telling can support the power of daily interaction. The more useful approaches are discussed from page 115.

- However, a topic approach to 'doing' emotions one at a time, creates a life-by-lesson-plan approach, and I have rarely found active recognition in such materials that adults express feelings as well.

LOOK, LISTEN, NOTE, LEARN

It will be really useful to children if you are willing to reflect. Here are three ways of exploring issues around emotional literacy and use of an emotional vocabulary. You can use these ideas for personal reflection or, in a supportive colleague or student group, as the basis for further discussion.

1. Your own childhood and adolescence

◆ When I was younger, I realised that it was all right to show that I felt…

◆ But I realised it was not so OK to let my family or friends see that I felt…

◆ How did you work this out?

2. Your observation of a child or adolescent

◆ Recently when… (recall an event or experience) happened to (name), I am sure that he/she felt… (identify emotion).

◆ I came to this interpretation because… (words, facial expression, behaviour…).

◆ Did any follow-up conversation confirm your interpretation?

3. Your own experiences as an adult of expressing your feelings to a child or adolescent

◆ Recently when… (recall an event or experience) happened, I felt… (name the emotion)

◆ And I showed (names) how I felt by…. (your words or body language)

◆ Looking back, I feel… and I think…

TAKE ANOTHER PERSPECTIVE

Just because a set of photos or dolls is marketed with the claim that they will promote understanding of emotions does not mean it is true. I encountered one set that I call 'the Botox dolls', because their faces look frozen.

Look at visual materials of this kind, ideally with colleagues or fellow students.

▪ Without looking at the label or accompanying booklet, can you work out the emotion allegedly portrayed in this photo, poster or on the face of this doll?

- If you are perplexed, or colleagues come up with different emotions, discuss whether this resource is going to be of value for young children.

- Consider whether these materials would support a discussion with older children about how tough it can be to read emotion from facial expression alone.

Using a puppet to support talking about 'How I feel today'

Emotion coaching

John Gottman and Joan Declaire (1997) studied the preferred style of parents for dealing with emotions within family life. Gottman and Declaire looked especially at different parental styles of handling the 'negative' emotions of anger, sadness, envy and so on. They distinguished four broad styles, which are equally applicable to any adults closely involved with children and adolescents:

- A dismissive approach when parents ignored or trivialised children's emotions. Children took the message that their parents did not notice their feelings or that such feelings were silly and unimportant compared with proper adult concerns.

- Active disapproval when parents gave the clear message that showing emotions in general, or these particular feelings, was unacceptable in this family. Children were criticised for their emotional expression and sometimes actually punished for what they had said and shown.

- In the laissez-faire approach parents were accepting of their children's emotions, even when they had a negative impact. The downside was that these parents failed to guide their children in the expression of strong feelings and did not set limits to behaviour.

- A fourth group had developed a style that Gottman and Declaire called emotion coaching and this style was judged to be the most constructive.

The parents who used emotional coaching accepted their children's expression of strong or negative feelings and let the children know that their emotions were heard and understood. However, unlike the laissez-faire approach, these parents took an active role about the feelings. They explored what children might do about the situation that had provoked the strong feelings. On other occasions parents acknowledged the emotion and guided their children towards ways of expressing the feelings that were less harmful to others.

MAKE THE CONNECTION WITH…
ADULT BEHAVIOURAL STYLES

Look at the discussion on page 30 about adult behavioural style. Can you see the connection of ideas between emotion coaching and an authoritative style for parents or practitioners? Children are not well served if responsible adults step aside from impulse control and emotional regulation. However, an authoritarian punitive style is likely either to drive emotions underground or increasingly lead to confrontation between child or adolescent and the adult.

The approach of emotion coaching is a direct attempt to help children develop a sense of self-worth without a self-centred imposition on other people. Adults are honest about their own emotions and share those feelings in a simple way, appropriate to the child's age.

There are links between emotion coaching and the practical approaches from the Adlerian tradition. For instance, emotion coaching stresses the importance of separating the child as a person from the behaviour, allowing an honest acknowledgement of 'I like you, I don't like it when you...'. Furthermore, an adult acting as an emotion coach does not manipulate feelings of affection to coerce good behaviour, as in, 'I won't like/love you any more if...'

Simple talking works

Parents in the family home, and practitioners in home-like early years provision, need to comment upon what is happening in front of their eyes and ears. Adults need to be comfortable to say right from the baby year, 'You look happy – I can see you giggling'. Children learn an emotional vocabulary because familiar adults comment, 'You look excited. I can see the big spider too.' or 'That was a big bang, have you hurt yourself?' and 'You've got your sad face. What's the matter?'

Kate Ripley and Elspeth Simpson (2007) identified that primary school programmes, like SEAL (see the Look, Listen, Note, Learn box on page 86), start with the assumption that children have a secure grasp of their own emotional life. So the materials focus more on understanding the feelings of other people. However, children will struggle when they have a shaky grasp of emotions as a whole. The First Steps programme of Ripley and Simpson was developed as a catch-up programme to help school-age children whose earlier experiences have not provided an emotional vocabulary. Similar programmes are also needed if children's understanding has been delayed as the result of a disability that affects social and communication skills.

Kate Ripley and Elspeth Simpson are clear that the aim is to encourage ordinary exchanges during early childhood – a remedial programme is not needed unless matters have gone awry. They describe an approach called Feelings State Talk that practitioners need to use in order to bridge the gap of experience for children in middle childhood. The ideas evolved from research by Judy Dunn in families. Their crucial recommendation is that familiar adults talk simply and spontaneously with young children at the time about how they are feeling. I would make the connection with the unnecessary problems that result for children if early years practitioners opt for very structured group work instead of using the opportunities of ordinary conversation.

LOOK, LISTEN, NOTE, LEARN

The SEAL (Social and Emotional Aspects of Learning) project was based initially on many of the ideas of Daniel Goleman (page 77).
Access the project home page of
www.standards.dfes.gov.uk/primary/publications/banda/seal/

Choose Posters from the attachments and resources section on the right-hand side. Look at the two 'Feelings Detective' A4 sheets and use the ideas to reflect on your own practice in supporting children to become more aware of their own emotions. Here are some starter questions.

- One sheet focuses on 'Understanding my feelings' and another on 'Understanding other people's feelings'. Do you give equal attention to both of these aspects of emotional literacy?

- How young are the children with whom you spend your days? If they are under-fives, they cannot be rushed through 'my feelings' to 'other people's feelings'.

- Explore the useful idea – for yourself, as well as with the children – about the difference between what you can feel inside and what other people can see from the outside. This focus is important when children (or adults!) are dealing with confrontation; only you know that your heart is beating faster.

LOOK, LISTEN, NOTE, LEARN

If children, for whatever reason, get stuck in one emotion, like anger or sadness, then supportive adults can help by catching the times when children show an alternative emotion, like happiness. They may appreciate friendly help to tune into, 'I feel happy when...' as well as, 'I often feel unhappy when...'

I think that adults can help children with the sense of a continuum. Many children and adolescents do not hurtle straight from 'not angry' to 'furious', or from 'not at all sad' to 'utterly distressed'. There is a specific problem when this pattern has been established and the individual has no middle gears of emotional expression. Adult support for emotional literacy links with your own use of an emotional vocabulary.

Children benefit from learning that there are steps of feeling along the way from irritated, a bit annoyed, getting cross, feeling angry, getting so angry that the emotion takes over completely and you 'go ballistic'. Some children need encouragement to distinguish the feelings that come between feeling a little bit sad and being overwhelmed by distress. It also helps when adults think about the alternatives to using a non-specific word like 'upset'.

Keep a note of the times you use words like 'angry', 'cross', 'sad' or 'upset'. Your observation can be simple, along the lines of:

- ◆ When… happened (brief description).
- ◆ I said to Gemma… (the words you used, as accurately as you can).
- ◆ Gemma reacted with… (words or body language).
- ◆ I think my words helped because…
- ◆ Another time, I could adjust what I said, because…
- ◆ Looking back over my notes, I realise that I use the word(s) a great deal. I could use words like… instead.

TAKE ANOTHER PERSPECTIVE

Practitioners are sometimes most concerned about children who are quick to show anger. Boys and girls need ways to express this strong feeling and not hurt others. Some writers are adamant that practitioners should never provide resources like a firm cushion or punching bag because of the implication that the only way to express anger is physically. I disagree.

In the end you want children or adolescents to use their words, to problem solve and catch their anger at an earlier stage. But this goal is in the distance for some of them: for now, better the cushion than someone's face. You can also explore a range of safe, physical ways to express boiling emotions. Perhaps this child needs permission to have a good stamp; this adolescent will experience release from a fierce growl and close to the body fist clenching. Explore what will help yet still be safe.

However, by middle childhood girls and boys who cry easily often need some help. Helen Woolley and her colleagues (2005) found that children were irritated by peers who regularly burst into tears over play disputes. I have observed sensitive practice when adults help with, 'There's no need to cry' – said in a patient not annoyed tone of voice – 'What could you say to…' More general conversation with the child could be about, 'What else could you do about…'

When emotions are a puzzle

Disabilities within the autistic spectrum complicate a range of communication and social skills. One of the struggles for children is to make sense of emotions. Children who live with autistic spectrum disorder find it very hard to learn about emotional expression from spontaneous exchanges. There is too much uncertainty about changing expression and subtle body language. However, Simon Baron-Cohen (2007) and his team found that some children were helped with recognition of emotions through a DVD that put human faces on trains and told stories about the characters through animation.

Talking with boys too

After useful experiences in early childhood – offered equally to both sexes – boys as well as girls will be able to talk about emotions and actions in a more reflective way. The suggestions within this section offer scope for children and adolescents to be themselves and there is no suggestion that they should be talking non-stop about their feelings. The objective is that both sexes are able to use words because they have an emotional vocabulary and the ability to talk about feelings and actions.

Dan Kindlon and Michael Thompson (1999) wrote of the problems for young males who struggle to regulate their emotions and redirect their own behaviour in times of stress. There can be a circular argument, starting in early childhood, when adults believe that boys are less able to process emotions. Some parents or practitioners are less likely to use an emotional vocabulary in conversation with boys, so they have limited experience of simple links between feelings and actions. Their inability to talk like many of their female peers is seen as further evidence that boys do not understand feelings and so on. There may well be some basic biological differences on average between males and females but such differences are accentuated when the social culture is more supportive of emotional communication for girls than their male peers.

Feeling angry: feeling sad

Nick Luxmoore (2006) describes his therapeutic work with young male adolescents, referred because they get angry about so many incidents and have great difficulty in regulating that emotion. They look furious to onlookers and yet Nick Luxmoore (like Kindlon and Thompson) points out that anger is sometimes the only emotion that these adolescents have learned to express. Some furious outbursts are actually driven by distress, hurt and anxiety. Also, familiar adults in the life of some adolescents have not taken much notice until the young person has gone emotionally over the top. Like other writers and observers, Nick Luxmoore comments on the high level of anxiety among young males that emotional expression, especially of the 'softer' feelings, will result in them being called 'gay'. Despite broad social changes over sexual orientation, this fear is still a reality within the younger generation.

However, problems over emotional literacy are not restricted to young male adolescents. Nick Luxmoore observes the opposite problem that female adolescents sometimes struggle with expressing anger. He describes how young women may cry, but these are tears of rage. In his therapeutic work he aims to help them to separate sadness, crying and anger – even to the point of having a crying chair and an angry chair. Troubled adolescents can distinguish their feelings by moving physically between the two chairs.

An important lesson within early childhood needs to be that everyone gets cross from time to time. Feeling angry does not make you a bad person. What matters is how the feeling is expressed; it is not all right to unleash anger on other people and hurt them – emotionally or physically. However, emotions have to emerge somehow and lack of emotional literacy stokes up problems.

Prosocial behaviour and social skills

Chapter 4 covered the emotional underpinning to behaviour. This chapter explores the concepts and choices around prosocial behaviour and supporting the development of positive peer relationships. Children and adolescents can learn and be motivated to use social skills so long as adults coach and model those skills in daily life.

> **The main sections of this chapter are:**
>
> ✳ **The elements of prosocial behaviour**
>
> ✳ **Learning social skills**
>
> ✳ **Social relationships**

THE ELEMENTS OF PROSOCIAL BEHAVIOUR

Practitioners – and parents too – can make a significant impact by guiding children towards prosocial behaviour and a strong motivation to use social and problem solving skills. Adults need to:

- Understand the elements of prosocial behaviour. Practitioners have to be able to recognise what prosocial actions look like, to acknowledge and appreciate instances and to hold developmentally realistic expectations for different ages.
- Commit to using the skills of problem solving and conflict resolution. Children and adolescents need to observe you applying these skills in daily exchanges, not only within special sessions or lessons. Be a good role model, set a clear example to children in your nursery, home, class or club.
- Work with colleagues in a team to make it easy for children and adolescents to behave in a prosocial way and to use social and problem solving skills. Ensure you are all consistent in welcoming a prosocial approach.

What is prosocial behaviour?

Practical researchers like Nancy Eisenberg (1992), Judy Dunn (1993) and Ronald Slaby et al. (1995) have described the ways in which children's early experience can support them to develop a prosocial orientation. This pattern arises when children have learned to tune into the feelings of other people. They develop the skills of empathy. Additionally even young children can start to behave with a selfless concern for the well-being of others: a behavioural outlook of altruism. The combination of empathy and altruism leads to patterns of prosocial behaviour. Children show intentional, voluntary actions that are supportive of another child, such as offering comfort, making space, sharing toys or ensuring that another child gets a turn.

Prosocial behaviour does not evolve simply with the passage of time. I have read naïve developmental materials claiming that by middle childhood children 'instinctively' act so as to help others. If this behaviour were instinctive, then all children would show the pattern, because experience would be irrelevant. A more accurate description is that, by middle childhood, children who have been guided towards prosocial behaviour regard this pattern as the obvious and right way to behave. You observe the result of a learned habit of behaviour that does not require lengthy 'shall I – shan't I?' reflection. The behaviour is not instinctive – far from it; it has become part of this child's ordinary repertoire of actions.

WHAT DOES IT MEAN?

Empathy: the ability and willingness to tune into the feelings of other people, whether they are peers or of a different age.

Altruism: acting with a selfless concern for the well-being of others, putting the concerns of somebody else before one's own wishes and preferences.

Prosocial behaviour: voluntarily chosen patterns of actions when the intention is to care for or benefit someone else, or avoid hurting them.

Antisocial behaviour: patterns of actions which harm, or could potentially harm others, when the direct motivation is to cause distress or there is lack of concern about negative consequences.

Adult guidance towards the prosocial option depends on commitment to and consistency over values. Alertness to what someone else is feeling does not necessarily lead to considerate behaviour. If you are adept at tuning into the feelings of others, how do you use that insight? The pivotal point is whether a child, adolescent (or adult) feels it is acceptable to use someone's emotions or concerns against them. A bullying approach by someone of any age rests upon exploiting vulnerability rather than acting to help someone feel emotionally safe.

In a friendly atmosphere, children usually get along well together

How do you help?

Children learn from familiar adults and their peers, but they also make choices within the possibilities and constraints of the environment(s) where they spend most of their time. You will help by the following actions.

- Create an emotionally warm and nurturing environment. Young or older children, who have to compete with peers for the attention and affection of adults, have little emotional energy left to give to each other.

- Ensure that prosocial behaviour does not mean that children lose out to their peers. Does he who shouts loudest get to be heard first? Does she who shoves hardest get to keep the favourite bike or control this space?

- Have simple ground rules that provide a clear focus on the considerate or helpful choice (page 168). Be ready to give children simple explanations of why 'we ask – we don't just grab'.

- Explain rather than direct. Just telling children, 'You mustn't be nasty to people' is less effective than alerting them to the consequences, for example, 'I think you hurt Sam's feelings when you were rude about his drawing.' In this exchange you also help Sam to express how he feels.

- Allow time and plenty of opportunities for even very young children to be helpful within the usual routines of the day. Be appreciative of what they have done and focus on praise 'Thank you. That was such a good tidy up job'. (More on encouraging wanted behaviour from page 186.)

Promote assertiveness

It is unrealistic, even counter-productive, to imply that prosocial behaviour requires a constant focus on the needs and feelings of others.

- In a harmonious atmosphere for home, nursery, school or club there is a two-way, reciprocal quality to interpersonal relations.
- It is a laudable goal to encourage young children towards sensitivity to the personal needs, views and feelings of others, but...
- ...with this social responsibility comes a legitimate personal right that children can expect generous attention to their own feelings. Sometimes it is fine that they put their emotional needs at the top of their personal what matters list.

Such actions are not selfish; they show assertiveness – it is not always 'me first' but neither is it always 'me last'. There is often confusion over the difference between assertive and aggressive behaviour. The distinction is explored in Chapter 9 in the context of adult working relationships. Effective use of social and problem solving skills depends upon assertiveness, rather than a submissive or passive approach, and is also undermined by an aggressive pattern of behaviour. It is impossible to guide children and adolescents towards an assertive style unless you set a good example day by day. Please use this section to reflect on supporting children and adolescents to behave in an assertive way, but also consider how far your own behaviour models what you want the younger generation to imitate.

When people talk and act in an assertive way, then there is a sense of 'we first':

- You stand up for your own rights within a conversation and when faced by a someone else who wants to push the boundaries. Yet you also behave so as not to dismiss the rights and contributions of other people.
- You communicate your wants, opinions, feelings and beliefs in a direct and honest way, still allow space for the ideas and experience of others. You also recognise that all rights carry with them associated responsibilities.
- You acknowledge that you make choices and need to accept the consequences of those choices. The adult style with children or

adolescents communicates that you want to alert them to their choices – also with fellow adults.

- Frustrations are not handled by believing it is somebody else's fault. However, you do not apologise, when problems were not your responsibility.

People who take an aggressive approach are motivated by the desire to win and are unconcerned if this is at the expense of other people's rights or emotional well-being. Their outlook is 'me first'.

- An aggressive approach pushes forward this person's opinions or wants. People may be convinced they are refreshingly honest. In fact they steam roller over everyone and probably become angry about bluntness in return.
- They may be keen to blame others or find ways of avoiding responsibility for their actions. Distressing consequences for other people may be dismissed as unavoidable, just something that happens.
- People who take an aggressive approach may criticise others for being 'oversensitive' and exploit the reluctance of non-assertive peers to seem 'rude' or 'pushy'.

People, who behave in a submissive or passive way, fail to stand up for their rights – the message is 'you first' most or all of the time.

- Their aim is to avoid conflict, to please others and to feel liked. Children may be anxious to be seen as a 'good' child. Adults may worry about being called 'hard', or 'self-centred'. They act as if they believe that other people's rights are more important and their own contribution is less valuable.
- They may express their opinions apologetically or offer a contribution or preference in a self-effacing style that almost invites dismissal. They may defer to others, inviting 'What do you think I should do?'
- Once the decision making power has been placed with someone else, it is less likely that an individual with a submissive style will accept the consequences of their actions. It was not their fault, they only did what someone else told them, somebody else 'made' them take this line of action.

Helping children and adolescents
Supportive adults reflect on their own level of assertiveness, rather than an inclination to take an aggressive or submissive style. You also need to take account of what children and adolescents have learned from their family.

- Ensure that you are not swift to view children or adolescents as 'confrontational' when they have learned to express their opinions and been encouraged to disagree, even with adults. Help, when necessary, with social skills of courtesy and finding a considerate way to be honest.

- It is unacceptable adult behaviour if children or adolescents are caught in the middle between different practitioners who are unable, or refuse, to distinguish between a child who is expressing an opinion and being 'cheeky'.

- Be observant of children or adolescents who have learned to avoid confrontation at all costs. Are they actually 'well behaved' or are their habits of non-assertion making their life more difficult than necessary? Do you have to 'rescue' them on a regular basis from minor conflicts with their peers?

LOOK, LISTEN, NOTE, LEARN

Access the home page of the SEAL (Social and Emotional Aspects of Learning) project
www.standards.dfes.gov.uk/primary/publications/banda/seal/

Choose Posters from the attachments and resources section. Look at 'If things go wrong – be assertive' and use the ideas to reflect on your own practice. Here are some starter questions.

- The A4 sheet does not have an image for being assertive. Talk with children about what that might be.

- The sheet is a reminder of the language of assertiveness – 'I feel… when… because… I would like…'. In what ways do you model that emotional honesty for children when you are less than happy about the way they have behaved?

- The message of the sheet is about reciprocity – my rights and your rights – and the close connection between rights and responsibilities. How do you bring alive this abstract concept for children, especially at the younger end of primary school? The concept of 'fairness' will probably make sense to them.

- In what ways do you help children and adolescents to understand that rights are not a shopping list of 'I demand', but come with responsibilities. Children have a right to a clean and safe environment, but they need to take on the responsibility not to litter or otherwise spoil their environment.

LEARNING SOCIAL SKILLS

Understanding and using social skills are part of prosocial behaviour and depend upon choices around values of kindness, courtesy and respect. Children need practical help, and some need a great deal, about how to operate successfully in the social situation of play, conversation and daily routines. Life in the school classroom requires additional skills (see page 173).

LOOK, LISTEN, NOTE, LEARN

You are more likely to help children learn and adolescents to fine-tune social skills when you are alert to what kind of skill is at work here.

◆ Over at least 2–3 weeks keep personal notes of social exchanges in which children, or adolescents need your input.

◆ What kind of social impasse or problem has arisen?

◆ In what ways did you need to help? What form of words or actions do children need to learn and make their own, so as to ease the interaction next time?

Sharing and turn taking

Early in my professional career I was struck by how much I heard the 'share' word in nurseries and that a common problem raised by parents was that their child would 'not share'. On reflection I identified three broad types of behaviour that adults call 'sharing'. Each is a fair pattern to want children to learn, yet these are distinctly different social situations from the child's perspective.

- Sharing one-time possessions like sweets is about giving and the fair message is, 'If you're not prepared to hand the packet around, then don't eat it in front of people'. I was taught this ground rule in my own childhood and I continued to agree as an adult. What do you think?

- Children are asked to share their own possessions with siblings or other children who visit the family home. The ground rules should be that toys or books are returned to the owner. So adults are really asking that children 'lend' and 'borrow'. Please discuss other fair ground rules, given that children are sometimes ask to 'share' possessions that matter a great deal to them.

■ One of the puzzling features to young children in their first experience of out-of-home provision is that everything belongs to everyone but nothing belongs to one person in particular. This concept applies to the home of a childminder just as much as to a nursery or children's centre. This situation can be described as possessions in common.

Children learn how to share resources and help each other

TAKE ANOTHER PERSPECTIVE

Some group settings still ask that children never bring in any of their own toys or books. However, it is more usual now that ways are found to respect the importance children place on their own possessions. Perhaps:

- Children can bring in items from home and are welcome to show and talk about them, perhaps at group time. The item is then put safely in a child's personal drawer until the end of the day or session

- A designated shelf or top of a low storage system is for special items that belong to someone. Practitioners might also bring in something that is important to them. Everyone understands that items on the special shelf are, 'Look, touch carefully but do not remove'.

- A day or session within the week is the 'bring from home' opportunity and the item(s) are for sharing. These settings have clear ground rules about 'taking good care of our toys and books', so this respectful behaviour applies to personal possessions on the special day.

- Sometimes primary schools have a special time when children can bring toys from home. This session is often at the end of the week and is part of an open-ended play time. Similar ground rules apply as in early years provision.

Possessions in common

Children need to learn the social skills of taking turns on limited resources like the wheeled vehicles and of sharing out a store of materials like blocks or crayons. They also need to negotiate sharing space and adult attention – and those are also issues within the family home.

Ronald Slaby and his team (1995) were concerned to redirect young children away from aggressive patterns. They usefully redefined their goal as an adult task to coach children in specific social skills. The project worked to identify the kinds of behaviour that children needed to learn if they were to develop an assertive way of dealing with ordinary disagreements and conflict of interests in play, rather than turn to aggressive methods. The team focused on how practitioners could shift away from telling/directing behaviours, such as, 'You must share' towards modelling ways that young children could manage the social demands of taking turns. The team was also keen to enable children to handle ordinary play situations without adult help, when that became possible. So, the practical focus is to suggest and problem solve rather than step in with an adult play direction like, 'Let him have a go'.

Since grab-and-run or grab-and-hold-on-very-tight can be successful strategies, adults have to model and encourage alternatives.

- The main non-grabbing option is to ask, and adults who are regular play companions model with their own words: 'Can you spare some bricks?', 'Have you finished with the string?' or 'Can I get my car on the road too?'
- You can start these strategies with children younger than 2 years, but you do not expect them to be able to use their words in this way yet. With older twos, and increasingly with over-threes, you guide by, 'We use our words; we don't just take. How about you ask Donna...?'

It is no fun, if being a 'good' child around here means that you have to hand over a toy as soon as someone asks. Ronald Slaby and his colleagues noticed that cooperative children sometimes gave a toy, or significant amounts of a resource like bricks, and brought their own play to a sudden stop. These children looked unhappy and when asked what had happened, they explained along the lines that, 'He asked me nicely, so I gave it to him'.

- Adults need to model what I call a 'nice no': friendly phrases like, 'I'm using it', 'I'll tell you when I'm done' or 'I can spare some... but not any...'
- Show how to offer deals and trades, for instance: 'I need lots of blue bricks, but you can have any other colour', 'I'll swop you this car for your truck' or 'Your train can go on this track. But I'd like my trains to run on this line.'

These practical ideas also rest upon how you resource and organise the physical environment indoors and outside.

- It is far better to have generous amounts of good quality materials, like building blocks, that can be used in many different ways, than to buy single toys, especially plastic battery-operated ones, that can only be operated by one child at a time. Under-threes especially need plenty of simple resources and containers with interesting items. They cannot wait ages for a turn.
- If you have plenty of simple play resources, then turn taking is less of an issue. You can focus on support for those times when children need to wait for a bike to be free, manage to follow the rule of 'one

99

child on the slide at a time' or occupy themselves until there is space at the sand tray.

- Sand timers provide a simple measure of time passing and the children soon take responsibility for their operation. Adults no longer have to clock-watch or police items like bikes. Children are eagle-eyed to spot a child who turns over the sand timer for an extra run for a friend. You would not have sand timers all over your nursery, club or playground. Pick and choose, with the support of the children, those resources for which this device would work.

Sharing space and territory

Sharing issues within play often revolve around space and territory. Adults can reduce the likelihood of disputes by thoughtful organisation of the physical environment and children can soon help you with what is working better, or not.

- In early years provision, any group time should be kept to a small number of children. They need to be able to sit comfortably, not be squashed up against another child (unless both of them want to be close) and see the adult, a book or puppet clearly all the time. Such times should not last so long that children exhaust their ability to concentrate and find amusement in fiddling activities.

- The considerate adult strategy is to create more space, and there is no reason why children, especially in early years, should not lie on their stomachs, resting on their elbows. For some children, this comfortable position enhances their ability to concentrate. Cushions are also a welcome addition. I have encountered primary school classrooms where comfortable areas are available.

MAKE THE CONNECTION WITH... COMFORT AND CONCENTRATION

The whole idea that 'good sitting' for children involves being cross-legged arises from there not being enough space. Some 7-year-olds in Sun Hill Infants explained that sometimes, 'You have to cross your legs and sit up straight. There wouldn't be enough room if you stuck your legs out and you'd trip people up.'

- In primary school, it may not be possible to resolve the problem completely. Considerate adults recognise what they are asking of children. Few adults – especially those unused to yoga – would choose to sit cross-legged for the length of time required of some children on an unforgiving floor surface.

- Ensure children do not have to sit for very long and accept that it is unreasonable to ask them to remain completely still. (I recall the bouts of 'pins and needles' in my feet and legs from my own primary school years.)
- Some children may need something to hold: Penny Tassoni's (personal communication) idea of a box of 'fiddlers' provides simple items like ribbons or small soft toys to occupy children's hands.
- Make sure that whole class discussion enables as much comfortable sitting as possible and that class time is broken up with physical movement (page 60).

Sharing territory and sorting out enough space for everyone is part of play and practitioners help by recognising that this issue is important for children and needs a problem solving approach. One option is to create turn-taking systems that ensure that children have sufficient space in popular areas or on favourite equipment. For instance, there will be limit to how many children can get round the water trolley and everyone still has an enjoyable time. If four children are the limit then four aprons or overalls can hang nearby. If the space around the tray is full, then children may like to use a queuing system by placing their personal name (plus photo) card on an agreed nearby shelf. You want to avoid multiple queuing systems, so always consider whether you actually need additional water resources besides this trolley. You will find another example on page 120.

When social skills are more difficult
In a well resourced environment, with plenty of time for relaxed play, children sometimes learn the social skills necessary for playful interactions without much obvious adult support. Their repertoire of skills only becomes obvious in contrast with the behaviour of children who struggle with relationships in play.

These 'cubbies' for personal items let children know they are valued

---

LOOK, LISTEN, NOTE, LEARN

Observe children's spontaneous play and look for examples of how they use social and communication skills, for instance:

◆ By 4 and 5 years of age children, playing with familiar peers, are usually able to pick up the social cues that tell the difference between something that is fun or serious, words that are a joke or a telling off.

◆ They are able to step mentally in and out of pretend play. Watch children literally pause the action, thrash out the next steps in the story, iron out problems over roles and start again from where they stopped.

◆ Collect examples of games in which children have generated their own rules.

Questions

Reflect on, and ideally discuss with colleagues or fellow students:

◆ What do your observations tell you about children's repertoire of social skills in play when all is going well?

◆ In what ways do your observations highlight the gap of understanding for some children?

Social play skills and disability
Children within the autistic spectrum struggle with the social cues of play and their confusion shows how much adults sometimes take for granted in the flow of undisrupted development during childhood. Children with autistic spectrum disorder unknowingly 'break' the social rules of play interaction and need focused adult support to unravel the mystery of what is going wrong. Jannik Beyer and Lone Gammeltoft (2000) explored practical ways to coach children at the mild or moderate end of the spectrum in social skills to enable them to operate as a play companion. Their work focused on managing a shared focus on objects of interest, imitation and mirroring in play and simple play 'scripts' that help children to grasp the rules of social interaction within play. See also the idea of social scripts discussed on page 218.

Theresa Casey (2005) describes the need to demystify what is meant by 'inclusive play' and shows that it has much in common with general good practice. Her report (Casey et al., 2004) of work at The Yard in Edinburgh shows how sensitive adults operate as play companions for children whose disabilities complicate their participation. Practitioners help with social play skills when they:

- provide an opening for a child to join in, when the child will not manage without this support
- provide a role for a child, for instance by joining in pretend play together
- model the play so the child can see and hear what is expected in this kind of game
- pair up with the child for play when a knowledgeable companion is needed
- make the play rules of any game sufficiently clear that child can keep up
- provide a way for children to leave a game, to ease out when they are ready.

Helen Woolley et al. (2005) observed that school teams are sometimes more aware of blocks to inclusion for physically disabled children and less sensitive to learning disabilities that have an impact on communication and social skills. The team also noted that specialist input was sometimes scheduled for break times. The children needed the sessions, but it cost them their playtime and chance to socialise with their peers. Specialist learning assistants needed to see their role as enabling children to become included in play. Without this sensitivity, children had the company of a familiar adult but became isolated from peers.

Children need time for friendships to develop

The etiquette of play

Helen Woolley et al. spent time talking with children in primary school playgrounds and showed, like other studies of play (Lindon, 2001) that girls and boys have an expert view about the social skills that matter for good play. Some children, without specific disabilities, have serious difficulty in managing an entry into play without a swift ejection by the other children. They show what their peers regard as bad manners for play: shouting and not listening, breaking the rules or being rude about the game. Children could explain the difference between being a good 'boss' of a game, when a peer had more skill or knowledge, and being 'bossy' in play, which was telling peers what to do for no good reason.

David Brown (1994) made similar observations. When children are regularly rebuffed by their peers, the explanation is sometimes that they have not learned socially acceptable techniques for joining play. They barge into on-going games because they do not know how to ask by words or hovering body language. They have not learned how to sidle in quietly or establish play relationships with individuals who may ease their entry. David Brown noticed that children with limited social skills were more likely to communicate by body language that they did not care about being ejected. However, they cared very much indeed. The 'couldn't care less' non-verbal message was sometimes supported by shouting rude comments from the sidelines or physical invasion of the play. These children were even less likely to be welcomed next time. Jackie Nunns (of Kids City, personal communication) described to me how she coached primary school boys in constructive play strategies, alternatives to 'I don't care, I'm not hurt' rejection by words and body language.

LOOK, LISTEN, NOTE, LEARN

When individual children lack social skills for play, it is unreasonable for practitioners to insist, 'You must let Mike play' or 'Don't be unkind to Ria, we are all friends here'. Perhaps if children cooperate in letting Mike play, the game will be disrupted yet again. Ria is not behaving like a friend and her peers are exasperated; they are not being deliberately unkind. Responsible adults observe what is actually happening when a child seems to be excluded from play. Practitioners will not help by assuming that the ejectors are being unpleasant or even concluding that this situation must be logged and treated as bullying.

Download the research study of Helen Woolley and her colleagues www.jrf.org.uk/knowledge/findings/socialpolicy/0016.asp and discuss the points of play etiquette that the team describes.

Collect examples when you have observed with an open mind and have some ideas about what is happening within the play.

- What was going on in the game before this child tried to join?
- How did he or she attempt to get into the game? What were the strategies?
- What was the reaction of the other children? Did they let him/her into the play and then eject after disruption?
- How did the child behave and look after the ejection?
- Does this pattern happen on a regular basis? Or was this a one-off? Will it be helpful to use the ABC method of observation (page 198).
- Does this child need some discreet help with how to join play?

SOCIAL RELATIONSHIPS

In a warm emotional atmosphere children can be ready to help each other. Practitioners simply need to create the opportunities for this mutual support to develop and spread.

Welcoming peer support

In happy early years provision it is not at all unusual to see even 3-year-olds helping out a baby or toddler. Boys and girls of 3, 4 and 5 years of age are willing to gather in a child who is new to the setting. Sometimes you do not even have to ask; individual children will move towards the new arrival, suggest what they might like play and show them where different play resources are located.

Buddy systems

Some primary schools have developed a system of 'buddies', in which children volunteer for the regular role of playground supporter, wearing a special hat or badge. Girls and boys are given support to understand the buddy role and responsibilities. Some buddies are additionally conflict busters (page 127). The playground may also have a Friendship Bench or Bus Stop: an idea developed by the school grounds charity, Learning Through Landscapes. This location is designated as the place to rest if you are temporarily without company, and the buddies keep an eye out for children sitting there. Adults are still ready to help, but this system draws on the social skills of peers.

In my visit to Sun Hill Infants I saw the Happy Hats in action.

- These are children in Year 1 or 2 (so still no older than 7 years of age) who have chosen to be on the break and lunchtime rota as play supporters to their peers. The Happy Hat children are introduced to children in reception (4- to 5-year-olds), the youngest in Sun Hill, towards the end of the summer term. The aim is to support these boys and girls when they start in the larger outdoor play space, leaving behind the boundaries of the reception play area.

- A further development, started in summer 2008, was to take reception children back to visit their early years setting. One aim was to help children with their transition into Year 1, reminding them of their early childhood roots. But the aim was also to enable children in the nursery or playgroup to meet slightly older children who could be familiar faces soon. In the autumn, the Year 1 children buddy up with children new to reception from their 'old' nursery.

- Sun Hill also has the Lunchtime Leaders, who wear a badge. These Year 2 children have chosen to commit to a term of being responsible for helping reception children in the lunch hall. The older children sit with the younger – therefore away from their own friends – and help them in any way to ease the transition to eating in a large space.

In my visit to Thongsley Fields Primary School I saw the Playground Friends.

- These are usually Year 6 children (11-year-olds) and they apply for the role. Existing Playground Friends are part of the interviewing process as it is made clear what the role entails. The training includes plenty of ideas for play and the talking and simple problem solving that goes on within the play process. The children spend time, on a rota, in the playground for the Year 1–3 children (5–8s). So the Playground Friends commit to some break and lunchtimes when they will not be with their peers.

- These older children act like mentors to the younger ones, who are pleased to have some 'big' children giving them generous attention. Some of the Year 6 pupils also volunteer to spend some lunchtimes with the Year 1–3 part of the school. They keep them company for lunch, eating their own lunch with the younger children and help in any way that is needed.

LOOK, LISTEN, NOTE, LEARN

When children struggle to cope in the social situation it is often necessary to make some structured observations to get a perspective on what is really happening. Suppose you are concerned that Stefan is often 'rough' with the other children and rarely 'kind'.

◆ Specifically, what kinds of behaviour do you regard as 'rough', perhaps deliberately causing another child physical hurt? What will be counted as 'kind'? Perhaps when Stefan deliberately behaves in a way that shows consideration for someone else.

◆ Draw up several sheets, with Stefan's name and the date at the top. Then a run of headings across the page to cover When, Where, Other Children, What.

◆ In the first column put the time and the shorthand of R (rough) or K (kind). Then add a brief description of where Stefan was at the time, the other children with him and in brief what he did that was rough or kind.

◆ Keep an accurate tally of these two kinds of behaviour over at least a week. If more than one practitioner is involved, then initial each observation.

Look at the observations and see what they tell you. Ideally discuss them with a colleague if you work together in a room. For instance:

◆ Is Stefan actually being rough or does he have a limited idea of how to join play?

◆ Will it help to have a personal photo card that reminds with, 'I ask "Can I play with you?"' If he barges in, you can remind with, 'Stefan, do you want to play with Gayatri? What do you say?' and show his personal card.

◆ Does Stefan know the names of the other children, does he use their names?

◆ Does Stefan gain acknowledgement when he behaves in a kind way? Are adults noticing by words, 'Stefan, that was kind when you…' and non-verbal messages like smiling?

◆ Are there times of the day or particular activities when Stefan has extra trouble making the right choice? Does he need an adult close by or, with help, can he follow the lead of a child who can cope?

The Circle of Friends

This phrase is used in different ways (see page 126 for another example). The strategy of creating a circle of potential friends was developed in Canada as one way to promote the inclusion of children with disabilities.

You can read about applications in the UK for autism in Penny Barratt et al. (2003) and the inclusion of visually impaired students on the RNIB site www.rnib.org.uk

The Circle of Friends is established for a child or adolescent who has serious difficulty in making friends in school or another setting.

- The Circle is led by an adult, who may be the child's key person/support assistant. The focus child needs to understand how the Circle could work and give informed consent; the approach is never imposed.
- The other children who join the Circle are volunteers who understand their role and the time commitment. Their parents are also informed about the initiative and what is involved for their son or daughter.
- The Circle meets regularly, usually weekly with the adult and focus child. The aim is to offer friendly support to the focus child in social situations and to provide the specific help needed by this child. The meetings are a chance to discuss progress and resolve any problems.

The adult is crucial as a facilitator to welcome positive but accurate feedback from the Circle about the focus child. Reports of Circles describe that the focus child's peers are adept at giving credit for positive behaviours. This ability means that, with the adult's continued help, problematic behaviour from the focus child was discussed in a constructive way.

Intervention groups

Some primary schools offer direct help to children who have difficulty in building positive relationships and whose struggles spill over into problems shown through their behaviour. The Durham County Council Behaviour Support Service developed the *Getting Along* initiative for primary schools. I am grateful to Sue Walker who showed me the materials in 2003.

Getting Along was a weekly programme lasting ten sessions in which a group of children experienced stories and other activities. The aim was to show ground rules of communication and courtesy and encourage friendly relationships between the children. The crucial planning element was that the group was not exclusively children who had trouble making friends. The Behaviour Support team worked with children's teachers to identify children who were able to provide a positive role model over turn taking and talking comfortably about feelings. The advice from Durham is to create a ratio of two children with relationship difficulties to four children who are at ease socially. This ratio helps, along with the way that the group is introduced, to establish that the special group has positive status and is not for social losers or 'bad' children.

Inclusion for all

Schools and other group settings are required to make reasonable adjustments to enable inclusion. However, the impact of emotional and behavioural difficulties (EBD) can be significant and sufficient resources are not always provided. Please read this section carefully, more than once if necessary, and discuss the issues with your colleagues and fellow students. See also Lindon (2006b) for a thorough discussion of a holistic approach to equality, with all the dilemmas that can arise, and see page 213 of this book for further discussion of EBD.

Children and adolescents can be understanding and insightful of the difficulties of a peer whose disabilities show through communication, emotional or behavioural difficulties. It is not, however, acceptable for adults to expect them to tolerate high levels of disruption, nor to be scared because the adults cannot contain this child's unpredictable outbursts (as happened in one primary school I knew). Nor is it acceptable that a school has to cope without necessary additional practitioners. In another primary school (described to me) the only way to ensure safety, let alone calm play enjoyment for all, was for the head and deputy to take turns as the close companion of one child in the playground.

Children and adolescents in school or out-of-school provision are reasonably accepting of adjustments to expectations of behaviour when they know their peer cannot meet the usual standards. But there are limits to tolerance if a disabled peer is judged to be given more than fair slack. Some years ago I listened to a group of secondary school students who wanted staff to 'sort out' the careless driving of male peers in their motorised chairs. Exasperated students were not making offensive remarks about disability. They objected to being run down in the school corridor: with disability rights come responsibilities.

Children or adolescents who are keen to be thought well-behaved can be concerned about objecting to the behaviour of a disabled peer. I encountered wise practice in one primary school where the staff had noticed that Anya (not her real name) with Downs Syndrome frequently poked and shoved her peers. All the indications were that Anya understood this was not acceptable. The children on the receiving end were loath to comment. They needed to be told it was right to speak to Anya as they would to any other peer: with the hand up 'Stop' gesture and words of, 'Anya, don't poke me' or 'Stop it, Anya. No shoving.'

TAKE ANOTHER PERSPECTIVE

It is appropriate that children and adolescents understand the impact of specific disabilities on their peer, for example that 15-year-old Danny lives with Tourette's Syndrome. Danny's peers need to understand that he cannot control his frequent verbal and behavioural tics, nor the rare outbursts of offensive language. It is not acceptable that they get angry with Danny for something he cannot control.

However, it is fair that his fellow students can sometimes express their feelings – in a courteous, assertive 'I' statement – and this release may help them be more patient. It might be, 'Danny, no offence, but I'm going to have to go to the other table. I just can't concentrate with you moving about next to me' or 'Danny, I know you haven't got that Stop button in your head. But I have to say, it really hurts when you call me a...'

What do you think?

Help with social skills for everyone

Primary and secondary schools have always had a strand dedicated to personal and social development, although that part of the formal curriculum has varied in official label and prominence. More recent national initiatives have come in through the focus of emotional well being and/or concerns about the behaviour of children and young people.

PSED in the school curriculum

The Social and Emotional Aspects of Learning (SEAL) project started in English primary schools but has now extended into the secondary years (DCSF, 2007d and 2007e). Evaluations of programmes like SEAL (OFSTED, 2007) highlight that good materials alone will not overcome a mental barricade that PSED is not part of a teacher's job. Without strong leadership from a senior member of the team, the risk grew that the programme was dismissed as 'yet another initiative'. Teachers in secondary school appeared to need even more convincing that such a programme would not take time and energy away from academic achievement.

Programmes like SEAL work when practitioners have been given thorough guidance in not only the details but also the concepts underlying this kind of approach. Over time the most significant impact in the successful programmes is the change in adults' outlook, which in turn makes a difference to daily life for pupils or students. There were changes in how behaviour was approached, including the greater involvement of pupils/students in how behaviour policy worked. Where practitioners became more able to adjust their style to acknowledge the social and emotional aspects of behaviour, they developed more constructive teaching methods. (Access the examples on pages 14–15 of the OFSTED evaluation).

Circle Time

The idea of the Quality Circle was one part of the approach William Deming used to establish total quality throughout a commercial organisation. Deming was an American statistician whose ideas about quality in production were initially embraced by Japanese companies when he went there in the mid 1940s. Deming's Quality Circle is a group of 8–10 people who meet regularly to discuss improvements for the workplace, production and motivation of the workforce. Jenny Mosley (1996) developed the concept of Quality Circles as part of her whole school approach to quality in this kind of organisation.

Jenny Mosley describes a holistic model which includes regular meetings of the staff and similar Quality Circles that include representatives of the children and parents. The Circle Time experiences for children were part of this whole approach and 8–10 children was also proposed as the maximum group size. The original aim was to provide regular (weekly) listening times when children could talk about what mattered to them currently. The Circle Time games and exercises were designed to foster a sense of community within the primary school class. However, much like William Deming's original vision, the Circle Time approach in school has sometimes been thinned beyond recognition. In the rest of this section I have written circle time in lower case, to make it clear that I am talking in general about this kind of approach.

LOOK, LISTEN, NOTE, LEARN

Access the home page of the SEAL (Social and Emotional Aspects of Learning) project
www.standards.dfes.gov.uk/primary/publications/banda/seal/

Choose Posters from the attachments and resources. Look at 'Are we ready for circle time?' and use the ideas to reflect on your own practice. Here are some starter questions.

- ◆ Notice that the language is that of 'our classroom'. How young are the children with whom you use a version of the circle time approach?
- ◆ If they are younger than the first year of formal school, then have you adjusted your expectations to be developmentally appropriate?
- ◆ The ground rules sum up respectful communication in any group situation. Are these guidelines noticeable in practice outside circle time sessions?
- ◆ One issue listed is, 'What targets and goals will we agree?' How much input do the children have into the goals? Does the forward plan for circle time change in the light of what concerned or enthused children this week?

A great deal depends on adult behaviour and realistic expectations.

- ▦ A thoughtful gathering time can support a positive approach to behaviour with children who are at least 3 to 4 years of age. Group discussion is not suitable for under-threes. I have seen alleged circle time with a large group of 2- to 3-year-olds and the result is mayhem, with completely avoidable 'behaviour problems'.

- ▦ Practitioners need to be sensitive to the basic skills needed for three to fives. If children struggle with communication in a group, it means they need more personal approaches, not that they are posing a behaviour problem to the adults.

- ▦ Any focused time has to be carefully facilitated and the group has to remain small. Even older primary school children will struggle to maintain attention in a large group or recall what it was they wanted to contribute when they originally put up their hand. When practitioners try to run discussion with a huge circle of children, then positive social skills are not promoted. Children learn persistent shouting or to remain quiet and daydream.

- ▦ You help children learn the skills through your good example, by recapping and encouraging children and through the range of activities (not too many) that occur within circle time.

- ▦ When children feel comfortable in the group they sometimes reveal confidential family matters or concerns that need a one-to-one conversation. Practitioners need to be adept at thanking a child for a contribution but closing that line of conversation, for instance with, 'Tracy, that sounds rather personal to your mummy. You and I can talk some more about that later.'

Hilary Cremin (2002) describes the potential value of well-run circle time. However, she also points out the disruptive effect if practitioners fail to set a good example about listening and respecting everyone's contribution.

- Hilary Cremin gives examples of practitioners who disobey the circle time rules of communication. I have watched group times in which the practitioner has interrupted children or broken off the discussion without warning to talk with a colleague. Such behaviour is disrespectful and children soon lose interest, even those who are keen to make their contribution.

- Small group times can be shaped by a flexible adult plan and there are now many books with ideas for circle time activities. But resources have to be used wisely. Hilary Cremin observed that circle time was counter productive when practitioners persisted with their session plan regardless of children's interest and unkind behaviour between children within the circle that needed to be addressed.

Talking about events and behaviour

Vivian Gussin Paley (1998, 2004) described in observational records of her kindergarten how much young children were motivated to talk about what happened in their play, including problems. These 3- to 5-year-olds were keen and able to talk around issues with a supportive and listening adult. A come-together time can be enjoyable as children reflect on what has happened today. In Sun Hill reception class the key groups came together at the end of the morning and the afternoon. Children shared highlights of their play and what they judged they had learned from it – the times were called Learn-its – and the practitioner made notes for the child's personal file.

In Sun Hill this small group time was also children's opportunity to raise anything they wanted to discuss. During my visit, the children in one key group wanted to talk about a confrontation between two children that had happened earlier in the day. The disagreement had become heated and an adult had needed to intervene to resolve the conflict. This event was important to these 5-year-olds and they really wanted to explore issues of what was right, what was wrong and why. The adult leading the group was flexible to the moment and supported a discussion. She was also sensitive to the fact that the conflict had been resolved; the conversation was respectful to the two children directly involved.

Small group time should never be used by adults to criticise children for how they have behaved earlier that day or week. I once watched a mat time, with many three to fives squashed on to the surface, and became increasingly uneasy as the practitioner used the opportunity to complain about how named children had been troublesome during this session. If no firm words had been expressed at the time (I had not observed the actual incidents), then now was too late. The two children in question (boys) looked unmoved about the nagging. The rest of the group became increasingly fidgety and was less than enthusiastic when the practitioner finally got around to something pleasant.

I think it is also important to be careful about highlighting individual children for positive behaviour within circle time. This approach can work, so long as you ensure that every child gets a positive mention on an even-handed basis. Any visual like a 'kindness tree' needs to have everyone's name on for something in the end (page 194). Circle time discussion is an ideal opportunity to make positive comments for the group as a whole. You might say, 'I was very proud of you yesterday. You showed all those grown-ups that James Street Club knows how to behave in a theatre.' You can also flag up improvement like, 'I've been watching the chase games at break time. You're all taking good care as you play. No more crashing into people – well done!'

Once children are confident about how a small group conversational time works, they may want to raise issues that need resolving in an early years setting. This discussion – which would be a 'kitchen table' conversation in the home of a childminder – is complementary to individual conversations. The guided conversation of small group time enables five to eights to become more at ease in open discussion. Older children are then able to raise issues in classroom or club meetings. They can problem solve their way through disagreements and diverse points of view in school council, even serious problems like bullying.

Puppets, dolls and stories
Circle time may offer open discussion but is often used for what I call the step back approaches to emotional literacy and social skills (page 81).

- Sometimes younger children find it easier to talk through a familiar puppet. I have known older children who still like to hold on to the puppet, although they may no longer speak through this prop. Sometimes Teddy evolves into a constructive way to show, 'I've got the floor for now. It's my turn' and works like the Talking Stick that passes around some groups.
- Story telling sessions need the same ground rules as circle time. In the story creation that I watched in Sun Hill, the practitioner was careful to ask for quiet, 'to show (name of child) that we are respecting her idea.'

- If you use a puppet to tell a story or special characters like an Empathy Doll (www.earlyideas.co.uk) then make sure that the fictional experiences are balanced. It may be counter-productive if their stories are full of Big Problems and Worries. Adventures and narrow escapes are a different situation.

- Persona Dolls (www.persona-doll-training.org) were developed with explicit anti-bias aims. The dolls, with their personal back story, can be used to help children (minimally 3- to 4-year-olds) to consider the perspective of children who look different from themselves or whose life is not the same. However, the wise approach is to create some common ground, alongside exploring that this doll faces situations that are frustrating or distressing. The aim is to evoke empathy and not pity.

TAKE ANOTHER PERSPECTIVE

A favourite puppet or set of soft toys can be an important addition to a nursery, school or club. In Sun Hill Infants children told me how much they liked the chance to take the class puppet back home for the weekend. In Thongsley Fields Primary, the head Rachel Meyer has a basket of soft toys in her office. Children are welcome to borrow them and even the oldest boys have been known to clutch one throughout break time. A favourite large puppet took his SATs (national tests for England) with the 11-year-olds in summer 2008.

Some materials make ambitious claims for boosting self-esteem or positive behaviour from the combination of props and ready-made lesson plans. It is wise to recall the difference between talking about moral judgements and values (page 25) and what a person actually does when faced with a similar situation.

- I have encountered unwise practice in schools where adults regularly patch up, rather than problem solve conflicts in outdoor play. The justification is that there is never enough time in the playground, so practitioners postpone any discussion until a later circle time.

MAKE THE CONNECTION WITH...
ACTUAL EVENTS

There is a phrase used in playwork that:

Play enables children to learn what cannot be directly taught by adults.

Relaxed time for play seems to contribute to children's social understanding. Many schools have embraced indoor social skills programmes and ideas from the range described in this chapter. Children need significant opportunities to apply these social and problem solving skills within non-classroom life. Play is a prime focus of when children need to use skills of turn taking, leading and following, negotiation and talking out 'How can we solve...?'

Practitioners need to take the classroom let's-talk-about ideas into the playground now-we-use-it environment. If the adults in the playground are a different part of the staff team, then these practitioners have to be fully involved in the whole school approach to behaviour. They need to understand and use the same listening and problem solving skills that are promoted in classroom life. They need to be confident to deal with events as they arise.

6

Problem solving and peer relationships

The ability to take prosocial options depends upon learning problem solving skills and being able to draw on that strategy, even in times of conflict. Children and adolescents will fall out and some disruption in relationships evolves into a pattern of bullying. This chapter covers positive approaches to this unacceptable behaviour that remain consistent with a focus on problem solving.

The main sections of this chapter are:

✶ **Problem solving and conflict resolution**

✶ **Disruption in relationships**

✶ **Bullying**

PROBLEM SOLVING AND CONFLICT RESOLUTION

Children can be supported from the early years to 'use their words' rather than their fists and to feel pleased and proud that they have 'sorted it all out'. This conversation or group discussion, sometimes calm but sometimes lively, is not all about problems with a capital P. However, similar skills apply when the emotional temperature has soared and the key issues are of conflict resolution.

WHAT DOES IT MEAN?

Problem solving: using the skills of speaking, listening and thinking to identify, talk around and resolve a problem.

Problem solving skills

These steps are sometimes part of a relatively short conversation, especially once children get the hang of how to resolve ordinary problems at the time.

1. What is the problem?

You need to talk, listen and think around, 'What is going on that makes a problem? What is happening or not happening?' A supportive adult has to listen to the children or adolescents. Be honest when you feel there is a problem; the children may not think there is any problem at all. Be attentive and hear when children tell you, to your surprise perhaps, that there is a serious issue they want to resolve or that their main concerns are very different from your own.

2. What might we do?

Effective problem solving is regularly derailed because people want to find an answer quickly, or else there is competitive solution-giving. Once you have agreed what the problem is, then you can have a meaningful discussion about what you could do about it. You need to generate a range of possible solutions to the problem – ideally always more than one – rather than jumping at the first proposal.

Children often have good ideas and one suggestion may lead into another. You ensure that everyone can be heard, even the quietest ones. In a wide-ranging group discussion, the ideas may need to be noted down or drawn. Some practical problems lend themselves to sketches or use of little figures.

3. What is the best idea?

Decide on the best solution out of those discussed. Talk through the possible options, 'How will this solution work?', 'What would we need to be prepared to do to make it work well?', 'What's on our side to make it work?', 'What might get in the way of this solution?' and 'How can we deal with those possible blocks?'

You reach an agreement on the best way forward. Both children and adults have to be committed to this solution, even more so when a problem is entrenched. The situation will not change for the better if an adult imposes the solution or lets one subgroup impose on another.

4. Put that idea into action

If you have a proper discussion, then there is a much better chance that the agreed solution will work for improvement. Support the children or adolescents to put the proposed solution into action and make sure you have all agreed a realistic timescale. Even good ideas do not necessarily work straightaway. Remind the children – or other adults – if necessary, what was agreed and the need to persevere and be patient.

5. Revisit

Follow up what has happened: you can discreetly monitor by keeping your ears and eyes open. But there will almost certainly be opportunities to ask,

'How do you think our idea about… is working out?' Be ready to evaluate progress with the children and discuss again as necessary. Sometimes the agreed solution to the agreed problem has worked smoothly. Then all you need to do is to be pleased with the children, alert them to the fact that, 'You had great ideas' or 'We've solved it, haven't we?' If there are still difficulties, then work through the steps again, or tackle the next stage of the problem, now that everyone feels motivated.

You have scope for active problem solving with children as young as 3 or 4 years.

- Raise with children – perhaps in small group time – that, 'We seem to have some problems in the construction area. I came across three times today because I could hear people were unhappy about something. What do you think is happening there?' You are not being critical of individuals, your approach is to bring a general problem into the open.
- Be constructive and convert comments like, 'Freddie's mean! He won't give me any room' to 'It sounds like we don't have enough space for all the builders' or 'It seems to be easy to knock over buildings when you try to move'. If there are issues around Freddie's typical behaviour, then mentally note that for later.
- Suggest that very soon, probably later today, 'I would like to do an experiment with you, so we can all find out the right number of builders for our construction area.' Then, so long as the children are intrigued (obviously), try adding one child at a time to the construction area, which is set up as usual. Let the experiment get a bit crowded and then ask individuals to step out until everyone has agreed that five builders are the limit for this area.
- Then make a notice with the children giving the visual and written reminder that no more than five builders at a time are in the area. It is also useful to have meaningful items, for example five yellow builder's hats, close to the area. As children enter they take, and maybe wear a hat. Then they replace it as they emerge. It is easy for other children to see if there are spare hats at this moment.

Bear in mind that a sensible adult response will sometimes be to say, 'Do you know, I think we need more space for our construction area. Stand here with me and let's see how we could make a wider area.' There may need to be further discussion of, 'So, if we get some more space from this side, what shall we do with this cosy corner?'

MAKE THE CONNECTION WITH...
ADULT PROBLEM SOLVING

The same process applies to problem solving between the adults.

■ Can you recognise the steps from your team meetings?
■ Can you identify some tips for better team meetings?

Problem solving and peer relationships

The basic steps of problem solving also apply to times when disagreement has moved into open conflict. The emotional temperature has risen, along with the volume of the argument. Young children cannot be expected to resolve this kind of situation without help; they run out of words and patience very quickly. However, they can be supported towards an increasing ability to problem-solve even quite serious disagreements.

TAKE ANOTHER PERSPECTIVE

Some practitioners – in early years, school and out-of-school provision – direct children to 'tell an adult' or 'come and get me' whenever there is any kind of argument or dispute.

- Practitioners want to avoid the shouting and hitting which can follow when children have run out of peaceful options, perhaps rather quickly. However, simply 'telling an adult' is not a good long-term strategy.

- It is also unhelpful if 'telling' adults means that they try to sort out the dispute, including who had what first, without finding out what actually happened.

- Increasingly, 'telling an adult' feels like the weak choice of losers. Children run the risk of being ostracised by peers as someone who 'tells on them'.

- Adults, who have not sorted out the details of 'telling', accuse children of 'telling tales' or 'always complaining'.

In contrast, children need to be confident to call on an adult when their own strategies are not working. You want a situation where even young children have learned the confidence to resolve some problems themselves. In a school or club where problem solving is established, enlisting the support of an adult is an acceptable back-up strategy. In Sun Hill the Year 2 children (7-year-olds) explained to me that adults were pleased when children 'used their initiative', meaning that 'We wouldn't run to the adults, we'd sort it out ourselves' and 'If you were in a fight (they meant verbal), you wouldn't ask "Can you help me?" straightaway. You'd try first'.

Practitioners who view themselves as partners in problem solving will be able to help children with talking through what has happened. If necessary you arrange a sit-down time with children whose disputes are not easily resolved in today's conversation (page 220).

The High/Scope approach for young children
Betsy Evans (2002) describes the High/Scope approach to dealing with conflict resolution within early childhood. This constructive model has adjusted mediation skills (page 125) and blended them with skills of emotional literacy (page 79) to be appropriate with young children. Like

other skills-based support, the High/Scope six-step approach requires that adults understand and commit to using these skills. Your aim is to help children with the immediate problem. But equally importantly you support them to learn skills of resolving problems for themselves, even when emotions run high. This section describes the process; you can see it in action in the High/Scope DVDs (page 257).

LOOK, LISTEN, NOTE, LEARN

Look through the description of the process of conflict resolution.

◆ **To what extent can you recognise some aspects of your current practice?**

◆ **Look at every part of the process. Are there some steps you tend to rush or do not reach?**

◆ **What do you judge gets in the way, or could disrupt the process? Is it time: thinking 'I have to sort this out quickly'? Do you feel uneasy, or self-conscious because other adults are watching you – or you believe they are?**

Step 1: Approach swiftly and calmly
When you hear the raised voices or see the grabbing or shoving, move across to the children. It is impossible to support conflict resolution with children from across the room. Be calm and do not raise your voice. The only good reason to shout is to catch children's attention to 'Stop!' a dangerous action. Get down to the children's eye level and do not loom over them. You may need to say firmly, 'Stefan, no hitting'. You use touch, your adult strength, wisely to prevent any hurtful behaviour between the children.

Step 2: Acknowledge children's feelings
As children become calmer (and they will not necessarily be emotionally distraught) offer simple, factual statements, ideally using each child's name, 'Tasha, you look cross and Patty, you look cross too.' Use reflective listening so children know you have heard them, 'Yes, Patty, I heard Tasha call you a rude name. Yes, it's true we don't use that word here, no matter how cross we are.' You may also need to acknowledge, 'Yes, Tasha, I understand that you were really cross with Patty. I'm going to listen to both of you. What happened here?'

Even if the reason for arguing seems minor to you, recall what it was like to be a child and what could really matter. With younger children, who do not have enough words, you use your emotional vocabulary to name the likely feelings.

Step 3: Gather information from the children

An effective problem solving process is led by listening; you show that you will not jump to conclusions about who started it or who had it first. The High/Scope model gives the sensible suggestion that the adult mediator holds on to a small item under dispute, while the problem solving conversation unfolds. A larger item can remain secure, while everyone involved keeps a hand on it.

You are impartial, so children feel confident they will all be heard. You ask open-ended questions like, 'What has happened?' or 'What's the problem here?' With very young children you describe what is happening, 'You want the bag and she wants this bag too' and you explain, ' We have a problem here'.

Step 4: Restate the problem

The information gathering moves into a clarity around what exactly is the problem. Notice how this process reflects the steps of ordinary problem solving (page 118) in that the adult does not rush to the solution. You use the children's words to reflect, 'So the problem is that you want to play shops, but you both want to be the shopkeeper?' You help them talk to each other with, 'Tasha, I think Patty felt hurt that you didn't like her idea about…'

If you are not sure, you can say, 'Patty, have I got that bit right?' If a child tells you, 'No, that wasn't it at all!', then say, 'I'm sorry, Tasha, have I misunderstood here? Please explain again.' You help children to communicate, to talk and listen their way out of this dispute. When you reflect what they say to each other, you reword hurtful language or avoid using words that are unacceptable here.

Step 5: Ask for solutions

You ask, 'What can we do here to solve this problem?' or 'What do you think we could do? We need some ideas.' Listen to what children suggest and avoid filling natural pauses with your ideas. Of course, you do not all sit there for ages in silence. You can ask, 'Are you still thinking?'

If children struggle to come up with any ideas, which may happen while they are still new to the process, the High/Scope model suggests that you offer, 'I have a idea. Shall I tell you my idea?' This approach may also be useful if children are competing over their preferred suggestions. The aim is to create calm time, so that children can find a way out of this situation and nobody feels like the loser.

Step 6: Be prepared to give follow-up support
Some situations can be left, maybe with a friendly eye and ear from the adults. Others need a bit more help and sometimes it feels right to say, 'How is it going with your idea about…' On a regular basis, maybe not every single time, make sure that you show you are proud of how well they talked and listened, 'because that was a tough problem to solve about…'

LOOK, LISTEN, NOTE, LEARN

Wise adults keep observant about the pattern of this kind of problem solving. It is not all right if disputes regularly get resolved because one or two children are willing to compromise and others scarcely give any ground. You can comment factually without being critical of individuals. Perhaps you say, 'Ciaran, that's a possible idea. But I think we've solved quite a few problems this week by you saying Tom can have first go. Let's see if we can find a different way today.'

The skills of mediation
The High/Scope model starts from early childhood and, in settings that use this approach, children of 3 and 4 years become able to sort out their own minor disputes. They are still likely to need adult help with major or long-running confrontations. The adult role is that of an impartial, trustworthy mediator (Lindon and Lindon, 2008). Mediators are seen to be fair because they offer an opportunity for each person in a conflict to be heard in turn and to listen to the other person. The mediator does not take sides so individuals are supported through the steps of problem solving and reach a solution that everyone agrees to be a mutually acceptable way forward.

The children of Sun Hill Infants usually start school with a confidence in language that makes them ready for talking out problems. However, children do not manage to sort out every dispute and the adults are ready to help in an active way. If the problem has become quite serious then the head, Kim Owen Jones, explained that she speaks separately with the children involved, who are sometimes friends who have fallen out with each other. Attention is given to both children and their views of what happened. Children who, given the facts as gathered, seem to be the source of troubles are encouraged to realise the impact of their behaviour. However, children on the receiving end are also asked how they have handled the problem so far. If a child has done nothing other than put up with the problem or get distressed, alternative strategies are now discussed. Then there is a meeting with both children with a chance for the child on the receiving end to express their feelings about the incident of unkindness or other trouble. There is then a discussion about what will happen next.

Older children are effective
playground helpers

A slightly different approach is used in Sun Hill when a child's behaviour has annoyed or distressed several children. This disruption in relationships, often in play, is handled within a group meeting, which the school calls the circle of friends (a different meaning to page 108). For example:

- The group is composed of all the children who are named by a child as not being willing to let him or her play, or children who have complained about the play behaviour of this child. The focus child sometimes disrupts play because of limited play skills or bringing in worries from family life.

- The group meets several times, facilitated by the head. Children are helped to talk around their different perspectives on what has happened, how individuals could behave differently, including possible strategies to use next time. Later, children can discuss how their alternative strategy is working.

In the Sun Hill circle of friends approach Kim Owen Jones is willing (and I think this is wise for the adult role) to raise the tough issues for children about how much do you want this child for your friend in play if s/he does not behave like a friend. The focus child is helped to see the consequences of continuing on this path: that other children will not welcome her/him as a play companion.

Support for problem solving through guided conversation can work even with older children and adolescents whose life has been far from easy. Belinda Hopkins (2008) offers a set of questions which guide conflict resolution in residential care settings where the team has made a commitment to the restorative approach:

- What's happened?
- What were you thinking as this happened? And now?
- What were you feeling at the time? And now?
- Who else has been affected by what happened?
- How can the harm caused be repaired?

Peer mediation and problem solving

Conflict resolution initiatives with children and adolescents started in the UK in the 1980s with the work of the Kingston Friends Workshop Group (Rawlings, 1996). Mediation skills have successfully been taught to children and young people, often as part of the personal and social element of a school curriculum. Look at summaries from William Baginsky (2004), Hilary Stacey and Pat Robinson (1997) and Hilary Cremin, previously Stacey (2000). The approach extends into additional support for older primary school children, still as young as 9 and 10 years old, to become effective playground supporters enabling their peers to deal with conflict in a non-aggressive way.

The playground buddies who are conflict busters often work in pairs and are available for peers to ask for help in resolving a dispute. Or the mediators may offer their help when they see problems. In some schemes, the mediators are available on a predictable basis in a room for peers to come and talk about an ongoing problem. The conflict buster role is not restricted to children who have always been well-behaved. Some very effective conflict busters have previously been the source of playground problems. They can be more effective for their insight into how hard it can be to make the right choice under pressure.

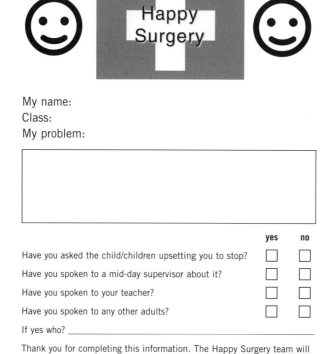

My name:
Class:
My problem:

	yes	no
Have you asked the child/children upsetting you to stop?	☐	☐
Have you spoken to a mid-day supervisor about it?	☐	☐
Have you spoken to your teacher?	☐	☐
Have you spoken to any other adults?	☐	☐

If yes who? _____

Thank you for completing this information. The Happy Surgery team will investigate your problem and we will be in touch with you very soon.

☺ ☺ ☺ ☺ ☺

The Happy Surgery form

Peer mediation schemes in secondary schools are often linked with specific support for younger students in the transition into secondary school. Look at the materials on www.betterbehaviourscotland.gov.uk Examples include organised buddy schemes with S5 and S6 students (15- to 17-year-olds) linking up with S1 new arrivals (12-year-olds), or additionally making contact with P7 (11-year-olds), the last year of primary school. These schemes aim to use peer support and mentoring to ease the transition. They may also identify young adolescents who may need help with friendships and in one school the S5 students set up a lunchtime games club.

Talking out problems

In Thongsley Fields Primary School the whole school approach to behaviour is supported by an active role for the pupils themselves. The School Council representatives explained to me how it worked.

- The Council meets regularly to discuss any issues of importance to the school. In summer 2008 they had focused on ideas for the outdoor classroom and fund raising for their trip to the seaside (a very successful event).
- They are also ready to problem-solve – an ongoing issue was about a gate into school grounds that local teenagers used without permission. A resolved issue was the football game in the older pupils' playground that 'had got out of hand'. The problem had been discussed and resolved by organising council representatives to take turns to referee the game.
- The children were in full agreement that bullying was a minor problem at Thongsley Fields 'because our school tries to sort it out'. One boy lingered behind after the end of our discussion; he was keen to ensure that I fully understood that any problems 'usually get sorted out in the end'.

The Happy Surgery idea at Thongsley Fields evolved from a council discussion about incidents between children. The Happy Surgery team are chosen by their own class and are supported by a Year 6 teacher. Children can fill in a form with any concern and post it in the Happy Surgery box. An appointment is made and the child is supported to talk through the problem. The team will have already talked with the child's teacher and in the meeting(s) they explore what their peer could do. As they described, 'We're here to listen – not to tell.'

Children explained to me that sometimes it is a case of friends falling out. More complex problems can bring in adult help and, if the problem is outside the school, then it is parents' responsibility. They were trialling a new form that enabled peers to tell and then talk about 'If you've done something wrong and feel bad'. The Happy Surgery had a few problems with pupils writing 'silly' or 'untrue' things on the forms. This event was rare but the team expressed confidence in spotting the 'pranks' and dealing with that misuse of their service.

Children are able to resolve some issues in play without adult help

---

LOOK, LISTEN, NOTE, LEARN

Access the home page of the SEAL (Social and Emotional Aspects of Learning) project
www.standards.dfes.gov.uk/primary/publications/banda/seal

Choose Posters from the attachments and resources. Look at 'Problem solving' and 'Peaceful problem solving' and use the ideas to reflect on your own practice.

◆ Notice how the two A4 sheets distinguish between times 'when you don't know what to do' and times 'when you just can't help falling out'. That second sheet links with the description of conflict resolution in this chapter.

◆ In what ways do you help children tell the difference? Are there ordinary problems (minor blips in any day) and are there Problems (with a capital P)?

- Look at the dustbin in the bottom left hand corner of 'Peaceful problem solving'. This visual message acknowledges feelings that it is understandable to have but which mess up the problem solving if you say them out loud.
- Dustbin feelings are wanting to identify whose fault it is (not mine!), or sweeping language about 'you always' or 'you never'. Does the dustbin image work for children with whom you spend your days?
- Do you and your colleagues need to use the dustbin too? What adult phrases should you 'put in the bin'?

WHAT DOES IT MEAN?

Conflict resolution: use of problem solving skills to deal with and resolve disagreements that have become short- or long-term confrontations.

Mediation: a process in which people involved in a dispute voluntarily come together to resolve the problem with an impartial third party.

Peer mediation: schemes, often in school, when children or adolescents have been trained to mediate disputes between their peers.

DISRUPTION IN RELATIONSHIPS

It is crucial that adults take bullying with seriousness (page 142). However, part of that responsibility is to avoid stretching the definition so wide that it encompasses minor skirmishes that children and adolescents are able to resolve, maybe with a bit of adult help, in the ways described so far in this chapter.

Temporary troubles

Tim Gill (2007) raises the problems for children when they are given an adult language model that defines even fleeting wind-ups as bullying. I agree with his stance that, 'Tackling bullying is a risk management problem *par excellence* (italics in original), and an explicitly balanced approach is needed at the outset. Blurring the distinction between bullying and the less serious conflicts hinders rather than helps this' (page 45). It is not being 'soft on bullying' to require genuinely reflective practice. Adults need to avoid the over-protection that leads children to believe they are incompetent to deal with peers who are less than kindly today, but may be fine tomorrow. Childhood and adolescence is seasoned with squabbles, even between friends who may swiftly get back on a friendly basis, so long as the current problem can be resolved.

Responsible adults do not abandon positive approaches to guiding children's behaviour as soon as the situation is labelled as 'bullying'. An unhelpful rhetoric around some advice, especially the aura of zero tolerance (page 143), can tempt practitioners into what feels like a decisive adult reaction. Sometimes they are anxious to avoid accusations that they condone ill-treatment. The consequence can be that adults believe they should intervene over minor altercations that children could deal with themselves and possibly were in the middle of resolving, until this grown-up insisted on taking over the situation.

Thoughtless remarks

Children need to be confident that their familiar adults understand words can hurt your feelings just like punches hurt your arm. Sometimes it makes good sense to say this phrase (similar to one used by Balham Nursery School) in conversations with children of 3 years or older. Name calling and unkind remarks deserve your attention, but also reflection about what kind of adult reaction will best help. Boys and girls whose feelings have been hurt do not usually want the other child just 'told off'. This adult strategy does not help children on the receiving end next time. Also they may be blamed by peers for telling, and not only by the child who hurt their feelings today.

Children are often told 'just ignore it' and sometimes that advice is sound (page 143). However, as a single strategy, this adult direction is unwise, because it can foist a submissive, non-assertive role on to children or adolescents. They need the option to use some verbal repartee, because this approach can help with minor wind-ups. However, it also lays a foundation of assertiveness which might foil, or at least slow down, children or adolescents whose experience has told them that empathy is only useful to identify your peers' weaknesses.

Assertive replies

There may be a connection with small group discussion or stories that have explored, 'What you could say, when…' However, helpful adults offer direct advice about the current situation faced by a child:

- A child may directly ask for help with, 'I don't like it when…'
- Or an observant adult can ask discreetly, 'Are you okay about being called "Ginger"?' You might add, 'I'm asking because your face looked "not okay".'

Unless there is very good reason to go up the gears of adult intervention, your first step is to help children with a phrase they can say in this situation. The best format is simple yet assertive and children ideally decide between a few suggestions. It might be, 'I don't like you saying that' or 'Stop calling me Ginger ' or 'That's not my name and I'm not replying to it', followed by non-response to the unacceptable word.

Straight, assertive comments will frequently work when there is a friendly atmosphere in nursery, school or club.

- Even 4- and 5-year-olds can learn the next level strategy of, 'Stop! I don't like you saying (or doing)…!', with the option of holding up one hand with the palm outwards. Rather like adults, children need the option of asking nicely once and then asking more firmly.

- Initially, you may offer to intercede for a child with, 'Tamar, please listen to us. Rory doesn't like it when you call him Rory-Pory. His name is Rory and that's what he wants to be called.' However, your aim is that Rory soon feels confident to speak up in an assertive way without your intervention.

- A considerate adult takes seriously that Rory feels picked on and does not want Tamar to call him a 'silly' name. Being picked on can lead to more sustained unpleasant name calling. But in this kind of example nobody is helped if Tamar's behaviour is immediately logged as a bullying incident.

Ground rules and values

In conversation with an adult, a child may raise what they see as a potential problem such as, 'Well I have got ginger hair, so…' You need to add, in language appropriate to the age of this child, that just because people have particular physical features or come from a particular region of the country, they do not have to accept being known by that shorthand. It is different if you have chosen your nickname. You may need to go up the level of seriousness with the child who made the remarks.

- Sometimes it will be appropriate to say, 'In our nursery (class, club) we find a kind way to say something'. Alternative words for older children or adolescents might be 'courteous', 'constructive' or 'honest but not hurtful' – which needs to be recognised as a tough balance on occasion.

- Say firmly that this word is a 'discourteous', 'rude' or 'unacceptable' way to refer to someone who is female or has this skin colour. In a conflict situation, you acknowledge a child's frustrations, whilst confirming, 'It's still not all right to use that word to Wai'.

- Children may honestly say, 'But my mum says… all the time'. Practitioners are responsible for what happens in nursery, school, club or your own home as a childminder, so you reply with something like, 'I know some grown-ups use that word when they talk about people who are disabled (or go to that church). But we don't use that word in nursery (club, etc.) because…'
- Avoid stopping with shorthand labels like 'racist' or 'sexist'; they fail to address what has arisen within the current interaction. Also you lack shorthand for hurtful behaviour that does not fit an equality heading, or you get mired in unhelpful ism-ing on every issue.

LOOK, LISTEN, NOTE, LEARN

Sometimes, unacceptable use of words between individuals raises broader issues in class or club. Then there is good reason to use circle time, a class or club meeting for a general discussion. If the connection to an earlier incident will be obvious, then ask involved children or adolescents for their informed agreement.

You can introduce the discussion along the lines of, 'You won't have missed that Maya and I had a disagreement yesterday about her use of words. We had a long conversation afterwards. Maya made some points that made me think. We both decided that it would be good for our club to have a general discussion.' Perhaps Maya is even confident to take the lead, in which case the practitioner would chair the club meeting and facilitate even-handed discussion.

Questions
- In your practice what opportunities of this nature have arisen?
- Looking back now, were there incidents that could, responsibly, have been used in this way?

Teasing or taunting?

Gael Lindenfield (1994) suggests that teasing is not meant to be taken seriously nor intended to hurt and it can easily become a two-way process. At the heart of teasing there is the desire to have mutual fun. Whereas at the core of verbal bullying is a one-way process that aims to distress or create fear. Barbara Coloroso (2005) makes a similar distinction: that taunting is underpinned by contempt for the other child or adolescent. Teasing another child can be friendly and part of a give-and-take repartee.

Adults need to listen to the verbal exchange and look at the body language, as well as check, 'Is everything OK here?'

Dennis Lines (2008) argues from his work in secondary schools that trivial teasing and banter is part of relational behaviour between adolescents and is often part of social bonding. Practitioners have to be observant and listen to the young people involved. Alert adults should be able to identify what Lines calls 'strategic name calling', when the verbal attack is relentless and the adolescent on the receiving end is clearly not part of the exchange. Then the words have crossed the line to become a 'venomous verbal assault'. An original embarrassing gaffe or local gossip about 'your mum' is now ammunition to torment and the adolescent feels laughed at and despised by 'everyone'.

Saying or showing 'sorry'

When relationships have been disrupted, the aim is that the person who hurt or mistreated a peer feels sorry, shows regrets and a willingness to make amends.

I think there should be a choice about words and actions.

- If 'sorry' is turned into a magic word then children will regard saying it as enough. They will not sound sorry because they are not at all regretful. I have known children who are starting the 'sorry' word as their fist pulls back. Or else you hear the irritated, 'I said so-rry!' with the implied message that the incident is over, so stop nagging me.
- If adults judge successful resolution by the actual word, then they can create avoidable power battles, when – long after the actual incident could have been resolved – everyone is 'waiting until you say "sorry"'.
- Effective conflict resolution is undermined if, after children feel satisfied that everything has been resolved, the adult harks back to the beginning to ensure that 'sorry' is said. This insistence is also disruptive because the mediation process so often reveals that fault is not neatly apportioned.

You can help the process of genuine regret and wanting to make some restitution through open-ended suggestions. If you use a friendly tone of voice, these comments will come across as an invitation to make amends, not as nagging.

- 'How do you think you could show Sachin that you are sorry about…'
- 'What could you both do to make things better now?'
- 'How can you put things right?'

■ 'Eva, what would help you feel better?' or 'Perhaps you could ask Eva what would help her feel better'.

It is also crucial that a 'sorry', however expressed, is accepted graciously. It is mean-spirited of adults to reply with a sharp, 'That's more like it!' or seize the apology as the opportunity to nag, 'Well I hope that means that you're not going to do it again'. Adults set a good example with any version of, 'Thanks' or accepting what a child or adolescent has done to make amends.

Some school teams ask for a written apology for behaviour that has distressed a peer or an adult. If you establish this policy then practitioners must be prepared to write in their turn when they make an equivalent misjudgement in behaviour. Also, if you require this permanent record of responsibility and regret, you must be sure of your facts. I have encountered examples, where children or adolescents have been required to write a letter of apology. Then it has later emerged that blame was far from clear cut, or they were falsely accused.

LOOK, LISTEN, NOTE, LEARN

Some adults – probably because of learning in their own childhood – feel strongly that children should be made to say 'sorry' when they have done wrong. Clearly, I believe that problems are created by taking this uncompromising line.

◆ What do you think?
◆ What are the views in your team or group of fellow-students?

BULLYING

Constructive materials place strategies to deal with bullying within overall policy and practice for guiding behaviour. Responsible adult behaviour is compatible with the problem solving and conflict resolution approaches described in this chapter. The DCFS *Safe to Learn* guidance (2007c) defines bullying as, 'Behaviour by an individual or group, usually repeated over time, that intentionally hurts another individual or group either physically or emotionally' (paragraph 4, Executive Summary). So bullying is a non-trivial pattern of unacceptable behaviour, not justified in response to the behaviour of the individuals who experience this ill-treatment. The same individual(s) may be persistently targeted or the bullying behaviour may be directed at a series of different individuals.

WHAT DOES IT MEAN?

Bullying: persistent ill-treatment, by an individual or group, that is intended to hurt the individual(s) on the receiving end, physically or emotionally.

MAKE THE CONNECTION WITH... AGE AND UNDERSTANDING

The materials referenced in this section are all about middle childhood and adolescence. I question that under-fives are capable of the deliberation that is part of genuine bullying. Young children undoubtedly act in unkind or physically hurtful ways to each other and that behaviour needs to be dealt with at the time. But the direction to step aside from terms like 'bully' and 'victim' applies to an even greater extent for early childhood. I have read magazine articles in which a writer labels 3- and 4-year-olds as 'bullies'. The suggestions for practitioner responses are then as negative as the labelling.

The dynamics of bullying

Michele Elliott (2002 and her organisation Kidscape) describes that there are no easy answers to 'why?'. Children and adolescents get into the bullying pattern for many different reasons. They are not all, as some materials claim, working off a base of low self-esteem and fragile personal identity. Some, as Michele Elliott identified, are the original 'spoiled brat', who sees no reason to moderate demands for space or possessions. Some children start on the receiving end and later start to bully in their turn. Often they were unsupported when they were harassed; now they are larger and stronger and it is time to pay back the hurt to someone else.

A problem of relationships

Dennis Lines (2008) echoes the restorative justice approach of Belinda Hopkins (2008) when he argues that bullying is a problem of disrupted or distorted relationships. The problem therefore needs a relationships solution, rather than an emphasis on punitive sanctions. He analyses bullying from the perspective of systems theory (page 25).

- This positive perspective pulls adult energies back to the interpersonal dynamics: what happens within a given bullying interaction. There is no such creature as an individual problem; there is only a problem in the system of peer group relations within a context like school.

■ Helpful intervention looks at the relationship between the child or adolescent who does the bullying, the individual(s) on the receiving end and the context in which the bullying takes place. Bullying patterns of behaviour can be changed by finding the lever into the cycle of bullying: breaking the habit of bullying and addressing the factors that support its continuance.

TAKE ANOTHER PERSPECTIVE

Dennis Lines (2008), like some other commentators, argues against creating stereotypes of 'innocent victim' and 'bad bully'. His key concept is that bullying is an activity and not an enduring personal characteristic. Please think about that idea and discuss the implications with colleagues or fellow students.

Keith Sullivan (2000) explores the triangular relationship between the observer, the 'victim' (I prefer 'target' but will stay with Sullivan's term) and the 'bully'.

■ A setting like a school is unsafe, and not operating as a community, if observers (adults or peers) do nothing or actually support the 'bully'. The 'bully' has personal power and the 'victim' has none.

■ If observers take over and rescue the 'victim', then the 'bully' loses some power. The 'victim', although safe for now, has no additional personal power or skills of assertiveness to deal with future troubles.

■ In what Sullivan describes as the genuinely safe school, the observer supports the 'victim' and enables him/her to resist the intimidation. Individuals who act as a 'bully' are involved in a process to enable them to change behaviours.

Given peer mediation and a conflict resolution approach, older children and adolescents can be active in this process.

Power and control
Jon Sutton (2001) points out that children who take to bullying are not all aggressive individuals unable to process the signs of other's distress. Some children who bully are far from being socially unskilled, in fact they use their high alertness to manipulate their peers. They are not all 'thugs'; some are very effective 'thinkers' and the problem arises from how they use that

knowledge. Jon Sutton suggests that training in greater empathy is not effective with this motivation towards bullying. The question is less, 'How would you feel if someone did that to you?' and more, 'How would you feel if you did something different instead?' There are parallels with the mistaken goals approach (page 71) since bullying may satisfy desire for power and control.

Children may feel powerless in their life, perhaps especially lacking control and autonomy in the classroom. Then they find an easy route to a sense of dominance by bullying their peers in the playground. Dennis Lines (2008) highlights the over-control and dominance motivation behind some bullying behaviour. He points out how schools, especially those with unreflective teams, offer fertile ground for bullying to develop. Schools are hierarchical institutions and power dynamics operate within the staff group and between staff and students. The schools, or other group settings, that are most effective in dealing with bullying operate more like a community than an institution (page 142).

MAKE THE CONNECTION WITH...
WHO IS PULLING THE STRINGS?

Bullying by its nature involves an imbalance of power: one person successfully intimidates or distresses someone else. However, the child or adolescent who bullies does not necessarily look powerful to the outsider adult.

Sharp observation, the perspectives of different adults and listening to children and adolescents can all show that the dynamics of a situation are very different from surface appearances. The moving force in a bullying situation may be a child or adolescent who operates behind the scenes; he or she stirs up or misinforms the peers who instigate the actual bullying. Some socially adept, but highly manipulative, children or adolescents operate almost like a puppet master.

Targets of bullying

Behaviour that one person claims is 'teasing' can indeed cross the line into intentional unkindness, even a distinct pleasure in creating embarrassment for the targeted child or adolescent. Rough and tumble play can slide into, or be subverted into physically aggressive actions. The significant difference is whether peers stop, when a child or adolescent says they do not like this teasing or horseplay. An insistence on continuing then crosses the line into the bullying zone.

Verbal cruelty can be a direct attack on a child's ethnic group identity, an adolescent's gender or presumed sexual orientation. But verbal bullying or physical attack may target wearing glasses, being adopted, having a parent with mental health problems, a relative in prison – the possibilities are endless. This form of persistent attack may be face-to-face, but may also be carried out in a covert way by spreading gossip, rumours and outright lies. This kind of behind-your-back attack now uses the many technological possibilities (page 151).

MAKE THE CONNECTION WITH... WORDS HURT TOO

Previous generations of children were deeply unimpressed with the adult cliché starting with 'Sticks and stones'. This poem was part of the South Lanarkshire pack *Bullyproofing our unit: addressing bullying in children's units* (2000, Hamilton: South Lanarkshire Council) and is reproduced here with permission.

Sticks and stones may break my bones,
but words can also hurt me.
Sticks and stones break only skin
while words are ghosts that haunt me.
Pain from words has left its scar
on mind and heart that's tender.
Cuts and bruises now have healed,
it's words that I remember.

Dennis Lines (2008) points to the inconvenient truth that there is a role of 'provocative victim'. Responsible practitioners should not ignore this possibility.

- Some children and adolescents show a pattern of almost inviting trouble. Observational tracking by practitioners may show that this child or adolescent is frequently on the receiving end of bullying-type behaviour from peers.
- Serial 'victims' may show a pattern of learned helplessness, seeming to be pleased for any full attention, even from peers who treat them in a contemptuous way. Unreflective anti-bullying practice can reinforce a 'victim' role for the child or adolescent who is constantly being rescued by adults.

A responsible focus on the dynamics of the situation can point to a lever for change. Understanding the complexity of some situations does not lift responsibility from children who have chosen to bully this peer. However, some children have great difficulty in distinguishing lively banter, which may still be close to the edge, from socially unacceptable remarks. Adult help is often best aimed at support for some repartee and for social skills of interaction. Sometimes children or adolescents who have been very distressed by unacceptable behaviour from some peers need sensitive help to distinguish now between trivial wind-ups and intended unpleasantness.

Bystanders

Sandra Fowler (2004) shows that different types of peer support initiatives can make a significant different to behaviour that children regard as unacceptable and bullying. Peer pressure can work towards taking responsibility for the consequences of unkind or cruel actions and the separate responsibility of every member of a group that bullies. Peer pressure can also be mobilised for the responsibility of bystanders: that members of this school or club do not watch and do nothing or simply enjoy the excitement of a physical dispute.

LOOK, LISTEN, NOTE, LEARN

Practitioners need to move away from simple categories of 'bully' and 'victim'.

Some materials focus usefully on the role of the 'bystander' (for instance Sue Ball, 2005). Anti-bullying work in a school or club works better when the atmosphere is that of a community:

- Here we share the responsibility to do something about ill-treatment.
- You cannot be a bystander; if you do nothing you collude in this unacceptable behaviour.

Jon Sutton (2001) studied the dynamics of bullying and highlights the different roles that can be involved – not only 'bullies' but their 'assistants' or 'reinforcers'. There are not only 'victims' but also 'outsiders' and 'defenders'.

Questions

- Reflect on and discuss these ideas for your practice.
- In what ways can these roles – not labels – help you and your colleagues to get to grips with the dynamics of bullying?

Dealing with bullying as a community

Wise advice leads through application of all the social skills, problem solving and conflict resolution approaches that are described in this chapter.

Take bullying seriously and listen properly

Children and adolescents have the right to feel and be safe in an enclosed setting like a school, club or youth centre.

- Individuals who are being bullied need reassurance that adults in whom they confide will take them seriously and help them resolve the situation. They do not want thoughtless reactions that only make matters worse.

- Individuals who are accused of bullying have the right to be heard, to put their side of the story. You take it seriously when a child says, 'Martha and her friends are bullying me'. But you do not take that statement as final evidence and now refer to Martha and the other named children as 'bullies'.

- You are talking with children and adolescents – not interviewing them as if it is already agreed that bullying has taken place. You talk promptly so that you can get a clear idea from all angles. You do not assume that the children who are accused of bullying will fabricate additional information to put a better light on their actions – although this dynamic can occur.

- Children or adolescents who bully may well say they did not act in this way, or that, if you will only listen, then you would understand how everything got out of hand earlier this afternoon. Sometimes they will be spinning you a tale, because they know that what they did was inexcusable.

- Sometimes you need to challenge explanations as they are voiced. Claims of 'it's just a joke' or 'we were only messing about' do not hold up if the target visibly did not enjoy the 'joke' and was trying to escape from the 'messing about'. The pranksters did not listen or look with any attention, so chose to continue with an unwilling partner.

- 'Borrowing' is when you have asked for the temporary use of something, the person concerned has said a genuine 'yes' and the property is returned in the same condition. Taking without permission is stealing.

- However, sometimes what happened was not so serious and children who 'told' have overstated their case, having learned that 'they bullied me' brings instant adult attention. There have been cases in schools where older children or adolescents have knowingly misrepresented ordinary disagreements.

MAKE THE CONNECTION WITH...
WHAT IS 'ZERO TOLERANCE'?

The phrase 'zero tolerance' became relatively common from the end of the 1990s and has been applied to different types of bullying, as well as applied in some antisocial behaviour initiatives. The phrase is far less prominent now in materials about bullying and its absence may reflect greater awareness of the problems generated by unreflective practice. Russell Skiba et al. (2006) reported to the American Psychological Association on the negative impact of this uncompromising approach in US schools.

Adult-child relationships are disrupted if the rhetoric of 'zero tolerance' boils down to adult posturing of, 'Look how tough we are about bullying!' It can slip into a punitive, no lower gears approach in which adults effectively bully in their turn. If the phrase and practice is applied disproportionately to prejudice-driven bullying then individuals from that group can find themselves accused by peers of being treated in an unequal fashion.

I also think 'zero tolerance' is not a constructive phrase, because it has been part of political initiatives in the UK about antisocial behaviour that have some seriously antisocial implications for the younger generation. If you really want to use the phrase, then make very sure the message is about kinds of behaviour that are 'not welcome here' and that no adults will simply let the situation pass without comment or problem solving.

Help with assertive responses

Children are sometimes told 'ignore them and they'll stop'. The truth underlying this cliché is that bullying needs a target. However, if there is no other easy target, the intimidation may go up a notch. Adults need to offer some constructive help.

- There is sad ignoring with drooping body posture and maybe pleading, 'Leave me alone' and there is assertive ignoring with upright body posture, steady stares and dismissive shrugs.
- Helping children and adolescents with more assertive verbal and non-verbal responses is never a judgement that they brought the problem on themselves. However, it is a social reality that individuals or groups who bully are less likely to target a peer with confident body language.
- Children are sometimes told to 'walk away' or 'leave the area' where they are troubled or actually threatened. This advice is sound for

independently mobile older children and adolescents when there is
no supporting adult close.

■ However, it is not acceptable for children to have to leave what
should be shared club or playground space. Adults should intervene,
and problem-solve if some spaces have become the personal territory
of specific groups.

Children or adolescents are sometimes advised not to show they are angry
or distressed to a peer who is bullying them. This advice is sound, but only
up to a point. Children on the receiving end need to avoid giving the fuel
of satisfaction to the other child(ren). However, assertive expression of
feelings can make a child feel stronger than trying to pretend they do not
care, when their body language will probably betray them.

Verbal repartee

Ground rules are that children do not use physical means, nor hit back.
However, they cannot be denied some verbal responses, even raising their
voice on occasion. Children and adolescents are often advised not to say
anything, because that may lead to an escalation of insults, and that advice
is sometimes valid. However, I have known situations where peers have
been stopped in their unpleasant tirade by a sharp reply. Also children and
adolescents can feel more in charge of an exchange when they seize their
own feelings and use them.

TAKE ANOTHER PERSPECTIVE

Children and adolescents need to be able to reply assertively to teasing
that is close to taunting and to verbal harassment. When peers have
behaved in a deliberately unkind way, then they have given up,
temporarily, their right to full kindness in return.

■ Of course, I am not saying you encourage children to insult each
other. You also still remind children that, no matter how the other
child has behaved, nobody here uses that kind of offensive
language. You may need to explore when does legitimate verbal
repartee become retaliation?

■ Children on the receiving end may get so creative with their words
that they are tempted to start proceedings with the other child.
Alert adults need to be ready to say, on the quiet, 'Erin, I think I
understand why you want to wind up Daria, but, come on, you're
better than that. You've done really well; you've stopped Daria
upsetting you. Leave it be now.'

■ Children are less likely to go for payback time if they feel their troubles were taken seriously at the time and if adults are generous with positive feedback about how Erin walked tall and talked strong.

Younger children need the simpler, 'Stop' or 'That's a horrid thing to say' but older children and adolescents can shift the power balance (in non-violent exchanges) with remarks like, 'Did it take you all day to come up with that?' or 'You're really pathetic. You think it makes you look big to say disgusting things about my dad.' Sometimes it shifts the balance to agree with facts by, 'Thanks for stating the amazingly obvious', 'Yeah, pity I wear glasses. It means I can see you properly' or 'Yes, I am black (or whatever). You've known me for months, have you only just noticed?'

It is often more effective to dish out the sharp repartee and then walk away. You can help children to realise that nobody can see inside. If they look and act confident, then children who are trying to distress them cannot hear their heart pound. Once children have walked tall away from the situation, the children who sought to bully them cannot know that afterwards, hopefully with their friends or a supportive adult, this child is taking their ten calm breaths or is close to tears.

Children are in a stronger position with friends standing by their side in support rather than rescuing them. A group of children sound stronger when saying, 'Stop that!' or 'Go away. Don't bother us again!' – or just standing and staring in unison. Practitioners need to keep an eye on whether they regularly have to deal with another child or group. Children without friends are more vulnerable and adults need to tackle isolation as a priority.

> ## MAKE THE CONNECTION WITH...
> ## DOES IT GO OUTSIDE YOUR SETTING?
>
> Minor incidents will be dealt with and, since the problem is resolved, everyone moves on. More entrenched or serious problems would need clear communication with parents. Outside authorities, like the police, should not be involved unless the behaviour is extreme and poses a genuine safety threat. Some kinds of bullying behaviour risk stepping over this boundary: theft, wanton destruction of property, physical or sexual assault, stalking or cyberbullying that moves into libel, harassment or pornographic images. Children, adolescents and their parents need to know that this behaviour is seriously unacceptable and perhaps how close you are to an obligation to bring in the police. But this warning should be genuine and not an empty threat.

Blame or consequences

It is not judged acceptable to resolve the situation by excluding target children for their own safety. The focus is on keeping children safe but also on repairing harm, enabling the child or group who has bullied to change their behaviour and to make reparation. Punitive disciplinary actions can disrupt this process and use of consequences (page 201) have to be proportionate to what actually happened.

No blame?

What has become known as the 'no blame' approach has both supporters and critics. The approach is described by Barbara Maines and George Robinson (1991) and is led by a wish to solve the problem of unacceptable behaviour and bring the feelings of the child on the receiving end to the fore. There is a clear element of encouraging children who bully, or bystanders, to recognise the results of their actions and to make amends. However, Kidscape has expressed concern that the process lacks effective adult exploration into what exactly has happened and that incidents more serious than falling out between friends may not be resolved in a safe way. Children or adolescents can be left vulnerable, when they have expressed their hurt in some detail, yet their peers are left to decide what, if anything, to do in order to make amends (www.kidscape.org.uk/info/noblame.shtml).

Restorative justice

In explaining the restorative approach, Belinda Hopkins (2008 and www.transformingconflict.org) makes the crucial point that behaviour management policies frequently focus on unacceptable actions in isolation.

The related emphasis on sanctions can become punitive and loses sight of the main goal to repair relationships that have been disrupted by this incident, or series of problems. Restorative methods, along with conflict resolution models as a whole, do not brush consequences to one side. The aim is still that harmful behaviour will change, but the route is to enable children and adolescents to repair or build a relationship in this school, club or residential community.

The restorative approach puts a strong emphasis on accountability, but defines this as 'miscreants' understanding the impact of their action, acknowledging the consequence of their choices and helping to decide how to put it right. Miscreant accountability is not defined in terms of receiving punishment. The restorative approach emerged from the youth justice system and is a robust approach that can deal with seriously wrong choices in behaviour. The approach is used with children and adolescents in schools (Gwynedd Lloyd et al., 2007) but also with seriously troubled individuals in the care system (Hopkins, 2008). Part of the process is that children or adolescents are given options, from which they can choose, about how to make amends, such as over their destruction of property.

Prejudice-driven bullying

Different guidance documents have increasingly focused on unacceptable behaviour that rests on targeting individuals or groups on the basis of their group identity, or presumed group identity. The DCFS guidance (2007c) uses the term prejudice-driven bullying for this pattern of behaviour. Single strand guidance documents have been issued with the rationale that practitioners welcome extra help with certain forms of prejudice-driven bullying, like homophobic, or feel ill-informed about new developments, like cyberbullying. Uncertainty among practitioners can combine with anxiety about 'saying the wrong thing' when equality issues are also a feature. Such doubts can tempt practitioners to believe that there is no problem, or that their intervention would only make the situation worse for the child or adolescent by putting the spotlight on their troubles.

WHAT DOES IT MEAN?

Prejudice-driven bullying: sustained ill-treatment of an individual or group targeted because of their group identity, or presumed identity.

Hierarchy of hurt: the concept that some forms of ill-treatment are more reprehensible than others, because of the established power relations between groups in broader society.

Once adults are fully aware of different types of prejudice-driven bullying, it is preferable to avoid putting behaviours into different categories.

- The main plot should be to achieve an inclusive approach. In this school, club or youth centre, it is unacceptable to target anybody and this community does not accept there is ever a good reason to attack or exclude other people on the grounds of their group identity.

- This obligation to focus on the individual, and how they behave, applies to everyone. Nobody from whatever group however defined can effectively whip out a card embossed with 'it doesn't apply to me'.

- It is also crucial that practitioners do not abandon their responsibility to find out what actually happened, once prejudice-driven bullying is involved, or assumed to be involved.

- Altercations between two children, when one is disabled, are not necessarily fuelled by contempt for the child's disability. Some children and adolescents from minority ethnic groups experience inexcusable ill-treatment from their peers, but some have been in the bullying group in their turn.

There is a serious problem around implying, or actually promoting a hierarchy of hurt approach, namely that some kinds of attack are – given the group identity of the person on the receiving end – more pernicious than others. Some tragic cases of bullying that hit the headlines because adolescents killed themselves in despair have been vicious targeting of individuals, unrelated to their group identity. The clear message in the DCSF guidance is that, 'There is no "hierarchy" of bullying – all forms of bullying should be taken equally seriously and dealt with appropriately' (paragraph 1.10, page 12, 2007c). The materials that focus on different types of bullying are even-handed: that offensiveness or intimidation travels in all directions. However, the no-hierarchy message is undermined to an extent by the requirement that racist forms of bullying have to be recorded by schools and the data submitted to the local authority. Recording of other forms of bullying is recommended.

MAKE THE CONNECTION WITH...
PROPER FACT FINDING

Schools are required to record all incidents that are alleged or perceived to be racist. However, the DCSF 2006 guidance on bullying around racism, religion and culture is clear (page 38, within the DCSF *Safe to learn* guidance, 2007c) that the obligation to record also includes the obligation to investigate. The DCSF are most concerned about under-reporting, but acknowledge that investigation sometimes supports a judgement that an incident was not racist.

There are subtle issues about good practice and need discussion within the team.

Look at the frequently asked questions and replies page in the guidance.

Sexual bullying

In terms of prejudice-driven bullying, sexual bullying on the grounds of gender has been relegated to brief mentions or subsumed under homophobic bullying. Plans for guidance were announced by the DCSF in late 2008, but this offensive behaviour deserves a section now.

Womankind is the only site (www.womankind.org.uk) that I have found to address sexual bullying directly. They define this problem as, 'Any kind of bullying behaviour, whether physical or non-physical, that is based on a person's sexuality or gender. It is when sexuality is used as a weapon by boys or by girls. It can be carried out to a person's face, behind their back or by use of technology.'

The few studies, like Nan Stein (1999) in the USA and Neil Duncan (1999) in the UK, are clear that routine sexual harassment, deeply inappropriate touching and invasion of personal space are serious problems in secondary schools where this kind of bullying is not seen as an issue or priority. However, children sometimes import offensive language and attempts at unacceptable intimate contact into primary school or after-club. Some of this behaviour raises concerns around safeguarding (Lindon, 2008a), because of the age of the child or the extreme nature of behaviour. Other levels of sexually based bullying need to be addressed within the context of unacceptable behaviour and ground rules of courtesy and respect. They also need to be couched in a balanced discussion about physical contact, accepted touch and respect for personal space. Certainly a positive environment and community atmosphere will not be created by rules that demonise all touch as 'inappropriate behaviour' or which ban consensual hugs.

Like any other kind of ill-treatment, sexually based bullying needs to be addressed as disrupted relationships, with a recognition of different levels.

- Verbal sexual attacks go from boys/young male adolescents to females, but also in the opposite direction and both are equally unacceptable.

- Some incidents are clod-hopping attempts to make contact with the opposite sex and need to be handled as a failure of social skills. Adolescents are sometimes able to deal with socially inept crassness but want a considerate hearing over words and actions that are not stopped by a fierce, 'Cut it out!'

- Some misjudged adolescent behaviour in mixed-sex school or youth club is about displays of affection that should be private, not a spectator event. Practitioners have to keep a perspective on raging hormones and poor judgement calls, whilst being ready to check appropriately for imposition and abuse of power in non-consensual relationships (Lindon, 2007 and 2008a).

TAKE ANOTHER PERSPECTIVE

Observant adults soon realise that offensiveness can become rife within one sex.

- Young males verbally trash each other: as sexually or otherwise inadequate or attracted to their own sex. Policy and practice over use of offensive terms has to acknowledge that the word 'gay' has become a generalised insult in the younger generation, even a wind-up term.

- Some young females are extremely mean-spirited in their descriptions of each other. Responsible adults have to address the subculture that normalises personal ridicule and rumour mongering within the female gender.

These issues need to be addressed alongside mistreatment between the sexes.

- Everyone has the right to secure personal space. Schools or clubs need to address aggressive propositioning or unwanted groping, otherwise such behaviour becomes established as normal.

- Neil Duncan (1999) described the toxic atmosphere when 'sexualised interpersonal conflict' and casual, offensive language becomes the way older children or adolescents deal with the insecurities of puberty and ordinary frustrations of daily life.

Cyberbullying

This term covers use of mobile phones, email, use of social networking sites and any form of technological communication with the aim of creating severe embarrassment, distress or disruption in relationships as the result of lies and innuendo. Cyberbullying needs to be taken very seriously (Peter Smith, 2005 or DCSF, 2007c). This technique of bullying has created another kind of bystander/colluder, who feels innocent because they only passed on the email or distressing photo or simply enjoyed the entry on the social networking site. The other significant aspect of cyberbullying is the swiftness with which a written example of toxic unpleasantness, let alone a filmed physical or sexual assault, becomes a matter of public property, spread over great swathes of cyberspace.

Shaheen Shariff (2008) describes the digital literacy of many older children and young people today. However, this skill base so often comes with an emotional illiteracy about the bullying nature of a posting, that is viewed as 'just a prank' and which feels anonymous and temporary. Some young people behave naïvely about the permanent nature of many postings: for the person attacked but also for the attacker who has left their trail of deliberate harassment, slander or libel.

WHAT DOES IT MEAN?

Cyberbullying: sustained ill-treatment using words or images through the technology of mobile phones, email or the Internet. Cyberbullying may run alongside face-to-face harassment of the same individual(s).

TAKE ANOTHER PERSPECTIVE

Another aspect to consider (with thanks to Lance Lindon) is that digitally literate older children and young people are speedy on the keyboard or mobile phone texting. Adults may think that written communication must have involved more thought and deliberation than what is said face-to-face. Some cyberbullying shows significant planning and a stalking mentality. However, some email postings and text messages are the digital form of blurting something out – they are typed and sent without much reflection.

This recognition is not an excuse. When adults are unpacking the consequences of thoughtless, but still hurtful, cyber communication, you need the firm response of, 'Well you typed it' or 'You forwarded this photo and you knew what it showed' just as much as, 'Well the words came out of your mouth'.

7

Adult reflection and choices

Practitioners, along with parents, need to weigh up the more constructive strategies and part of this reflection has to be their own behaviour and choices, sometimes from contradictory advice.

The main sections of this chapter are:

☆ **Reflective practitioners make choices**

☆ **Setting up the ground rules**

☆ **Understanding life in school**

REFLECTIVE PRACTITIONERS MAKE CHOICES

The main plot is that children and adolescents learn to guide themselves, that they make the right choice rather than waiting for adults to direct them, stop them or catch them out in misbehaviour. This key goal requires that adults become aware of and are willing to reflect on their own active choices.

The language of choice

Using the language of choice is the foundation of the more constructive approaches towards guiding behaviour within the school community, not only classroom behaviour. The approach is also directly applicable to any other setting for children and adolescents.

Adlerian theory – choices and consequences

All the ideas within the concept of 'language of choice' were established over the middle decades of the twentieth century within the Adlerian framework. The ideas were developed by Rudolf Dreikurs for family life (Dreikurs and Soltz, 1995) and by the 1970s were being applied to school (Dreikurs et al., 1998) with the objective of creating a democratic, rather than an autocratic, atmosphere in the classroom.

■ The approach draws on the Adlerian concept of 'social interest', a feeling of belonging within a group. When children feel a sense of social interest, they act out of choice in ways that are not exclusively about their own self-interest. They are keen to make a contribution to the group, of which they feel a welcomed member.

- For children to feel that they belong, their familiar adults need to be on the same side as children and adolescents. Adults need to recognise the rights of children while acting as a responsible, and kind, adult. There is a shared responsibility for what happens within the classroom, any other part of the school environment, or any group setting.

- Children's behaviour is seen as dependent on the decisions that they have made at a choice point. Children may be unaware of making an active choice; they may feel as if the flow of behaviour is inevitable – what else could they do? It is the adult role to help children recognise that they are at a choice point and their decision could lead them in this direction or another.

- The adult role is to offer choices and help children gain a sense of alternatives. The choices are not endless and part of being a responsible adult includes making it very clear what is not acceptable. The offered choices are genuine and any linked adult behaviour is followed through in a consistent way, with a calm use of consequences (page 201).

This approach to guiding behaviour turns away from systems of symbolic reward (page 189) and sanctions (page 201). It turns towards how adults act and talk at the time when children can make a choice. The adult role is to voice those choices, along with the consequences of options. The adult has to use their words, backed up by consistent body language, to express the options open to a child and what will follow. The adult uses the language of choice, rather than the language of coercion, pleading or nagging.

The Choice Theory of William Glasser

The ideas of choice theory (Glasser, 1998 and Glasser and Glasser, 1999; Rowe, 2008) have common ground with the Adlerian approach. William Glasser also applied the ideas to relationships in general, not only the school environment.

- The key concept is that the only behaviour you can directly control is your own. You cannot make someone else behave in a specific way. All you can do is to give them information about the choices they make – or are about to make – and the consequences of those choices.

- Adults need to recognise that they also make choices in how they deal with children and adolescents whose behaviour they find tough to handle. Adults have direct control over how they behave and can make the active choice to react in a different way when they feel challenged by how a child behaves.

- Attempts to control children (or anyone else) lead through what William Glasser calls the 'seven deadly habits'. These are actions dominated by criticising, blaming, complaining, nagging, threatening, punishing and bribing/rewarding to control. Some of these patterns of behaviour are regarded as unacceptable if children act in that way.

- On the other hand, a focus on highlighting choices leads through William Glasser's 'seven caring habits' of supporting, encouraging, listening, accepting, trusting, respecting and negotiating differences. These adult choices focus on building a positive relationship and mending problems within that relationship. In contrast, the deadly habits lead to disconnection and disruption of a personal relationship.

Choice theory proposes that everyone's behaviour is made up of four basic components: acting, thinking, feeling and physiology (body chemistry and reactions like sweating). You have direct control over your own acting and thinking. You can only control the feeling and physiological components through how you choose to act and think, including positive self-talk. You cannot stop yourself feeling challenged by an adolescent's behaviour; you can make a choice over how to express that feeling through visible actions and choice of words.

William Glasser also proposed that all behaviour is driven by five basic needs laid down in our genetic makeup: survival (basic physical needs), love and belonging, power (from a sense of competence and self-worth), freedom to take control of our own life and fun (satisfaction and enjoyment). His discussion, of what happens when needs are blocked, has much in common with Adlerian theory about mistaken goals (page 71) and Abraham Maslow's hierarchy of needs (page 68). Love and belonging is the most important, since human beings need to feel connected with people who matter in order to satisfy the other needs. So, choice theory has a strong focus on building relationships with children as individuals and not as objects of an impersonal system of control.

Adult role and style

Many adults have become confused about a suitable role in their relationships with children. Unreflective discussion often poses two stark options: strong adults lay down the law or weak adults let children run wild. Practitioners need to reflect on the style of adult behaviour that offers a constructive middle course. A useful approach originated with studies of family life (page 30).

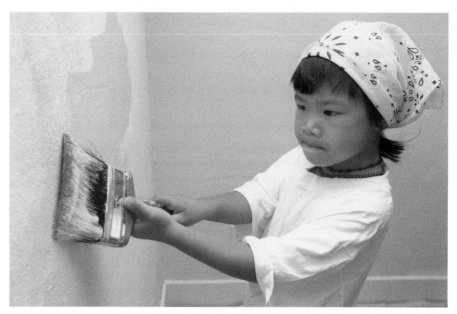

Children and young people flourish when given responsibility

The authoritarian style

The temptation of this model is that practitioners are the Big Boss in the classroom, the playground or club. Their views count and respect is due to them regardless of what they do. Taking an authoritarian stance can look promising, when practitioners want to feel and look powerful and doubt their ability to achieve this aim through their own qualities. The authoritarian stance says, 'I have authority and you should do what I say because I am a teacher (in charge of the playground, the club leader and so on)'.

The potential problem here is that power and control become the most important issues for the practitioner who takes up an authoritarian stance, just as much as a parent in the family home. You can easily slide into classroom and club power battles with children or adolescents over minor issues, because winning – or not obviously losing – has become the most crucial outcome. Serious problems result when an authoritarian practitioner runs out of effective threats and is faced down by an older child or adolescent who wins dominance.

TAKE ANOTHER PERSPECTIVE

Children bring their family experience with them into nursery, school and club. They experience a relative match or mismatch between the adult style with which they are familiar and how the adults behave in this new setting. Reflect on how children might feel, think and behave if:

- Their family life is dominated by an authoritarian style of parenting and nursery life is led by firm-but-fair adults. Might the children initially be confused? How might you help?

- They face the opposite situation and have been used to reasons, they expect to discuss decisions with adults, express doubts or ask 'why?' Might they be regarded as 'cheeky' by practitioners who take a more authoritarian line?

- What about children whose parents take a permissive approach – what may happen when girls and boys join a setting where there are ground rules?

Think over situations that you have faced and discuss the issues with colleagues or fellow students.

Permissive approach

Authoritarian practitioners create frightened or silently rebellious children and adolescents. There is also the strong possibility that some children will copy the punitive role model and fight for dominance over their peers, if they do not yet feel ready to take on the adult. Nevertheless, children do not relish permissive, uncertain adults; they want grown-ups to take appropriate responsibility. A permissive style may be preferable to a practitioner who yells and threatens. However, a practitioner who is uneasy about taking charge will not deal effectively with boys and girls who are a persistent trouble to their peers – disrupting nursery or classroom life or play in the break times.

Practitioners take up a permissive style for different reasons.

- Perhaps you do not relish being in charge, because you do not want to seem like a bossy grown-up – perhaps like someone from your own childhood. But you can lead, without being an overbearing, humourless taskmaster.

- Some practitioners are uncomfortable being part of the older generation and want to be a 'mate'. This confusion over role can arise in playwork and youth settings, but is also possible within classroom dynamics that have gone awry. You should be friendly with children and adolescents, but your adult responsibilities mean you cannot be a friend in the same way as their peers.

- Some advice has focused on the spectre of restricting children's spontaneity or squeezing their personality into a narrow adult-pleaser. Children deserve nurturing, but they are not well served if their wishes run roughshod over everyone else. Other children do not like their company – never mind adults.

MAKE THE CONNECTION WITH... SAYING 'NO'

I am sometimes asked whether it is all right to say 'no' to a child: a question provoked by advice to remove this word from adults' working vocabulary. My reply is that 'no' is an appropriate word, when you have a good reason and you explain in terms that children can understand. You also avoid saying 'no' frequently or without thinking.

It is useful to track your own use of 'no', especially if you find a child's behaviour difficult to guide.

- Keep a discreet count – how often do you say 'no' to this child or young adolescent? Is it much more often than to his or her peers?

- Do you have a good reason for each 'no'?

- Does the child or adolescent understand that reason?

- What is the associated 'yes'? If children need redirecting, are you giving enough guidance beyond 'no'?

Authoritative approach – firm but fair

Practitioners who take this style offer emotional warmth and safety. They have a sense of authority, which they are prepared to use when necessary. If you are confident you can take control, then you do not have to flex your control muscles for the sake of it. Authoritative practitioners do not try to micro-manage every aspect of children's behaviour, even in the classroom situation. They set the broad parameters and allow even young children to make some of their own choices.

It is not easy for any adults to deal with children or adolescents who push the boundaries in front of an 'audience'. Practitioners in school or club can be acutely aware when there is another pair of adult eyes watching.

However, there are many more pairs of child or adolescent eyes and ears trained on observation of how you will handle this situation. It can be very tempting to be authoritarian with a child, in the hope of looking strong and reducing feelings of embarrassment. The most experienced and confident of adults – practitioners and parents – still experience those feelings; they manage to avoid letting the emotions derail a sensible approach.

LOOK, LISTEN, NOTE, LEARN

In discussion about guiding children's behaviour the options are far too often polarised between what is seen as strong adults laying down the law as opposed to weak adults letting children run wild. Think about the three styles of practitioner behaviour discussed in this section.

◆ What evidence of the different patterns can you recall from your own childhood – your own family or that of close friends? Looking back, what style do you think was mainly taken by your teachers?

◆ In what ways are you following an authoritative style of adult behaviour in your professional involvement with children or adolescents? Gather examples of how you handled actual events, not what you planned or hoped to do.

◆ In what ways might you move, with your colleagues if you work in a team, more towards the firm but fair?

Power and control

William Glasser's (1998) choice theory (page 154) evolved from study of what went awry when adults, in any relationship, became focused on control. The first edition of his book about classroom dynamics was entitled *Control Theory*. Andrea Clifford-Poston, writing about family life (Clifford-Poston, 2007) and playwork settings (2008) describes a slippery slope when adults feel powerless, because they cannot directly control a child's behaviour. Once 'who's boss?' has become the central question, adult emotions start to include anxiety and a sense of threat to self-esteem. The mistaken belief is that a competent adult would and should be able to control this child and that any onlookers are ready to think, 'How pathetic is this person!' Often the feeling of anger then overtakes the adult: anger with the child for behaving in this way, but often also hidden anger with oneself. My own observation is that feelings of resentment get entangled in the mix: how some grown-ups reach a point when they directly blame children.

Bill Rogers (2006) describes how fear of loss of control undermines teachers' behaviour when they slide into power battles with individuals. He warns about taking an 'over-vigilant' approach to minor classroom misbehaviour that is better met with minimal attention. Part of effective adult behaviour in the classroom is to deal simply with low-level disturbances and not to hurtle towards the barricades of confrontation for minor cheek or slow responding to instructions. I agree that this kind of non-compliance is, frankly, part of the job description of being a child, let alone an adolescent. An authoritative teacher role is not supported by inattention, but the middle ground is created by what Bill Rogers calls 'relaxed vigilance'. Adults know they are alert and, just as important, so do the pupils or students. However, adults have stepped aside from the mistaken belief that strength is demonstrated by rising fiercely to every little thing.

MAKE THE CONNECTION WITH... DEAL WITH IT AND CARRY ON

Bill Rogers (2006) writes of the need to be rid of 'the psychological junk mail', by which he means an unhelpful mental inbox of 'shoulds' and 'musts'. This clutter leads adults to be too hard on themselves.

■ Tell yourself, with the same kind of positive self-talk that you encourage in some of the children, that you defused a confrontation between Ayesha and Jerry. You did not rise to the emotional bait from highly articulate Greg.

■ Be pleased with yourself about what went well. Reflect, if it will genuinely be helpful on what you might do differently next time. But avoid endlessly revisiting in your mind what you cannot now change – it is the past.

■ Good practice in dealing with children's behaviour is to say or do what is needed at the time. You do not nag, hark back or drag out sanctions for misdemeanours. Treat yourself with equivalent consideration.

SCENARIO

Different choices by adults about their own behaviour are highly likely to make a significant and positive shift in the interaction. Have you been involved in, or observed, situations like this example?

- 13-year-old Marlon has dropped litter in the playground. You have noticed and go across. You say, 'Marlon, put the litter in the bin, thanks.'

Pause and reflect

There is a good chance that Marlon will walk over and put his litter in the bin and you can smile or wave your thanks. What is likely to happen if you start with, 'Don't be so messy, Marlon!' or 'Put that in the bin right this minute!'?

- But maybe Marlon decides to push the boundaries with, 'You put it in! I'm busy.' You reply with, 'That's not a good use of my time. You dropped it, Marlon. I'd like you to put it in the bin. I'll walk over with you. I've been wanting to hear about... (something of direct interest to Marlon) '

Pause and reflect

You offer Marlon a chance to do the right thing and refuse to go head to head with him. Compromise is a strong adult option when you offer it. If he declines to walk across with you, you give him, 'One more chance, Marlon (pause). Okay I'm not willing to have our playground messed up. I'll put it in the bin and I'll put your name down for clean-up squad tomorrow lunchtime.' This consequence is a logical link with Marlon's behaviour. Clean-up squad needs to be focused work to tidy the school grounds, but not a miserable experience.

- An alternative tack from Marlon might be (said with a grin), 'Are you going to make me, Miss?' You cannot make him go to the bin, so you might say, 'Good grief, Marlon, you're head and shoulders taller than me. Of course, I can't make you. I'm asking you pleasantly.'
- Regardless of your size, if you know Marlon has a sense of humour, you might say, 'I plan to use my incredible superpower of asking nicely.'

Pause and reflect

The aim is to give Marlon more than one chance to make the right choice and to avoid a power and control battle that you cannot win.

161

Emotional literacy for adults

Effective and considerate adults acknowledge the likely feelings of children and adolescents in school life and elsewhere. The mark of being professional in your work cannot be to claim that your own behaviour is unaffected by emotions. Of course you have feelings, and you cannot have an effective, personal relationship with children if you behave like an automaton. Being professional is about recognising your feelings – maybe not straightaway, and supportive colleagues can be a real help – and ensuring that emotions do not sidetrack you from a positive approach to this child or group.

Being 'angry' or 'upset'

Adults need to consider their own emotional vocabulary, just as much as help children with use of words (page 80). Adults, who are 'angry' about every little thing set a poor example to observant children or adolescents.

- Save the word 'angry' for when it is really needed. What is a more appropriate expression for this situation? Are you mildly annoyed that yet again…? Are you frustrated at the waste of good time and energy? Are you irritated?
- Avoid frittering away the power of 'angry'; then it has meaning when you have good reason to use it. When children or adolescents have behaved in a seriously unacceptable way, then it can be right to tell them, 'I am angry and so very disappointed that you…' or, 'I was appalled to hear that…'

The same need for reflection applies to 'being upset'. Are you taken aback, saddened, actually distressed or genuinely frightened by a child's behaviour? Strong emotions, like fear, need to be explored with a supportive colleague.

- Your discussion with bystanders in a confrontation may include, 'I accept that none of you used racist language towards Yasmin. But I'm shocked that you stood by and just listened to that tirade from Lorna and Kelsey.'
- There is no neat formula and adults as professionals must still be authentic. Perhaps, you say, 'Your reaction has really taken me by surprise. We need to talk about…' Sometimes it is appropriate to be 'saddened about the choice you've made to…' or 'disappointed that you have/have not…'

Class teachers or a tutor group leader should have developed a relationship of commitment. Children or young people feel confident that this conversation is going to move on to, 'What are we going to do about this situation?' However, it can feel, and be right, sometimes to say, 'We're going to talk about how you can make amends on this one. But, Marlon, I have to get this out of the way first. I am stunned that you could behave in such an idiotic way. What possessed you to drop your trousers on the school bus this morning!' If you have an established relationship with Marlon, and your tone is exasperated, not furious, he will know you do not expect a 'sensible' answer. Since Marlon is a young adolescent, you will also understand how his brain is working (page 67). He may already be mortified at what he did and know that you have to tell his parents.

Social learning and choices

Despite greater equality between the sexes, young males and females are still treated differently over their formative years (page 88). These young people grow up and social learning is provoked by experiences within professional life.

Bill Rogers (2006) highlights that some males with whom he has worked want a get-out clause of 'I can't help getting angry when...'. Rogers' constructive reworking of this statement is that some men (not all) cannot seem to stop themselves showing anger in loud and physically aggressive ways. He points out that this kind of expression is learned, not an inevitable part of the biological package, so habits can be unlearned and acceptable alternatives put in their place. The professional response is to make a distinction between anger as the emotion and impulsive behaviours like shouting, being vindictive in words or intimidating through actions.

I want to add the other side of the gender coin. Undoubtedly, some young females learn a pattern of aggressive expression of anger and this learned pattern can be unleashed in their later professional life. However, I have also worked with female practitioners whose perspective on behaviour has been dominated by 'I can't help getting upset when...'. The implication is that the problem would be solved, if this practitioner could opt out of those aspects of the job that provoke the feelings. I have also encountered the rationale of 'They make me feel intimidated...' as the justification for severely limiting boisterous games of 4- and 5-year-old boys. Responsible adults own up to their personal emotions.

The professional response, once again, is to recognise the feeling and make choices about how the emotion emerges through visible behaviour. It is not acceptable to require children, or your adult peers, to be responsible for 'making' you feel anything. You do your own feeling and sometimes an honest acknowledgement of an emotion is the only way to move into grown-up problem solving and set a model of assertiveness for children and adolescents.

When it feels personal

Even when children or adolescents speak the word 'you', sometimes they are expressing general frustration with other adults who have annoyed them recently. These people are not currently present – but you are.

- You could say something like, 'Michael, it seems to me you're seriously cross this afternoon. Is it about something I've done?' (pause) 'Not me in particular, then? Do you want to talk about it?' If the answer is a 'yes' by word or gesture, then in the playground, after school club or youth centre, you may be able to say, 'OK you've got my full attention'.

- In the classroom, it may not be possible to talk immediately and the offer has to be more of, 'We can have an uninterrupted conversation at (time) in (place). Do we have an agreement to talk then?' If you have created a shared understanding in your class that 'we talk things through', then neither Michael, nor his classmates, will assume he is going to get a telling-off later.

Sometimes you actually have done something unacceptable – like not listened, jumped to conclusions or otherwise failed to meet your own high standards. In that case, you need to set a good example and admit it. However, you can still raise a fair objection to how your attention is being drawn to this error. You might say, 'You're right, I wasn't following our Listen First rule. I'm sorry about that. Please tell me again, but without the name calling. Thank you.' The whole sentence, including the implied reminder about 'our Courtesy rule', is said in a calm tone and there is a sense of equality with children or adolescents.

MAKE THE CONNECTION WITH…
USING THE GROUND RULES

Some examples in this section refer to ground rules and this aspect of good practice is covered from page 166. You may notice that examples of courteous adult requests are followed by 'thank you' and not 'please'. I came across this choice of words when first reading Bill Rogers' books in the early 1990s. It makes sense and, if the idea is new to you, take this chance to reflect on the difference.

- The emotional tone of 'please' is more that of asking, with a possibility that the child or adolescent may decline to follow a fair request linked with 'our rule'.

- In contrast, 'thank you' communicates a friendly confidence that this rule reminder will be enough for the child to redirect their choice of behaviour.

■ It is often appropriate to turn away slightly. You action is not a dismissal; the non-verbal message is that you do not need to stare them into cooperation.

Of course, you know some children and adolescents will need more guidance, but you continue to give them that chance to redirect first time of asking.

The adult role is to guide children and adolescents towards greater courtesy. It is unprofessional to retaliate with personal remarks or to go eyeball to eyeball with the 'how dare you!' approach.

■ It sets a far better example to deal with unpleasant remarks through reference to a shared ground rule in class or club meetings. For example, 'We agreed a ground rule of no put-downs to anybody and I'm included in "anybody"'.

■ There are times to admit to a partial truth. Perhaps a child blurts out, 'You're only an assistant! I don't need to do what you say!' You reply with, 'Helena, you're right, my job is called Support Assistant. But I don't come with an "only" tag. I'm responsible for keeping everyone safe in the playground (pause and a firm no-nonsense look). Now, I'm going to ask you once more to…'

In a warm emotional atmosphere, it can be normal for adults to make pleasant remarks to children like, 'That's a fine hat' and ask about their interests. Children and adolescents will often reciprocate with compliments and questions to you. A team needs to talk through any uncertainties over professional and personal boundaries. However, it is not fair to children and adolescents if their comments are always judged as intrusive and inappropriate behaviour. You want to keep children on-task within the classroom environment, so it is wise to avoid being drawn into conversation that distracts. For example, Gavin asks, 'Mr Mayfield, you're limping. Were you knocked off your bike again?' If the answer is 'yes' then questions might flow: 'What happened? Were you wearing your helmet – like you tell us to? Is it going to cost loads of money to get your bike fixed?' You can reply, 'Now's not the time, Gavin. I'll be on the Friendship Bench at morning break. I'll tell anyone the gory details then.'

It is not only young children who make remarks out loud without being aware that their comment is very personal and possibly discourteous. Older children and adolescents do not always engage their brain before opening their mouth and letting that unspoken thought become public. There is a difference between the remark of, 'Sir, sir, you've got a bald patch. Did y'know?' and persistent chants of 'Baldy!' or 'Egghead'. A humorous teasing tone might be met – and brought to a halt – with, 'Darren, keen powers of observation there but I had noticed', or 'Yes, talk about unfair, and at my age too. But what do I say to you guys, "Life isn't always fair!"', which can work if that is one of your favourite phrases. Further remarks, or a shift of gears to taunting shouts needs a firmer response of, 'Enough, that breaks our Courtesy rule and the rule covers me too.'

Older children and adolescents may subvert pleasantry and move into more intrusive comments. It is crucial that you do not ignore suggestive or offensive remarks. Highly suggestive remarks from under-eights should also make you wonder how they have learned such innuendo. Your firm response models how you want children or adolescents to handle similar situations (page 149). Examples are:

- 'Gareth, your complimentary remarks about my boots were fine and thank you. Your comment about my legs crossed the line between pleasantry and over-personal. Stop now, Gareth.' You might also use the palm up signal: a shared gesture for 'Stop' in your class and school.

- 'I don't make personal remarks about your body and I expect the same courtesy in return.' If children or adolescents push the limits with you, then intrusive personal remarks may also be an issue between peers. A new ground rule may work of, 'Compliments about clothes – yes. Personal comments on bodies – no', so long as you reach the wording through group discussion.

- 'Olivia, that last remark was well over the line. It breaks our Courtesy rule. You also used offensive terms that you know are not acceptable in our school. I'm booking you in for Serious Talk Time with me and your year tutor.'

Any practitioners dealing with routine harassment about their group identity, disability or (presumed) sexual orientation have the right to expect full support from colleagues. No setting will deal effectively with prejudice-driven bullying (page 147) if practitioners are expected to tolerate unacceptable behaviour.

SETTING UP THE GROUND RULES

It is considerably easier to guide the behaviour of children and adolescents when there is a shared basis of ground rules. You will have noticed that some examples have included reference to 'our rule about' or how 'we' behave in this setting.

Show as well as tell

Over early childhood, you have to do much of the boundary setting as a responsible adult. Some nurseries have a set of written rules on the wall, but this reminder is for the adults – practitioners and parents. Young children are guided through your acknowledgement, right at the time, of behaviour that is 'thoughtful'. You communicate, 'Well done for asking' or 'Good listening! I can tell your ears are switched on'.

Visual reminders are placed where they make most sense and this friendly memory jogger helps children to guide themselves. The best reminder notices are made with children's help and have a photo of boys or girls who are currently part of your setting or home as a childminder.

- A photo of a child closing the door to the garden with 'Please close me' can help to avoid the situation where an open door leads to a bone-chilling draft. If a piece of equipment can only be used when an adult is present then you create a notice, with the children's help, that gives that reminder message.

- An underpinning ground rule is likely to be, 'In nursery, we take care of the toys and books'. I am grateful to Frankie Stanton, head of Tarnerland Nursery School (Brighton, West Sussex), for sharing their idea to show what taking care, or not, looks like. Despite friendly reminders, the children were often leaving the book corner in a mess, so practitioners and children created two photos. One image showed books left in disarray with the caption, 'Our books are unhappy' and a downturned face. Another image showed children enjoying books with a few ready on the floor but the rest back on the shelf. The caption was, 'Our books are happy' with a smiley face.

- The head of Mayville (High School) Nursery in Southsea (Hampshire) described to me their visuals that show in action rules like respect and caring for others that apply across the whole school. They made a set of photos to communicate the right choice in recognisable situations. Practitioners can bring children's attention to the display, secured at child eye level. Sometimes, a child will take a peer to look together at the relevant photos.

- Helpful visual reminders do not cease with nursery. Sun Hill Infants School had a laminated notice that said 'Stop' and showed this reminder with the image of an open palm held up. This notice marked the edge of the part of the school grounds which Years 1 and 2 (5- to 7-year-olds) could use during playtime. There was no physical boundary and the space was used for other activities. Children understood, and most usually followed, the request that ordinary playtime did not go beyond this marker.

Ground rules that are likely to work

So long as their earlier experiences have shown the value of consistency, then over-fives understand in a simple way how a shared code of behaviour works. Ground rules work best as part of guiding behaviour when the rules are drafted as a joint enterprise with the children and adolescents themselves. Even if introduced in a conversational way, off-the-shelf laminated posters are an adult production from elsewhere. It is irrelevant that a group of children often come up with something similar: the visual reminder and wording should be theirs.

Discussion with children and adolescents

Part of forming a close relationship with a new class in school is to get to know everyone by name. Effective teachers ask for children's support by helping to create a written seating plan or wearing name badges during a familiarisation period. During the 'getting to know you' phase, the teacher, with any supporting practitioners, guides a discussion that reaches a group agreement about how everyone will behave in this class. You can break a large class into smaller groups who then report back but you need a whole group agreement in the end.

After school clubs and youth centres need to generate their own set of rules. This set would not last forever; it is valuable to revisit rules and to renew the process when there has been a significant turnover in attendance. If your provision occupies space on school grounds, you may consider the school rules. However, it is not appropriate simply to import that set into club life.

There is no exact formula for this discussion but useful starters can be:

- 'Let's get some ideas about what will make our school a happy place to be' or 'I want you to look forward to after-school club. What will help you all to have an enjoyable time here?'
- Another angle can be, 'How do we like to be treated?', which moves towards behaving towards other people in ways that you welcome in your turn.
- The ideas will emerge and you – or an older child – can write them on a large sheet of paper. Children who are not comfortably literate need to feel welcome to contribute their emergent writing and any drawings. Reassure everyone that the ideas are a work in progress and wording can be changed.
- You contribute your ideas as a partner in the discussion. Perhaps you say, 'Looking at our list, I think we're missing something about...' or 'I'd like something about how we treat each other – courtesy, good manners whatever we like to call it. Any ideas?'

It is important that adults are honest about a ground rule that they definitely want on the list. The exact wording may be open to discussion, but the creation of a rule is non-negotiable.

- For instance, 'I need to discuss with you the ways to get my attention when we're working as a whole class'. The ground rule is likely to be about putting up a hand rather than shouting out.
- Sensible health and safety for the whole primary school requires that everyone (adults too) wears a sunhat and sunscreen outdoors, whenever the summer heat goes above a given temperature.

Make sure the adult mental list is neither long nor dominates the discussion.

Content and choice of wording

The wording is led by 'we': rules apply to everyone, not just children. I read a notice in one 3–5s room in which every rule was what the children had to do, with no indication that this behaviour also applied to the adults. For example, one rule was, 'You will listen to the teachers' rather than, 'We listen to each other'. Young children could not read the rules but the list was used for practitioner reference, was visible to parents and as a whole gave an oppressive message.

The list of rules is no more than five or six items with younger children within middle childhood. Even with older children and adolescents, ten is a realistic maximum. Long lists get over-complex and are unwieldy as a constructive reminder. Most effective ground rules for school or club can be reduced to basic statements that revolve around a prosocial outlook:

- Taking care of other people – courtesy, respect for feelings and personal space
- Taking care of shared possessions – play and work resources, our environment
- Communication to support rather than disrupt – listen, avoid put-downs, use your words to resolve problems and ask for adult help if necessary
- Classroom life needs some ground rules that apply to communication and shared use of resources in this specific environment
- Keeping safe for yourself and other people – usually the place for a walking/careful movement rule inside the building.

> **MAKE THE CONNECTION WITH.....**
> **RIGHTS WITH RESPONSIBILITIES**
>
> All of these points for shared ground rules are about a balance of rights and responsibilities within the school or club community. For example, everyone has the right to expect their views and contribution will be treated with respect. In turn everyone has the responsibility, an obligation if you like, to show respect in their turn. Disagreements will arise, but differences of opinion need to be expressed without dismissive body language or verbal insult.
>
> ■ Can you think of some other right–responsibility pairs?

Choice of words matters, because ground rules become a public statement about what is important in our class or what we value most in our club. Rules are best phrased as a positive, as a 'do' rather than 'don't' or 'no...'

- A long list of 'don't do this' can leave the space for some bright spark(s) to identify what you have failed to ban and then use the annoying, yet reasonable, justification of, 'But you didn't say we mustn't...'
- If the first draft has negative phrasing, then it is worth discussing 'what do we do when...?' No hitting is a fair request, but what do you do instead?
- A 'don't' can be constructive, if it follows a clear 'do'. But it is unwise to have ground rules where every positive is followed by the flipside of 'we don't'.

Sometimes children ask for a clear prohibition on specific behaviour that bothers them. At one point the group at Balham After-School Club wanted a rule about, 'No cussing', which meant bad-mouthing peers, not necessarily swear words. The same group had thoroughly discussed that the best way to phrase their road safety rule was, 'We don't talk as we cross the road'. This rule ensured that everyone kept fully alert, even though they crossed at pedestrian lights. The club team heard that children generalised this safety rule to time with their family.

The final list of ground rules, or 'our behaviour agreement', is neatly written or typed and made into a wall poster. Younger children in middle childhood may still like some visuals associated with what they now feel to be 'our class/club rules'. Partnership with families is supported when you send a typed copy home with a covering letter explaining that this agreement has been agreed by the teacher and this (named) class, year group or club. Parents are requested to read the agreement with their son or daughter and talk about it in the family.

LOOK, LISTEN, NOTE, LEARN

Look with a fresh eye at the ground rules that apply in your own setting.

- ◆ **Are they brief and to the point?**
- ◆ **In what ways were children and adolescents involved in their creation?**
- ◆ **Is it clear that adults should follow the rules as well?**

Review and discussion

Ground rules need to have meaning day by day. Adults use them to acknowledge wanted behaviour and to guide children away from unwanted actions. So long as over-fives trust you, they will be confident to voice questions and comments around the existing code. Over-fives, even some fours, are able to raise and talk about a situation that needs a new ground rule, or some serious clarification of an existing rule. Perhaps there are territorial disputes over the willow tunnel or some children have a creative interpretation of 'one at a time on the slide'.

Thoughtful practitioners are open to rethinking a ground rule. Julian Grenier described ('To the Point' column *Nursery World* 3 July 2008) how the team at Kate Greenaway Nursery School and Children's Centre had taken a fresh look at the 'no running indoors' rule. Some team members had attended training about Developmental Movement Play by Jabadao (www.jabadao.org). They observed what was actually happening and noticed that most children, even the youngest, took care not to bump into each other, or the furniture, even when they were moving faster than the recommended 'nice walking'. If they bumped, it was intentional, playful bumping and not because the children could not control their movement. The team experimented with dropping 'no running indoors' and it was soon clear that the rule was not needed.

Over time, new aspects of behaviour arise, for example use of mobile phones.

- ▨ The *Learning Behaviour* working group chaired by Alan Steer (2005) assigned a section to the impact of mobile phones on school life and the potential problems if ground rules were not established and kept. The working group was concerned about behaviour like texting as part of harassment of peers, or contacting parents so that they would come into school to confront staff.
- ▨ However, the technology can be disruptive in more mundane ways: phones go off during lessons, texting can be the modern equivalent

of going off-task by passing notes. College tutors and professional trainers do not appreciate having to deal with young people who behave as if anyone on the end of their mobile phone is a higher priority than the tutor or fellow students.

■ In school break time, and in club life, practitioners need to encourage face-to-face conversation and enjoyment of a range of play or leisure activities. It is neither helpful, nor necessary, to accept the dominance of mobile phones with a passive, 'It's how it is now – what can you do?'

LOOK, LISTEN, NOTE, LEARN

Mobile phone technology is now part of life for most adolescents and so poses a practical issue for secondary schools and sixth form colleges. Many younger children are now given their own mobile, so primary schools and clubs increasingly have to discuss the practical issues.

Questions

◆ Is there a ground rule that applies in your setting? Options can be an agreement that mobile phones remain switched off, or secure in a bag or locker or simply do not come into school grounds.

◆ It should be obvious that practitioners do not chat on their mobiles while at work in school, nursery or club. But what about parents and other visitors?

◆ I have talked with settings who have placed at their entrance the visual of a phone with a line through and the message 'Please switch off your phone'. This decision was reached, because many parents continued to make and take calls while dropping off and picking up their children, who quite reasonably wanted their attention.

UNDERSTANDING LIFE IN SCHOOL

Behaviour that is regarded as problematic in the school context has common ground with the task of guiding children and adolescents in other settings. However, some behaviour experienced as a problem in school is specific to the educational aims of this setting and group teaching methods in the classroom. The *Learning Behaviour* report from the group chaired by Alan Steer (2005) confirmed, from all the evidence that they heard, that children and adolescents in schools across the country are mainly well behaved. The more common problems were what they described as low level nuisance behaviour that was inappropriate in a classroom

Classroom life requires particular habits of behaviour

environment: non-work related chatter, calling out and inattention. They did not confirm media headlines that paint a picture of a teaching force overwhelmed everywhere by an ill-disciplined rabble.

Behaviour habits for classroom life

The demands of the learning environment of the classroom shape the social role of being a school pupil or student. The classroom is a considerably easier environment for teachers when children have learned habits of behaviour that enable them to function within a group that is working to a shared purpose and where the typical ratio is that of one adult to many pupils or students. The main issues are that children are able to:

▪ Understand and deal with communication within a group. Children need to be able to listen to instructions and to understand that an instruction given to the whole group, or specific subgroup, applies to them, even when the adult has not said their personal name.

▪ Stay on task once they have been given an assignment and get themselves back on track if they are distracted by their own thoughts or the intervention of another child. They need to be able to focus on their work without non-stop reminders, but also to be confident to ask for help when necessary.

- Understand and follow routines within classroom life, without needing adult guidance at every turn. Children also need to be able to handle routine transitions within the day, from class time to playtime, the lunch break, the beginning and ends of the day – which for some children means a different form of provision, not necessarily going back home.

- Cope with the majority and then all of their self-care, unless they are judged to need a personal support assistant because of physical or learning disabilities.

- Enter and leave the classroom in a calm way without barging into other people or furniture. Part of this pattern of behaviour will include the ability to line up with other children to ensure that a large group of bodies passes safely through a narrow exit or entry point.

- Sit still or at least be relatively still for quite a lot of the time. It is expected that children as pupils do not move about the classroom without a good reason.

- Take turns within group discussion, wait for their chance to speak and not interrupt as a matter of course. Acceptable classroom behaviour means 'hands up' to show you want to ask or contribute, not shouting or calling out loudly.

- Commit to being punctual and be on time for school (a shared responsibility with parents) and for class. Children and adolescents need to be trusted not to 'get lost' as they move from one part of the building to another and to emerge from parts of the school grounds when playtime is over.

MAKE THE CONNECTION WITH...
HOW OLD ARE THEY?

The list of classroom skills of behaviour demands a lot of children, especially the youngest in primary school. It is unrealistic of adults to expect under-fives to behave as pupils in a structured classroom situation. It is unacceptable that some publications refer to 3- and 4-year-olds as 'pupils', solely because these young children have their early years provision located within school grounds. They are not yet in the role of school pupil and nobody should expect them to take on those specific responsibilities. Unreasonable and unrealistic adult expectations create avoidable problems for children (page 46).

LOOK, LISTEN, NOTE , LEARN

Children need to learn to control the loudness of what they say. This task is still a work in progress for some under-eights who genuinely have trouble recognising and controlling their volume. There are choices for adults other than snapping, 'Be quiet!' and I have encountered several considerate ways.

♦ Use the hand gesture that communicates, 'down a bit' as well as the words, 'Dan, can you speak a little quieter. Thank you'.

♦ The practical idea of an 'indoor' and an 'outdoor' voice – since one of the pleasures of generous playtime in school is that children can be livelier outside. One practitioner told me of a creative addition in her school. Children who especially struggled with their quieter, indoor voice were reminded, as they came from play into the classroom to, 'Put your outdoor voice in your pocket'. It was a friendly reminder and the practitioner would do the action of popping the imaginary voice into a pocket.

♦ Bill Rogers (2006) offers the concept of a 'partner voice', which is appropriate when working and talking on a joint project for older children and adolescents.

Questions

♦ What ideas have you encountered that recognise the need for relative quiet in the classroom, but are a friendly way of helping children?

♦ What do you recall of the options when you were in school yourself? Can you reconnect with the frustration if, as a child, the courteous ways are not working or the 'noisy ones' seem to get most attention?

Encouraging positive classroom behaviour

Clear ground rules, especially if properly discussed and agreed with the children or adolescents (page 168), mean that adults can deal with a considerable array of low-level unwanted behaviour through friendly reminders about 'our rule'. Behaviour is dealt with at the time and children are also acknowledged, by friendly words and body language, for following a specific ground rule. Children who are still struggling with how to get attention in class can be reminded of 'Our Communication Rule' for classroom. The adult guidance can be less of, 'Finn, don't shout out' and more of, 'Finn, hand up for attention, thank you. I will be across to you very soon.'

Focus on what you want to have happen, the choice you wish a child to make.

- Avoid asking, 'Andy, why are you looking out of the window?' or 'What's so interesting out there?' The answer takes you somewhere you do not want to go, because the point is, 'Eyes on the board, Andy. Thanks'.

- Acknowledge simply when children do the right thing, but especially when that choice has not been easy. You might say, 'Paresh, you need to put your hand up in group time.' If Paresh tries to continue, since he has got your attention, you say, 'Now I'm listening to Keisha's point.' If Paresh soon manages to raise his hand, then you say swiftly, 'Well done with the hand up, Paresh. It's your turn now.'

Children manage when expectations are realistic

Pitch your level of intervention

The point about establishing a friendly ongoing relationship with children or adolescents is that sometimes you do not have to say much at all, if anything. A firm look, what is sometimes known as 'the beady eye', may be enough to get pupils or students back on track. Once you know them well you may choose to do some selective ignoring, withdrawing attention for behaviour that you wish to fade away and which is no more than a low level irritation. You are not ignoring children as an individual; you are temporarily focused away from them.

MAKE THE CONNECTION WITH... CONSISTENT APPROACHES

The approach of selectively ignoring minor misbehaviour applies to playground life as well as the classroom. Of course other children may bring the behaviour to your attention. Another child may want you to know, 'Mr Mayfield! Darren's kicking the wall again!' You might reply in a voice that can be heard by Darren, 'It's all right, Tess. I think Darren will stop very soon. I hope so; I need a reliable arm to take over this skipping rope.'

Questions

■ Think over what approaches can be consistent between the classroom and playground times of the school day, or to settings like club?

■ What ground rules or approaches are specific to the classroom?

WHAT DOES IT MEAN?

Proportionate: a response that is pitched appropriately to the level of seriousness of the behaviour or situation.

A responsible adult approach to unwanted behaviour in any situation is to make your response proportionate to the actions of the child or adolescent.

■ You go steadily up the gears of guidance and intervention. Adults who rush straight to high levels of verbal confrontation and threatened sanctions have nothing left for the serious exchanges. Also they soon look like an ineffective windbag, because they wave verbal threats that never materialise.

■ Consequences (page 201) are linked in a meaningful way to what a child or adolescent has done, or not done. If pupils or students repeatedly disrupt classroom harmony then they will lose their right to participate in that classroom experience on a temporary basis. There will be some version of time out (page 207) and focused discussion with individuals about ways to enable them to get themselves back on track (page 218).

■ The emotional tone of classroom life needs to be that temporary exclusion from that shared experience is a loss for a child or adolescent. They want to earn their way back, to be trusted once again.

■ Clear ground rules can then be linked with clear consequences, sometimes two options, when a child or adolescent has chosen to contravene a rule. They are given more than one opportunity to make the right choice. Then they are judged to have chosen to accept the consequence of not following an agreed code of behaviour. This principle applies to settings other than classrooms.

SCENARIO

Suppose, the school rule is that students can have mobile phones but during classroom time the phone must stay, switched off, in a student's personal bag. Consider this example also as a way to deal with other kinds of misbehaviour.

■ Sasha (14 years) has her phone visible on her desk. You say simply, 'Sasha, phone in your bag, thanks'. Allow her a short pouting time, and do not rise to this non-verbal message.
■ Mentally count up to 10, looking expectant, then go to the next step, 'Sasha, our rule is no mobiles out in class. It goes in your bag or on my desk – your choice.'

Pause and reflect

What will probably happen if you get tetchy with Sasha at this early stage, 'Why on earth is your phone out, Sasha?' or 'What is your problem!'

■ Sasha may choose to go up the gears, 'It's my mobile, you can't take it away'. You come back, still with a level tone, 'Sasha, we have a class rule about mobiles. It applies to everyone. You put your phone in your bag (pause). Otherwise it spends the lesson on my desk.' Most likely Sasha will now put the phone in her bag. If she mutters and looks sulky, ignore that behaviour.

Pause and reflect

Effective handling of this kind of situation needs you to be the grown-up. What is likely to happen if you snap, 'Don't give me that sulky look, young lady!'

■ If Sasha grasps the phone to her, you respond, 'Sasha, you're now on last chance. You have chosen to take my time and attention away from your classmates. You're holding the phone; you put it in your bag.'
■ If Sasha now puts the phone away, you respond with, 'Thanks' and turn back immediately to the rest of the class.

Pause and reflect

You will lose the momentum if you are now tempted to complain, 'Who do you think you are – some kind of celebrity? Nobody's impressed, you know!' Unfortunately, Sasha may be a role model to some of the class and you will lose ground by being snide or trying to take her down a couple of pegs.

If Sasha still refuses either option, then you follow the whole school consequence for when students cannot be trusted in responsible possession of a mobile phone. A wise approach will not include wrestling to seize the phone, or any other item.

- It might be, 'OK, Sasha, you've chosen to lose mobile phone privileges for two weeks.' Sasha will know that this step means she will have to open her bag each morning and the head will remove the phone if she has brought it.
- Alternatively the whole team agreement may be, 'OK Sasha, you have broken our rule about mobiles, so you have chosen to leave class and go into the cool-down place. I will meet you at (time) here and you will do your missed classwork during the lunch break.'

MAKE THE CONNECTION WITH…
KEEP THE MAJORITY ON YOUR SIDE

When you are dealing with a group of children and adolescents, you really need peer pressure to work for you. You do not want to lose the support of the well-intentioned many as a result of taking cheap shots at the annoying few. In an ongoing relationship you can be safe to use humour with care and knowing the children well. But never single out a child or adolescent as the butt of your witticism, nor attempt to make them look foolish.

In his presentations, Bill Rogers highlights how teachers need to keep 'the good-natured majority' on their side. Unwise behaviour, from frustrated adults who may feel under attack, slides into sweeping whole group punishments or ill-tempered complaints that spatter everyone. Teachers (or any other responsible adults) then alienate the well-disposed children. If you behave badly towards this fellow student, who is to say you will not turn on other individuals? Bill Rogers describes the serious risk that the rest of the group will gravitate towards those individuals he describes as 'the catalysts' for disruption in a class.

Primary and secondary behaviours

It is not unusual that a child or adolescent will bring other issues into the current exchange – and not only in the classroom situation. For example:

- 'I wasn't the only one doing... Why d'you pick on me!'
- 'You've got it all wrong. I had it first; Kayleigh stole it!'
- 'He's always calling me a... I thought this school cared about bullying.'
- 'But Mrs Patel lets us...' or 'John definitely said we're not supposed to...'
- 'You have no idea how awful my life is!'

Some writers – for parents and practitioners - advise that you refuse to deal with secondary behaviours, because they are irrelevant excuses and self-justification, and focus on the main issue, the primary behaviour. I think it is wiser to acknowledge the other issue, very briefly sometimes. Children or adolescents may have a valid point. If you try to ignore their interjection, they simply redouble their efforts to be heard. Also, it is not courteous adult communication to announce, 'that doesn't matter' or 'you're just trying to get away with...' You need to make swift decisions about acknowledgement, for instance:

- 'Yes, Ansel, I realise you were the only one who didn't see me coming. That's why it's you and me having this conversation now.'
- 'Thank you Maria. I accept that I jumped to conclusions. Let's restart this conversation with a better question, "What happened here?"'
- 'I've heard what you said about... I am willing to talk with you about that, but not until we have dealt with...'
- 'I will check with Mrs Patel (or John), but for now I am reminding you of our rule that...'
- 'You can have my full attention later for what's going on in the rest of your life. But for now we're talking about...'

Some of these secondary behaviours raise issues, for instance about possible inconsistency in the team, that need to be explored and maybe resolved. Sometimes, it will be appropriate to get back with, 'You remember that Asif let me know he thought there were some mixed messages about.... I raised it in our staff meeting and we are all agreed the ground rule about... is that.... We are sorry if that was not completely clear before'.

WHAT DOES IT MEAN?

Primary and secondary behaviours: describing the difference between the action which is the current focus of the problem or dispute and actions or events which are at a tangent.

Changing the situation to help the behaviour

Thoughtful adults do not focus exclusively on how children behave. Practitioners (and parents too) need to look at the circumstances that appear to provoke certain patterns of behaviour, especially those actions that the adults see as 'a problem'.

I have learned a great deal from practitioners in primary schools where the head, and full team, regard the experience of the youngest children as the proper starting point for setting the tone of the school community.

Respect good early years practice

The team of Sun Hill Infants made me welcome for a visit in the summer of 2008. The head, Kim Owen Jones, describes taking on a school in 2000 that had a very good reputation but in which children were assigned the role of passive learner. A very structured approach started with reception class and the more lively children had trouble with high levels of adult direction. Perfectly normal 4- and 5-year-olds could not help but find ways to be physically more active and their bursts of exuberance got them sent to the head's office. Kim Owen Jones describes little lines of children, often boys, waiting to be 'told off' by her, for minor non-compliance to adult instructions and inability to sit still for ages.

In collaboration with Rosie Waring Green, the leader of the reception class, Kim Owen Jones took Sun Hill in a significantly different direction. Practice with the youngest children was changed to considerably greater choice for children in how they pursued their interests each day. The lines of children outside the head's door disappeared completely once being busy and on the move was no longer judged as a sign of being off-task. Any issues around behaviour are dealt with as they arise. Year 1, and not reception, is seen as a transition year towards the more formal classroom approach of Year 2.

Insights from nurture groups

Sometimes it becomes clearer what a given situation requires when you focus on those individuals who cannot manage. Marjorie Boxall (2002) first developed nurture groups in the 1970s for children whose inability to cope in primary school was likely to lead to exclusion. In a small group with a predictable routine led through play, children are enabled to learn social skills crucial to group life, such as taking turns, making choices and seeing an activity through to completion. Children are usually eased back into their class one step at a time and often need similar steady support to rejoin their peers in the playground.

All groups with the name of 'nurture group' do not necessarily operate in the same way, although they should share common principles. For example, the nurture group that I observed in Thongsley Fields Primary School was developed as a special session at the beginning of each school day for a small group of children. These boys and girls felt more able to cope because they had breakfast with the same group of other children in a special room and guided by the same practitioner. The children experienced a chance to chat informally, to enjoy a guided conversation about how they were feeling today, supported by the use of finger puppets and a story. They then joined their class for the rest of the day.

WHAT DOES IT MEAN?

Nurture group: a small, emotionally supportive group for children who cannot yet cope in the classroom environment.

Transitions within the school system

Many primary schools make serious efforts to engage with the children's early years experience, through contact with families but also with the local early years provision. In some areas, there is an additional transition between an infant and junior school. Many secondary schools have also made considerable effort to ease the move between the primary and secondary stage.

Even when the involved adults genuinely recognise the experience for children, the transition to secondary school is still a major adjustment. Children have spent half their life working themselves to the top of the age hierarchy, to gain a responsible and respected position in the school community. In primary schools with very good practice, these children have learned impressive social, problem solving and study skills. Then over a single summer, they are back at the beginning: the youngest and probably the smallest in a new school, where they have to find their confidence and a positive role all over again.

The *Learning Behaviour* report (Alan Steer, 2005) recognised that some secondary school practice could definitely be improved, noting their evidence that:

- Constructive behaviour policy and practice in primary schools is often applicable to students in secondary school. These teams could learn from their primary stage colleagues.

- Later educational stages have the responsibility to build on the skills that children have already developed and children learn respect by receiving it.

- When secondary school teams fail to take account of children's prior learning, the staff can deskill and demotivate these young students. For some young adolescents, this lack of acknowledgement results in avoidable alienation within a couple of years of secondary school.

School life as a whole

Key messages run through the most useful materials about guiding the behaviour of children and adolescents in the classroom. Linking with the language of choice (page 153), reflective practitioners are aware of the decisions they make about their own behaviour and attitudes within the professional role.

- Guiding children's behaviour is part of the job of being a teacher. Dealing with behaviour that disrupts the classroom is not a tiresome sideline that justifies complaints about 'not being able to do my proper job'.

- Good quality teaching matters. Some children will try to disrupt the most interesting of lessons. However, some behaviour that irritates teachers arises because well-disposed children or adolescents have not been fully engaged.

- Effective and friendly control within the classroom is closely related to the whole emotional tone of the school, as well as the rhythm of the day. The classroom environment is a specialist part of the school day. There should be continuity between values underpinning classroom behaviour and expectations for behaviour in break and lunchtimes.

- Children and adolescents need movement and physical activity. The classroom environment becomes stagnant, even oppressive, when there is no relief from the hard work (page 60). Wise school teams do not cut back on play and conversation breaks and they protect time to eat a decent lunch.

- School life is more than the classroom. Guidance of behaviour is led through building genuine relationships with children and adolescents. They should feel confident that familiar teachers ask about the netball team because they are interested or that they remember about this child's activities outside school.

Play in school

In many schools there is a division of roles such that teachers do not spend time with children or adolescents except in the classroom. Practitioners need their own breaks within the day, but teachers will build a more rounded relationship if they spend regular non-classroom time with pupils or students.

- You come to understand their games or the problems they want resolved in the playground and there is more opportunity for open conversation. I have visited, and heard of, primary schools where teachers, including the head, spend time out at break or lunchtime. They are ready to have relaxed conversations with children and cheer on the impromptu race.

- Some before and after-school provision on school grounds is truly part of the whole school team. I have known schools where teachers, and head, ensure that on some days they eat with the children who attend for breakfast club. There is real interest in what children do in their club time and an effort to make links wherever appropriate.

- Children's play has to be seen as something that is valuable in itself – that deserves time, space and adults who are a respected part of the whole school team. Some primary school teams have transformed their outdoor play space and ensure that adults are play companions rather than controllers. The change could best be describing as transforming break time into playtime.

Peter Blatchford and Sonia Sharp (1994) and PLAYLINK (1999) describe how much of discussion about play in school has been driven by the adult perspective. Anthony Pellegrini and Peter Blatchford (2002) point out that school teams want to promote social skills, yet overlook that much of the context and a great deal of potential learning occurs within spontaneous play within school grounds. Unobservant adults, in a huddle at the edge of the playground, complain that children are 'just hanging about', when they are not being 'disruptive' in unacceptably enthusiastic run-and-chase or furtive games with a football.

Adult anxiety around risk and play has further disrupted play in some school playgrounds and elsewhere (Gill, 2007; Lindon, 2003; Play Safety Forum, 2002.) However, children do not learn vital skills of problem solving when adults decide to solve playground difficulties by stopping specific games or restricting time outside. Children cannot learn to manage their own risk when adults impose judgements based on fear and worst case scenarios. A consistent message from the break time research and consultations with children is that they share many of the concerns of their school staff. However, children ground those concerns within a high value for play and a desire that adults address any problems as something to resolve, not to sweep away by bans and authoritarian sanctions.

The quality of school grounds matters a great deal. Children have informed views on what helps and what does not help to make the grounds a welcoming environment for play and social contact. Wendy Titman (1992 and 1994) described the expertise of children about their own playground spaces: what matters and should not be changed and what was a problem from their perspective. Marc Armitage's (2001) social historical research describes how over the 1970s and 80s the prevailing design of school grounds became more square or rectangular. The available play space for children offered fewer small spaces, which severely reduced children's ability to organise games within their own location. Different games and groups of play companions were more likely to have territorial problems and the accident rate increased within shared large spaces.

LOOK, LISTEN, NOTE, LEARN

Many problems over behaviour dissipate when children have sufficient time to play. Look at the *Play Today* report on St John Baptist Church of England Primary School in Hoxton, East London (*School: a perfect place to play* Issue 63, August 2008 www.playengland.org.uk/play/play-today-63.pdf). The school team tackled the poor reputation of the school through focus on the school grounds as equally important as the classroom. The team stepped outside traditional professional boundaries for teachers by addressing key principles of playwork (www.skillsactive.com/playwork/principles). They developed the outdoor environment as a place for learning, created play resources led by a consultation with the children and launched significant gardening projects. Children became enthused, attendance levels rocketed, scholastic achievement was improved and problems with behaviour and bullying incidents reduced to a minimal level.

Question

- Check out any play strategy documents for your area.
- Look for local primary schools that have created play-full school grounds or who are in the process of improvements. Arrange a visit: find out ways children were consulted and what has happened in terms of play behaviour.
- Follow up further reading in the Resources section, like Free Play Network (2005), Lester and Russell (2008), Lindon (2001) and PLAYLINK (1999).

Dealing with behaviour day by day

Adults have a responsibility to guide the behaviour of children and adolescents within a warm relationship and a positive framework of realistic ground rules. This chapter covers a range of approaches to supporting positive choices in behaviour and offers a basis for choosing between different approaches. Discussion then covers taking a proportionate response to behaviour that steps outside the ground rules or seriously challenges adult guidance.

> **The main sections of this chapter are:**
>
> ✳ **Catch them out being 'good'**
>
> ✳ **Responding to unwanted behaviour**
>
> ✳ **Ordinary or challenging behaviour?**

CATCH THEM OUT BEING 'GOOD'

Children and adolescents appreciate being noticed for what they have done well. They are disheartened and, in the end alienated, by an environment where adults only stir themselves to pick up on what has not been done properly. There are different ways for adults to show recognition of behaviour that they welcome and this section explores the ideas behind different strands of advice to practitioners.

Focus on encouragement

Rudolf Dreikurs, and other writers within the Adlerian tradition, explored the difference between spoken praise and encouragement.

- Spoken praise, or tangible rewards, focus mainly on the end result of what children have done, whereas encouragement by word and body language offers more scope for you to recognise effort and improvement.

- Verbal praise tends to stress a fixed quality about children, 'You are such a sensible boy'. In contrast, encouragement focuses on what a child has managed today, 'Well done for checking your landing place before you jumped.'

- Encouragement homes in more on the process. So it is possible to focus on how children have tried to manage something, even if they were not entirely successful. Adults express appreciation that a child has waited for her turn, even when she needed a bit of adult help with the waiting.

- A pattern of encouragement can boost children's feelings of satisfaction about what they have managed, 'Good job with the mopping'. Whereas dependence on spoken praise can seem unforgiving of times when children do not feel like being 'a helpful child'.

MAKE THE CONNECTION WITH...
BE FAIR, BE EVEN-HANDED

Reflective practitioners and teams need to keep alert to their personal communication. It is not responsible adult behaviour if some children are given positive comments of recognition far more often than others. It is possible to get into a negative loop with a child or adolescent (a fellow adult too) and then the responsible approach is to get yourself back on track.

Some years ago I came across the 'say three good things' approach, that can help when adults have developed a gloomy view of a child or adolescent. The grown-up commits to finding a minimum of three times per day or session in which the child is shown genuine appreciation for 'little things'. Adult attention and powers of observation are shifted to noticing, 'Good job with the brushing', 'Thanks for making space' or 'That is such an interesting question'. Little negative things are then more likely to pass without comment and adult nagging decreases. A positive cycle with this child has a chance to develop.

You have plenty of choices in how to encourage children:

- Spoken encouragement through sincere compliments, saying 'thank you' to a child and simple appreciation of their efforts. Non-verbal encouragement is given through smiles, nods and friendly touch.
- Verbal and non-verbal encouragement gives an immediate, clear message to children: what they have done and why you are pleased, like, 'Thanks for helping Josh with his coat – that was a thoughtful thing to do'.
- Do not wait for ages for something impressive; 'little and often' is a good rule of thumb. This approach is sometimes called crediting children (with thanks to Val Stothard) and can be a simple statement, with positive facial expression, of what children have

Children are keen to help

done: 'You put your shoes on by yourself' or 'Well done, you felt cross and you used your words.'

■ Some adults pick up on every little negative piece of behaviour from a child they find annoying. Reversing this process must be authentic – see the idea of 'say three good things' in the box. When you acknowledge the cooperative behaviour of a child, who is not usually cooperative, you must avoid the negative undertone of, 'why can't you always be like this?'

■ Acknowledge the behaviour of a child who is usually well behaved, do not just let it pass. Avoid the kickback of not letting a 'good' child have an off day; comments like, 'Now that's not like you, is it?' are very discouraging.

It works best to give encouragement close to the behaviour, as part of natural communication, rather than saving comments until later, maybe the end of the day or session. Younger children will have completely forgotten what they did earlier. Older children may remember the incident which you are now recalling with an encouraging remark. However, it is still more effective to make a brief verbal and/or non-verbal comment close to when the behaviour happened.

WHAT DOES IT MEAN?

Encouragement: positive feedback by words and non-verbal communication, as much for effort as for achievement.

Praise: positive feedback in words, usually for what has been done or achieved.

Reward: giving tangible items or special experiences as a result of behaviour or achievement.

Incentives: a promise of a reward in the future, as a result of particular behaviour or achievement – the element of 'if… then'.

Symbolic rewards: giving something that represents praise for behaviour or other achievements, such as stickers or certificates.

Using symbolic rewards

For many years schools have used symbolic rewards – a token that is a visible sign of approval, like the silver and gold stars from my childhood memories. However, in recent years, there has been a significant increase in the promotion of stickers, smiley faces, hand stamps and certificates. Some writers advise that these symbolic rewards are handed out for a very wide range of behaviour.

Earning stickers rather than choices over behaviour

There are good reasons to reflect on this approach with children in school. But it is developmentally foolish to institute a system of symbolic reward within early childhood. It sets up a wrong set of expectations of why it is worth behaving well. Additionally under-fives, let alone under-threes, have scarcely any idea why they have got this hand stamp or smiley face, other than they have been 'good'. They will not turn it down, since the adults seem to think stickers are so valuable. Even in middle childhood, parents recount that their son or daughter has only a hazy idea of how they earned this symbolic reward.

In behaviourist terms, the prospect of stickers or certificates is assumed to operate as an incentive and the earning of them as positive reinforcement: a reward that will increase the likelihood of wanted behaviour. However, there are potential problems as soon as you go more than a little way down this route. There is a serious fade-out effect, not best resolved by creating even more complex systems.

■ Once adults have placed the symbolic reward centre stage, children are motivated less by making an active choice in behaviour and more by whether they want and anticipate success in getting this symbol. If tidying up has become an activity that merits a sticker, children may decide that today they will opt out of tidying up and can live with no sticker or badge.

- It is possible to lose sight of the behaviour that the system is supposed to increase. Children judge their personal worth by counting the certificates rather than recall of actual events and the pleasures of achievement.

- Well-rounded advice about symbolic rewards emphasises the need to talk with children and not simply dole out the stickers. However, problems arise when practitioners have largely delegated the task of acknowledgement to the sticker or hand stamp. The feeling grows that 'just talking' is not enough, supported by an implicit message in some commercial marketing, that twenty-first century children will not behave well for simple verbal encouragement.

MAKE THE CONNECTION WITH...
REWARDS CAN BE UNPREDICTABLE

Social learning theory allows that reinforcement can be experienced as internal feelings (intrinsic), such as pride in achieving a task or skill. This development of behaviourism acknowledges that people observe, think and feel.

Any team needs to talk with and listen to children (and their parents too). Their responses will tell you if your system is working as you believe. Children and adolescents are the experts about the receiving end of adult strategies for guiding behaviour. Discussion with them highlights that events which adults believe are 'rewards' can have unexpected results. For example:

- A child who loves to be the centre of attention may be strongly motivated by the prospect of receiving a certificate during whole school assembly. On the other hand, a child who feels desperately self-conscious will find such public praise emotionally painful. The experience is not a reward; it is more like punishment. This child might welcome a quiet conversation from an adult.

- Older children in primary school, especially the boys, can be embarrassed by being awarded the 'good behaviour' certificate on a regular basis. They also risk having their playground credibility utterly undermined. They are happy you are proud of them, but would much rather you told them privately.

Questions

■ If you use a system of symbolic rewards, have you and your team checked recently how children and adolescents understand your system?

■ Never mind the theory, how do they believe it works in practice?

Monitor and track

If you choose to use symbolic rewards, or any kind of tangible payoff for behaviour, there has to be a consistent approach between all practitioners within one form of provision. It is unacceptable adult behaviour if some groups or classes have to meet much stricter standards. You also have to track very carefully who gets the rewards and for what specific behaviours.

A frequent problem is that stickers are given out disproportionately to children at either end of the spectrum: children who manage to be outstanding and children who have serious struggles. Parents, and children themselves, complain there is minimal acknowledgement for ordinary 'good' behaviour. Some advice is then to institute another layer to acknowledge children 'in the middle'. Sensible teams rethink a creaking system and significantly reduce or bin the symbolic rewards.

TAKE ANOTHER PERSPECTIVE

Are you well and truly stickered? Some ways to tell:

■ Children often check, 'Will you give me a sticker if I...?' before being helpful or other prosocial behaviour.

■ Children announce sadly, 'I've haven't done anything special today', because they have no symbol.

■ Some parents chase you with, 'Why hasn't my child got as many as...?'

■ The large bill from the company making all these stickers, smiley faces and certificates. They cannot sell you simple verbal appreciation and actual smiles!

Questions

■ Have you stepped back and reflected on the system as a whole?

■ Or are you tempted to home in on individual children as 'uncooperative', or a parent as 'difficult', when they are only being sharp observers of your system?

Simple approaches

Careful use of symbolic incentive or reward can work, so long as the approach does not overwhelm personal communication and common sense (I do not often use this phrase, but it is the best here). Keep the system simple and tune into how children understand it to work. In my visit to Sun Hill Infants School, the Year 2 children (6- to 7-year-olds) were able to explain clearly the difference between the Green and the Silver Smileys and generally that, 'I wouldn't be special if you had one all the time.' In the summer of 2008 the Sun Hill team were in the process of rethinking even their limited symbolic reward system.

These ideas, explained to me by practitioners from other settings, are examples of what can work well so long as a team fully discusses the what, why and how.

Almost blank stickers

One nursery changed to white sticky labels, which all started with, 'Ask me about...' and then something personal was added each time.

- These labels were used sparingly and with a care that all children had one over time. The message was sometimes about 'the big castle I built' and sometimes about 'how I helped to sweep up the leaves'.
- The written label supported communication with parents, focused on actual behaviour and helped young children to recall events special to them.
- Some parents chose to use the white label for communication from home into nursery. This choice helped children feel that their key person and parent were sharing important events from family as well as nursery life.

The example would work just as well in reception and the earlier years of primary school. Slightly older children could choose to write their own label with adult support and encouragement.

The group jar

I first heard this approach used with a reception class (4- to 5-year-olds) and that is the youngest age with whom you can sensibly use this idea. Under-fours do not understand the symbolic nature and the timescale is too long. The aim of this approach is to encourage and celebrate positive behaviour without getting enmeshed in rewards for individual children.

- You have a large jar on display so children can see it all the time. You also have a collection of large marbles or the larger pieces of dried pasta.

- Individual children gain a marble, or pasta piece, to pop into the jar. The adult acknowledges a wide range of positive behaviour from individuals. So, you can show appreciation for what might look like a small step to an unfamiliar adult but you know is a big effort or achievement for this boy or girl.

- The jar belongs to everyone in the class and the adult does not keep track of who earned how many marbles. It is a group effort and a group achievement.

- The jar needs to fill up relatively quickly, even when used with children into middle childhood. Standards for earning a marble should not be so stringent that the jar sits there for weeks before getting full.

- Once the jar is full, then it is traded for an enjoyable experience for the whole group. Children soon get the idea of the range of activities they can request. They also show an understanding of events that, 'we would really like but we know can't happen tomorrow, because you have to organise it'.

- I have heard examples of having a picnic, visiting a local park, having a cooking session, watching a video/DVD and other experiences that do not happen on a frequent basis and maybe would not otherwise happen here.

The whole tone must be positive and the jar must not be used as a vehicle for nagging or potential sanction. These points apply to any symbolic system.

- After a fraught day, the most that an adult says is, 'That's a pity, no marbles today. I'm confident tomorrow will be different.' You do not have to comment, but definitely use that kind of reply if a child raises the subject.

- The prospect of losing marbles must never be used as a threat. It is irrelevant if you rarely carry out this threat, as one room team wanted to reassure me. (Also they were working with 2-year-olds, so the system was not appropriate.)

- I was told of a primary school class in which the teacher regularly raided the jar as a sanction for individual children's misbehaviour. In this unpleasant atmosphere the group jar will not work as an incentive and the class was fed up with their teacher, whose behaviour was seen as very unfair.

The Golden Leaves and similar ideas

In one nursery I visited, they had drawn a large tree on to thick paper and fixed it to the wall. The team leader had started the Golden Leaves to encourage some practitioners to be more positive about individual children whom they regarded as troublesome. The adults had a store of paper leaves that they used to acknowledge specific behaviour. The adult wrote a short description on the leaf: 'good listening in story time' or 'helping Sacha with her coat buttons'. Children held on to their personal Leaf until the short group time each day and then it was fixed to the tree. Children could say, if they wanted, how they had gained this Golden Leaf. At the end of each week the group looked at the whole tree, the leaves went into children's personal folders and the process started again.

The Kindness Tree is a similar focus: adults are alert for specific examples of 'being kind'. Like the Golden Leaves, adults need to ensure that the kindness notes are distributed across the group. Practitioners discreetly keep track of who has already appeared on the Kindness Tree. Adults need to reflect on 'how have I missed Gary being kind?' and not assume that, 'Gary is never kind'.

TAKE ANOTHER PERSPECTIVE

So many schools use systems of symbolic reward that practitioners often assume this approach is the only, or best, way to guide behaviour. Thongsley Fields Primary School turned away from symbolic reward systems, when they rethought their entire approach in 2000 based on the language of choice (page 153).

- The main objective is that children take ownership of their own behaviour and become able to guide themselves. This outlook and ability to self-regulate become a positive habit – a skill that supports lifelong learning.

- The key underpinning value is stated in their school prospectus that, 'Good behaviour is not rewarded, it is expected'. Expectations are pitched at a realistic level for children's age and acknowledge that many local families experience a great deal of stress.

The team guide children's behaviour through warm relationships, clear rules and personal communication. There is a great deal of acknowledgement for positive behaviour, without a single sticker or pre-printed certificate. The celebration is by words, body language and a nurturing environment in which children and adults are comfortable with friendly physical contact.

Over a two-day visit, my notebook was full of examples of spontaneous kindness and consideration between the children. I regularly saw older children go up to younger ones in the corridor, to check whether they needed any help. I spent scarcely thirty seconds standing in one classroom before I realised two children were approaching from different directions, each with a chair to enable to me to sit. They had not been asked; it was a spontaneous act of courtesy to a visitor. With a 'thank you', I put myself on one chair and my heavy bag on the other.

Of course, the children do not behave positively all the time. Some of them really struggle with the pattern of behaviour needed in a school community. But their behaviour is addressed in a constructive way (page 218).

RESPONDING TO UNWANTED BEHAVIOUR

Of course you have to address behaviour from children and adolescents that you do not want them to choose. You are ready to talk, and listen, when a pattern of misbehaviour has developed or you notice this child or adolescent is struggling to make the right choice.

What is actually happening?

Part of the adult responsibility is willingness to step back mentally and consider that what you believe to be the dynamics of this situation is not the full story.

Negative reinforcement

A key behaviourist concept is that reinforcement (negative or positive) strengthens a response: makes it more likely that this behaviour will be repeated. The concept of negative reinforcement is a useful perspective for understanding why a given adult reaction has failed to dissuade a child or adolescent from a repeated pattern of behaviour.

SCENARIO

Owain is 7 years old and stuck in a pattern. He has realised that he cannot read like his peers; it is a mystery to him. He has found that clowning around in class distracts his teacher from persisting in asking him to read aloud. His teacher reprimands Owain for 'being silly' and other actions but is puzzled as to why Owain continues in this behaviour day by day.

Pause and reflect

Owain has been reinforced in his actions: he successfully avoids the anxiety provoked by a task which is stressful to him. He is unlikely to take a different course of action unless helped by his teacher. Adults understand the serious consequences of not being able to read, but Owain does not foresee the long term impact of his strategy.

Questions

- Do you face situations where you have not yet taken this perspective: a child's strategy is working, so why would she or he change?
- How might the Owain's teacher change her behaviour to step aside from the current pattern?
- Recall the effectiveness of partial reinforcement (page 19). Owain's strategy does not have to work every time; it has to work often enough.

Positive reinforcement – from the child's perspective

Sometimes exasperated adult reactions to a child's behaviour work as positive reinforcement: the addition of something pleasant and welcome. Whereas the adults believe they are behaving in a way that should be experienced by the child as punishment: the addition of something unwelcome by the child. The classic example is when a child, or adolescent, is desperate for personal attention and has learned a strategy of disruption, of 'demanding' instant reaction.

- Young children may fling things, throw tantrums or dissolve into tears at the smallest provocation. Older children in the classroom situation may call out, make undue noise with books or trouble their peers. These behaviours are often met with significant attention by adult words and actions.

- Practitioners are then perplexed about, 'Why does he keep pinching his classmates, when it always gets him into trouble?' or 'I get so irritated with her constant waterworks, why does she cry at the slightest thing?'

- Until adults stop and reflect, they are stuck in a repeating loop with the child, who is actually being reinforced for their action by full adult attention. If children have limited experience of friendly adult interaction, then being told off and moaned at by adults is worth their effort. Sometimes, practitioners (and parents) need fellow adults to point out the problem in a constructive way.

The way out is an adult strategy of tactical ignoring of the unwanted behaviour – a policy of non-reinforcement – and deliberate reinforcement through attention to ways that you wish children to act so as to get your attention. (See page 71 about mistaken goals.) You choose to ignore the behaviour, or to give it minimal attention; you do not ignore the child as a person.

LOOK, LISTEN, NOTE, LEARN

When you are puzzled or frustrated by the behaviour of a child, it can help to observe in a more structured way. One method is the ABC approach. I do not know who originated this idea; it has been around for many years.

- A is for antecedent – what happens prior to the behaviour that concerns you
- B is for behaviour
- C is for consequences – what happens immediately afterwards.

First of all, decide the focus of your observation. Suppose 9-year-old Hamid appears to be at the centre of many shouting arguments in your club. Ideally led by one practitioner, the club team needs to gather observations of the sequence, the events either side of Hamid's outbursts.

Head up a sheet with ABC, written in full if you like, to give three columns. Each observation should be dated, timed and signed by initials. After each incident, you swiftly write up what occurred before the outburst and how it was handled.

Within the team, look at your observations after about a week. For instance:

- Has sharper observation shown that the usual trigger is that Hamid is wound up by other children?
- Does Hamid have few strategies in between asking, almost pleading, to be left alone and then going into full shout mode?
- Are there times of the day or circumstances when Hamid's ability to cope runs out faster? If practitioners are alert, is it possible to intervene and redirect?
- What typically happens afterwards? Is Hamid simply being told off for shouting? Do practitioners problem-solve what has led up to the argument?
- What kind of attention does Hamid receive when he is not in full outburst?

Punishment is unreliable

In behaviourist theory punishment weakens habits of behaviour. However, adult punitive actions sometimes result only in the apparent disappearance of behaviours. Children and adolescents may become secretive and simply ensure that they are not observed or discovered.

MAKE THE CONNECTION WITH... AUTHORITARIAN STYLE

Highly controlling adults often behave as if reward is defined by the absence of punishment. The authoritarian rationale (page 30) is that children will behave themselves, because these actions are not met by shouting or loss of privileges.

The logic of negative reinforcement is that an action is strengthened when it leads to the removal of something unwanted. However, in real life that only works when the child, adolescent or adult has some feeling of control. A punitive regime is so disheartening that the absence of being punished is simply a temporary respite. It does not act as a motivating reward for active choices.

Even at the milder level, a punitive approach to children's behaviour is almost entirely negative: cross words, nagging or a long stream of 'don't you start!' and 'stop that'. Adults can develop bad habits as individuals, or within a team, and feeling very tired or stressed does not help. The serious disadvantages are:

- The message is limited, 'don't' rather than 'do', so children's opportunity to learn is restricted. A wholly negative approach leaves children to work out what is left once they have discounted all the 'not allowed's.
- Children are confused and sometimes upset; they may not understand why adults are exasperated or angry. Young children especially need direct guidance away from temptation and not just words.
- Knee-jerk punishments often have very little direct link to what a child has done, or not done. The adult action is driven more by their emotions – feeling angry, tired, embarrassed, fed up or incompetent to deal with the situation.
- By law, no practitioners in the UK can use corporal punishment: hitting or other forms of physical assault in the name of discipline. But when adults use verbal ridicule or threats, they are modelling negative behaviour. Practitioners should always consider, 'Would I like a child to imitate what I've just done?'
- Furthermore, adolescents increasingly rise to the confrontation and punitive adults back themselves into a corner where the only option appears to become even more punitive. A childhood dominated by this kind of adult behaviour soon becomes one of emotional and possibly physical abuse and safeguarding concerns are soon an issue (see Lindon, 2008a).

TAKE ANOTHER PERSPECTIVE

The misuse of the jar of marbles (page 193), removing marbles from a group jar for the individual misbehaviour, raises a more general issue for reflection. I have also encountered loss of Golden Time (see page 204) for a whole class as the result of misbehaviour of the few.

- Is it fair to insist that a whole group or class shares collective responsibility for the misbehaviour of one or two children?

The adult argument is that better behaved children, or adolescents, will exert pressure on their peers in order not to lose their own break time or privileges. In my own school years I thought this rationale was unfair: most of the class had done nothing wrong, so why were we being punished? Now an adult, I feel equally strongly about the faulty logic that presumes children or adolescents can control peers' behaviour, when the responsible adult has conspicuously failed.

The same objection applies when an adult threatens to cancel a special event for everyone until someone confesses to the graffiti on the outdoor wall of the club.

- If the culprit(s) are currently unknown, then adults need to be honest about the options. The money to pay someone to clean the graffiti will have to come from the club budget. That means something else will have to be cut and that could delay purchase of the basketball nets.

- The decision can be postponed for a week. Meanwhile the adult would most like that the 'artists' come forward and with a proposal for cleaning up the graffiti: their own efforts if this will be effective or some fund raising.

- Suppose nobody has admitted the defacing of the wall and ordinary efforts will remove the graffiti. Then a playworker, who shows commitment to 'our club' will also be part of the clean-up crew. The clear message is, 'I know most of you did not make this mess/create the damage, and neither did I. I'm saddened that nobody has spoken up. But the bottom line is – we're in this together.' A committed class teacher will take the same line.

Sanctions or consequences?

Rudolf Dreikurs developed the idea of using the consequences of children's behaviour. He applied this approach to family life (Dreikurs and Soltz, 1995) and the classroom situation (Dreikurs, Grunwald and Pepper, 1998). Don Dinkmeyer and his colleagues (1997, 2008) developed the ideas further in what they called the STEP approach to parenting. This approach resolves the difficulties raised by punitive sanctions, let alone fiercer approaches to punishment. I have used the term 'sanctions' to apply to adult-determined events, imposed following unwanted behaviour, but not necessarily linked meaningfully with those actions.

WHAT DOES IT MEAN?

Sanctions: adult-determined events that are imposed following unwanted behaviour from children or adolescents. These may be experienced as punitive by the child.

Using consequences: events that follow unwanted behaviour, but which are closely linked with what a child has done or not done.

Behaviour that you want to stop or redirect can be guided by ensuring that children experience the consequences of their actions. A great deal depends on how adults behave, because an apparently similar action can be experienced on the receiving end as punitive or a calm use of consequences.

- Whenever possible, adults pre-warn that a given consequence will follow, if a child or adolescent continues in this way. In contrast, punitive sanctions appear without warning, or with a threat only moments before imposition.

- The adult remains calm and children have the chance to change direction themselves. In nursery you might say to a 4-year-old, 'Jonas, you need to stop throwing blocks (pause). You can stay here and be a builder (pause). But people who throw blocks have to play somewhere else.' If Jonas cannot stop himself then his removal from this play space feels more like a 'fair cop'.

- Consequences need to be consistently applied, even when the adult is tired. Behaviour is dealt with at the time and the child is allowed a fresh start. There is no nagging, no harking back. Children are given chances in the future and adults offer a friendly reminder of 'how you behave when…' Children receive plenty of appreciation when they are behaving well.

Natural and logical consequences

Adults can sometimes let a child or adolescent experience the natural consequence of their choice. In fact, there are advantages for learning when adults do not rush around over-protecting children from consequences that are perfectly safe for them to experience. At home, adolescents who choose not to put their clothes in the washing basin will inevitably run out of clean items to wear. In after school club, if the children are uncooperative in searching for lost pieces of a jigsaw, then that item will be incomplete and less enjoyable. In a family home or out-of-home setting, the adults make a choice about how they respond. If parents seek out adolescents' dirty washing, they disrupt the natural consequence. Practitioners in club may decide they are unwilling to let resources be spoiled through lack of care and for the time being they will do the search.

It would be irresponsible to allow a child or adolescent to experience the natural consequences of the unsafe action of someone else. Ground rules are established for safe enough behaviour around tools or for use of equipment like hockey sticks. A child or adolescent, who is not behaving safely, is given the chance to recall 'what we do when…' and redirect themselves. If they persist, then they have shown they cannot be trusted today with this equipment or in this activity. The logical consequence is that they have to put down their screwdriver or sit out the hockey game for a time. In reality the ideas of natural consequences often flow into logical consequences.

Logical consequences are more adult-determined follow-on events but directly relevant to the behaviour. There is a meaningful connection between what children do, or refuse to do, and what then follows. For instance, in her school classroom, 9-year-old Gayle has been warned but continues to mess about. The natural consequence of her behaviour is that she will run out of time to complete the work that her peers have managed to finish. Since this result followed from Gayle's own behaviour choice it was avoidable, so she will have to put in the necessary effort over break time or her lunchtime. Gayle's teacher has to follow through with the consequence, without complaining about her own lost break time. In this school, leaving your work uncompleted is not a choice on offer.

In a school playground, children who do not take reasonable care in playing football will be invited to come up with ways to pay for the broken window. It is not inevitable that children have to pay for damage, although there are times when handing over a cash contribution will be appropriate. A logical consequence feels to children like a fair result (not necessarily welcome, but fair). The established values of the school community are that everybody is expected to make reparation for their own choices that have caused damage or disruption.

Bill Rogers (2006) uses the term 'behavioural consequences' to cover the same idea. He also covers the realistic concept of 'deferred consequences', allowing for the fact that sometimes everyone (adults as well as child or adolescent) needs to calm down before any conversation can happen. Ideally behaviour is dealt with at the time and everyone moves on within the day. Another meaning of deferred consequences arises when children are given a genuine choice that they can make reparation now or later. Timing is important, since a positive approach to behaviour is not established if the adult reaction is to keep postponing 'until later', when the links will be lost, given this child's timescale.

'Artificial consequences'

This term was used by Jillian Rodd (1997) to cover follow-on events that adults use but which do not connect with what a child or adolescent has done. The concept offers a bridge to the less constructive sanctions that adults impose.

- The footballers would experience an artificial consequence (or punitive sanction) if they were told they could no longer come on the school museum trip. Breaking a window is reprehensible and needs to be addressed but this action is not connected in any way with the kind of behaviour needed on a school outing. The footballers will regard such an adult action as unfair.

- In contrast, 8-year-old Marcia might fairly be warned that her place on the museum trip is in jeopardy if she continues to have serious trouble with controlling her outbursts of temper. Taking children or young adolescents into a public space and facility requires that adults can trust them. Adults will support Marcia and continue to help her to find safer ways of dealing with her strong emotions. However, one more outburst before this Friday's trip and regrettably Marcia will not be permitted to come with her class.

> **WHAT DOES IT MEAN?**
>
> **Natural consequences**: events that follow on as a highly likely result of a child's behaviour, unless the adult decision is taken to block or reduce the consequence.
>
> **Logical or behavioural consequences**: events which are determined by adults and are linked in an understandable and fair way with the behaviour.
>
> **Deferred consequences**: when there is a slight time delay for application of logical consequences, or the choice between equally applicable consequences.
>
> **Artificial consequences**: events which are adult-determined but do not link logically or naturally with the behaviour – what I call punitive sanctions.

Using loss of special time

One approach to unwanted behaviour is to use loss of a general special time to operate as a disincentive. The most popular example of this technique in primary schools is use of Golden Time. I am therefore going to discuss this specific approach but my serious reservations apply to any version of the system.

Golden Time is part of the whole primary school approach described by Jenny Mosley and Helen Sonnet (2005). This end of the week special time of play is available so long as children have not contravened any of the school's Golden Rules. If during the week children break a rule, then the teacher speaks quietly to them and gives them a warning card. If they break the same or another rule while the card is still there then they are told they have lost five minutes of their Golden Time and this is noted by the adult. They can continue to lose their Golden Time in five minute chunks. Children can earn back up to half of the lost time by meeting an earning back contract made with the teacher. Part of a whole school policy is that playground supervisors, not only class teachers, use this warning and time loss system for children's behaviour.

In behaviourist terms, the rationale is that:

- Behaving in line with the Golden Rules is rewarded by enjoyment of special time at the end of the week. However, when I have listened to children, they seem to view the session as a normal activity you can lose rather than a special activity you can secure through easily recognisable behaviour.

- Unwanted behaviour will be reduced because failure to follow the rules is sanctioned by threatened or actual loss of Golden Time. However, this complicated system has adults and children focused on losing and regaining time within a special event that could be as far as five days ahead. Practitioners' energy is focused on keeping track of the system, not on dealing with what the child has done now.

- Children sit and watch the sand timer during Golden Time on Friday for misbehaviour that could have occurred as far back as Monday. It is a long-winded way of dealing with actions that should be resolved at the time and not be a harking back when the sums are complete at the end of the week.

In Adlerian terms, the experience is presumed to work as a logical consequence.

- A class teacher will have explained the links that the adults have made: that following the Golden Rules is connected with holding on to, or losing, your Golden Time. However, the complexity of the system and the time delay disconnects children's behaviour from the consequences of their action.

- The same system is required both to encourage wanted behaviour and discourage unwanted actions. The most likely event is that Golden Time operates as an artificial consequence (see page 203). Loss of special time is the adult-determined, delayed result for a wide range of unwanted behaviours.

- Peers on the receiving end of unkind or disruptive behaviour should have the incident resolved at the time. Children may feel satisfied that the peer who hurt their feelings earlier in the week (if they recall) is now staring at a sand timer while they enjoy Golden Time. Pleasure at their exclusion is hardly compatible with school as a harmonious community.

MAKE THE CONNECTION WITH...
PLAY IN SCHOOL

The introduction of Golden Time to primary schools addressed the need to inject some play back into the week. This welcome aim is achieved by schools who protect generous time for break and lunchtimes in playgrounds that are full of play. Some primary schools, as I saw in my visits to Sun Hill Infants and to Thongsley Fields Primary, have also ensured that each classroom has space and time for play. Under these circumstances there is no need for a Golden Time.

Rachel Myer, the head of Thongsley Fields, explained her team's concern that operating a Golden Time implies that the rest of children's experiences in the school week are less than 'golden'. The aim in this school is that children are strongly motivated by their desire to be in class. The disincentive to these boys and girls is to take time from the activities of their group, even for a short while.

The issue around play is one reason why I disagree completely with the advice of Jenny Mosley and Helen Sonnet (2005) to use Golden Time in early years provision. Good practice with these young children is that the days are led by learning through play; a Golden Time of play makes no sense at all. My other objection arises from the time delay (even with the suggestion of a daily Golden Time) and the disconnection of behaviour from meaningful consequences.

Children need to play as part of healthy development

Using time out

The original use of this technique was with children whose actions had taken them beyond being guided by adult words and they could not stop themselves. The technique was used with behaviour that was well outside the usual pattern for this age, genuinely challenging behaviour. However, versions of time out existed in schools in terms of 'standing in the corner' or 'facing the wall' and in early years settings through the 'naughty chair' or corner. In family homes, the version was 'go to your bedroom'.

In behaviourist terms, this technique operates as an extreme form of ignoring, of refusing to give attention (reinforcement) for behaviour that is definitely not wanted. In Adlerian terms, time out is a good example of a possible approach for guiding children that can work positively as a consequence, or be sidelined into a punitive reaction by adults, who are most influenced by their own annoyance.

WHAT DOES IT MEAN?

Time out: a period of time spent away from the main action when a child's misbehaviour is unresponsive to other guidance.

Constructive use of time out

Creating a time out may be used when friendly guidance has not worked and the situation is rapidly worsening. Children have been given fair warning, been reminded of how they need to behave in this given situation. The usual advice, for instance Tanya Byron (2005) in writing for parents, is to say it once in a friendly reminder tone and once in a firmer tone – not unfriendly but more to communicate, 'I really do mean this'. Then, if the child does not cooperate in stopping how they are behaving, the adult says, 'Time out now'. They are taken somewhere safe, out of the immediate action, or sometimes placed outside the room, with the door held closed by the adult if necessary.

Advice about using time out is sometimes rather vague about the minimum age of children with whom the approach should ever be used. Tanya Byron (2005) advises that the technique should only be used for over-twos. I would raise that to a minimum of 3 years of age. It is crucial that children are not left for an indeterminate amount of time. The rule of thumb tends to be no more than one minute for each age of life up to a maximum of five minutes in total.

A major point about time out, used in a constructive way, is that the breathing space can help children calm down and the adult focuses simply on making sure they are safe. The adult also calms down, if necessary, so you are able to talk with the children when they are calm.

- However, it is a technique of last resort, not to be used as adults' first option to frustration with a child. Recall that time out was not originally developed for use with minor misbehaviour, nor for children who are just slow to cooperate.

- Sometimes it is essential to get children out of the immediate space, when their behaviour puts other children at physical risk. However, even with removals from the problem area, I agree with Andrea Clifford-Poston (2007) that younger children sometimes need 'time in' and not 'time out'. Enthusiastic use of the 'naughty step' (promoted in some books and television programmes) creates separation from the adult, so can disrupt the chance for children to learn other ways of coping.

- Nor should time out be a way out for adults who cannot be bothered to have what I call 'a quiet chat' about what is happening now. If practitioners have only a limited idea about how to talk then they may be tempted to dispatch the child somewhere else at the first sign of mild trouble.

- Time out should not to be used as a follow-up sanction after children have been willing to talk through what has happened. Children will feel rightly aggrieved if one or all of them now have to sit out of play for a given time. They might as well have carried on shouting and shoving.

LOOK, LISTEN, NOTE, LEARN

If some children experience a lot of time out, you need to track what is happening. Use the ABC observation technique (page 198).

- ◆ In a team, are you consistent about what behaviour is met by time out? Are some practitioners using time out more often and instead of other approaches?

- ◆ Is this child behaving so as to get time out – is the strategy working as an incentive, not a disincentive? So, what happens during time out?

- ◆ Does Francine get scooped up by the nursery manager and have personal attention in the office? This consequence is not necessarily to be avoided, but should be used as a deliberate incentive for specific behaviour from Francine.

You should be able to identify at least some opportunities for direct guidance towards alternative ways of behaving. Be clear for children what choice you want them to make instead, so you do not have to institute time out. Be ready to acknowledge every time they manage this alternative.

- It might be: 'Stefan, well done! You used your words. You've told me you're cross about... Now let's see what we can do about...'

- Make sure that a familiar adult is close to the child and can redirect, perhaps with, 'Stefan, stop' (hand up signal) 'listen to me' (gesture to your ear) 'what do you do when...?' You give a genuine, 'Well done, Stefan' even if you have had to guide quite a lot of his reaction to this difficult situation.

- Sometimes, it might be, 'Stop' (hand up) 'Look' (point to the focus of the problem) 'How do we... when...?'

Learning to do 'calm down'

Children benefit from being a part of the valuable calming down element of responsible use of time out. This opportunity is far more likely to arise when adults create a calm-down place, which avoids negative overtones. It is even possible, I have known it happen, that practitioners chose to use the area to do their own 'counting quietly up to 10' or 'I'm going to sit on our calm-down cushion. I need to feel better about my horrible bus journey this morning.'

I have known 4- and 5-year-olds who have been able to recognise, 'I need to start my day in the snuggle corner' or 'I just want to sit a bit.' A calm time out of the action is best guided by timekeeping shared by the children themselves. A sand timer not only guides a suitable length of time, but watching and listening to the flow of sand can in itself be a calming experience. I was told of one 4-year-old who had learned to recognise his own inner turmoil and sometimes chose to upend the sand for another run. Then he judged he was ready to rejoin play.

MAKE THE CONNECTION WITH... WORDS MATTER

Time out in a calm-down place, with a calm adult close by is a very different experience from the institution of the 'naughty' chair or step. This negative labelling has been abandoned, in the vast majority of early years provision, because the word is seriously unhelpful.

If children need a calming time out, then you want them to reflect on exactly what they have done, not the non-specific 'naughty'. Sitting on a 'naughty' chair or mat is distressing to children who would otherwise soon be ready to talk. Some children see their spell(s) on the naughty chair as a badge of honour.

In Thongsley Fields Primary School there is a strong focus on helping children to learn to direct themselves. This team had observed that children who struggled to control their own actions learned to use conventional 'time out' as a way to remove themselves completely from the classroom. Their strategy was successful because children extracted themselves from the situation they found such a challenge. However, they had also removed themselves from the class teacher who knew them and needed to help them to cope.

In Thongsley Fields the staff directly guide children in ways they can help themselves calm down. These practical ideas are seen as relevant for everyone and not just children who find behaving well a serious struggle. The ideas are presented as a range of strategies from which children choose what works for them. Suggestions include take a deep breath, stop and count to 10, have some time by yourself, close your eyes and think of a calm place, talk to a friend. Each room has a calm-down place and children use this option in a constructive way. In 2008 the eldest pupils had gone on a school residential trip. Some boys were very keen to telephone their head, Rachel Myer. Their message was that they had already sorted out a good corner for their calm-down place and all would be well.

Stay-back time
In school a possible consequence of misbehaviour is that children or adolescents lose some personal time as a result of how they have behaved in class or during break times. Serious conversations about their behaviour are unlikely to happen within classroom time so the pupil or student will have to give up some of their break or lunchtime – as will the practitioner involved.

A school team can make detention part of the behaviour policy, although there are legal requirements about giving notice to families (usually 24 hours). However, there is no obligation to use detentions and it is up to the school to determine the details of this approach. Old style detention is an artificial consequence, a punitive sanction, because it involves limitations on the free time of students as the follow-on of a wide range of misdemeanours. Detention is ineffective, and unacceptable adult behaviour, within a constructive policy when:

- It is used for minor misbehaviour like being off-task. Such incidents need to be handled at the time.
- Whole classes lose their personal time – a blunt instrument approach that loses the good will of well behaved students (page 200). If it is difficult to identify disrupters, then whole class meetings need to problem solve the issues.
- Students sit in silence doing nothing or they have to 'do lines'. The only suitable focus for writing is the incident that took this student into detention.

Stay-back time can be effective so long as there is a focus on what has happened and what is going to be different next time. Bill Rogers (2006) suggests that this option works as a helpful consequence when students are expected to consider:

- What happened? What has led you to be in stay-back time?
- What is your side of the story? (There is always a right of reply.)
- What rule or right was affected by your behaviour?
- What can you do to make things better?
- What can your teacher do to help you fix things now?

The teacher supervising stay-back time would be available to help, if requested, and a copy of the written account would go to the class teacher or tutor. The student would retain a copy and the whole point is to use this think-about time to move the problem along in a constructive way. However, a similar approach can be used with primary school age pupils when an adult is more active in helping the thinking out loud, followed by the writing.

Exclusion

Across the UK it is feasible that children or adolescents can be excluded from their setting for a fixed period or on a permanent basis. It is expected that every effort has been made to exhaust other ways of dealing with behaviour and that fixed period exclusions are linked with a clear plan for the child's return. Every effort should also have been made to work with parents over the behaviour that is causing problems and to keep them informed, even if they are reluctant to work in partnership.

Many of the references to exclusion are about schools. However, any team has to consider whether misbehaviour is so serious or persistent that exclusion has to be considered. After-school clubs and youth centres have ground rules and practitioners have to consider the well being of the many, as well as the personal struggles of the few. Clubs may operate a not-welcome period, linked with clear communication about the behaviour required to secure re-entry to club.

Permanent exclusion is the final resort and for children of school age the local authority must provide alternative education: a pupil referral unit if no other school will accept this child or adolescent. You can find information on www.teachernet.gov.uk and www.teachingexpertise.com (search 'exclusions' in the Behaviour Management section).

WHAT DOES IT MEAN?

Exclusion: a fixed period over which a child or adolescent cannot attend the setting. If there is no improvement then the exclusion may be made permanent.

ORDINARY OR CHALLENGING BEHAVIOUR?

Adults, as practitioners or parents, will have to deal with behaviour that is mildly or seriously unwelcome from children and adolescents. Part of the responsible adult outlook is to keep a perspective on realistic expectations. Even the most well behaved of children will push the boundaries at some point. In fact, considerate practitioners are aware of children, or adolescents, who seem so concerned to keep within the rules that they risk becoming anxious.

What is challenging?

Some children or adolescents behave in ways that are verbally and physically aggressive and highly disruptive. I have no objection to describing such patterns as 'challenging', because they genuinely challenge the approaches that usually work with other children and adolescents. However, it has become common to apply the word 'challenging' to children whose behaviour is ordinary 5-, 9- or 14-year-old boundary pushing. I think some usage of the word is to avoid using 'naughty' or 'bad'. If we need a general term, then I would rather use 'misbehaviour', still with adult willingness to discuss why this action is unwanted or an unacceptable strategy. Practitioners (or writers) who apply 'challenging' to behaviour within normal range should really address who feels 'challenged' and on what grounds?

WHAT DOES IT MEAN?

Challenging behaviour: actions and reactions from children or adolescents that, in contrast with their peers, are more persistent, extreme or resistant to ordinary methods of guidance.

Emotional and behavioural difficulties (EBD): patterns of serious misbehaviour and inability to cope from children or adolescents, in contrast with realistic expectations for this age group. (Sometimes the D stands for disorder or there is an additional S – ESBD - for social.)

Media headlines about behaviour often imply that disruption is rife in every school. Advice based on observation and overviews (Leaman, 2005; Rogers, 2004; Steer, 2005) describes the more accurate picture of a growing minority of children and adolescents whose behaviour disrupts classroom life and whose inability to cope has a negative impact of their peers. Supportive practitioners realise that the classroom environment requires specific skills (see page 173); with help and patience most children manage. However, some of their peers need considerably more personal guidance in class and other parts of the school day.

Louisa Leaman (2005) points to the strain of an inclusive policy that requires mainstream schools to cope with children who need one-to-one attention and a much smaller group than the typical class size. Intensive use of positive strategies will work over time, to redirect what Leaman calls 'misguided coping mechanisms', as will focused support for social and problem solving skills (see Chapters 5 and 6). However, a laudable attempt to avoid social exclusion too often comes with minimal additional resources for schools. Some early years provision faces similar problems from lack of appropriate support.

There are different routes to the challenging pattern of emotional and behavioural difficulties (EBD).

- Some children and adolescents who show EBD are living with a disability that directly reduces their ability to behave like their age peers. However, all children with a disability do not show disruption to their behaviour.

- Some children showing EBD do not have any specific disability. Some have been set adrift by their family experiences: a highly disruptive childhood, lack of nurture and inconsistent parenting or an indulgent approach that leaves children unable to regulate their own behaviour (see also page 31).

This section covers additional approaches that can be constructive for children or adolescents with entrenched problems in coping with what they experience as the challenges of daily life. All the issues over teamwork continue to apply for challenging behaviour; everyone on the team needs to share the responsibility to guide children. Practitioners need to be attentive to children with known EBD and, as Val Stothard described to me, 'have energy to go where the problem is'. If adults (parents as well as practitioners) wait too long, idly watching, then minor incidents become major and the final adult reaction becomes more severe, maybe finally going across to children then shouting at them. Some practitioners may be reluctant to intervene for fear of making the wrong choice for their action. In this case, team discussion is crucial, so that everyone knows what to do and a child experiences consistency rather than inconsistency and intermittent severity.

TAKE ANOTHER PERSPECTIVE

Disabled children will push out the boundaries and need ordinary guidance.

- Children or adolescents are not well served by excusing them inappropriately – and the differential treatment will annoy and alienate their age peers.

- Adults have to address a mistaken belief that a disabled child or adolescent, maybe with a charming personality, could not cause trouble to peers, disabled or otherwise. It is wise not to overlook the 'child' in favour of the 'disabled'.

- Children who are seriously ill, even with life-threatening conditions, do not benefit when practitioners or parents are motivated by sorrow that a child has so much to bear already. Children with a shortened lifespan need even more to enjoy that time in play with peers, who will struggle to be friends if the other child is excused unkind behaviour in play.

Ordinary guidance coexists with appropriate adjustment for a child's disability, like creating small steps in changing behaviour or using alternative systems of communication. It is often overlooked that some profoundly disabled children or adolescents are in almost constant pain and some of their apparent misbehaviour is alleviated by effective pain control.

Individual plans and agreements

Constructive strategies for guiding children and adolescents do not suddenly change completely, when their behaviour is genuinely challenging or categorised as EBD. However, help has to be more organised, once it is clear that ordinary methods of guidance have been given a fair chance, but have not worked. You need a process of problem discussion and problem solving that includes the child or adolescent, their parent(s) and additional professional help as appropriate to the difficulties. Depending on the circumstances, you might call on the special needs support for your setting, an educational psychologist or other specialists that can provide further information when a child's behaviour is affected by disability. The key points about an individual plan are:

- Focus on the behaviour that is at the centre of difficulties. If problems seem to be numerous, then everyone – the child too – needs to home in on no more than one or two specific behaviours.
- Like any other sensible discussion, you have to go beyond a label. What wrong choices is this child or adolescent making? Under what circumstances and with what usual consequences?
- What do they need to do instead? Are there steps along the way to reaching this end goal and do you need to create realistic sub-goals or targets?
- What support will this child or adolescent welcome? A personal visual reminder, a non-verbal or brief verbal reminder from a familiar adult, the option of taking brief time out?
- Which practitioner will most closely support this child or adolescent towards the target? Parents need ideally to be fully on board with the approach and follow appropriate targets at home.

Help within a relationship

Any adult in contact with the child needs to understand the approach and behave consistently with its aims. However, children who already have trouble making the right choice can feel overwhelmed if too many adults are directly involved. In provision, the help will be led by a named person:

the key person, special support assistant or class teacher. A named adult at the centre of special help is crucial, given the number of professionals, and possibly contradictory advice, that can be involved when children or adolescents have complex behavioural difficulties.

Val Stothard (1998) describes the development of an approach of 'intensive interaction' in work with children and adolescents with severe learning disabilities. The model developed from concern that behaviour modification methods could lead to very controlling adult behaviour and an impersonal approach that was reluctant to consider what behaviour was 'saying' once it was labelled as 'difficult' or 'inappropriate'. Val Stothard shows the strong parallels with teams who work in mainstream schools. The shift to greater empathy challenged practitioners to relinquish some adult control and to have a good reason to insist that a disabled child or young person had to follow an adult request. A more playful atmosphere, and avoiding triggers to misbehaviour, must shift from the negative interpretation of 'letting them get away with it.'

Tracking and review

This process works best when children and adolescents are fully involved in monitoring their own targets and progress. They appreciate systems like social scripts (page 218) and simple visual reminders. A common approach is to use tick or star charts (see page 222), but they involve trading symbolic stars for tangible rewards. It is better to approach struggles around behaviour as a problem that you, as the adult, and this individual child are going to resolve as a joint effort.

In Thongsley Fields the team operate the Ladders to Inclusion. This approach is made personal for each child, the details focus on the behaviour that he or she currently finds such a struggle. A child's individual ladder homes in on how s/he needs to behave under a given situation. The set of faces from 5 (all) to 1 (none) is the means for a child to monitor themselves against their ladder, as well as constructive feedback from the adult. 'Where do they think they have been today overall on their ladder?' The adult directly supporting this child helps the reflection and encourages with the expectation that it can be two steps forward and then one back on the ladder. Children work themselves off the need for a personal ladder, but they may need a different ladder as they become able to tackle the next issue about their behaviour.

Ladder to Lunchtimes

5	ALL ☺☺☺☺☺
4	MOST ☺☺☺
3	HALF ☺☺
2	A LITTLE ☺
1	NONE ☹

© 2008 Thongsley Fields Nursery and Primary School

MAKE THE CONNECTION WITH... PUBLIC INFORMATION

I disagree with public display boards showing the behaviour of children who struggle to follow the ground rules of a setting. Advice about Golden Time (see page 204) sometimes describes a public display of personal clouds and sun visual reminders. I have also seen other kinds of public tracking.

If children need a visual and written reminder, then it is more respectful and considerate to use a system they hold on to themselves. It might be a football warning card system or a personal booklet with their behaviour target reminders within a shared plan.

If nothing else, I think that adults should think very seriously about an approach that they would, I am sure, not welcome being used on them, when they are not up to standard in professional life.

Ladder to Full-time Inclusion

Full-time	8.50–3.15
Full-time am + lunch	8.50–1.15
Full-time am	8.50–12.15
am including break	8.50–11.15
am no break	8.50–11.00
One session	11.15–12.15

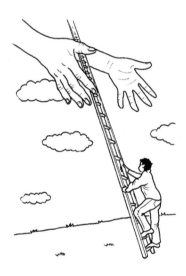

© 2008 Thongsley Fields Nursery and Primary School

Social scripts

The purpose of the story script is to guide this child towards an alternative way of behaving when faced with the situation that currently leads to difficulties. Children may have a disability that impacts on their behaviour. Alternatively their early experiences may have been so disruptive that they cannot cope without this more focused guidance. Ordinary reminders of ground rules, or 'what we do when…' have not worked. Like any method that goes beyond the usual approaches, practitioners need to focus on one, at most two, specific behaviours from an individual child. All practitioners in contact with the child know how to use the story script and you aim for full partnership with the family. If the approach works well in your setting, the child's parent(s) may welcome something similar for home.

You write a very simple story in the present tense, using 'I' for this child. The story is not more than four to five sentences long. It describes the situation and how this child will behave. Advice varies about the wording but I suggest that you avoid the word 'try'. You want to focus on behaviour that this child has a good chance of managing. She or he will not manage every time but you set a realistic aspiration. The goal is not to 'try'; the goal is to behave in the way described in the personal story. For example:

- Lisa finds it very hard to remain safe by an adult on local trips. Penny, her key person, might write this story: 'My name is Lisa. I like to walk to the market with Penny and my friends. I will hold Penny's hand when we walk. Penny and my friends will say, 'Well done, Lisa! Safe walking!'

- The personal story is illustrated by a few photos of Lisa, behaving in the positive way and being congratulated. The story can be made like a book, spread over a few pages. Lisa can be helped to recall and focus on safe behaviour on trips by looking at the book before the trip.

- Once Lisa manages to walk safely, no straining or running away, the script is adjusted to 'I will walk close to Penny' or 'I will walk with my friend, Razak.'

- A younger child might be presented with the book, with the explanation that, 'I made this special book for you. It will help you to stay safe with Penny when we go out.' An older child might be active in making the personal book.

If you want to find out more about this approach, access the paper 'Social Scripts' on www.leics.gov.uk/index.htm (search for 'Autism Outreach Team' and you find a range of resources.) The Camden Early Years Intervention Team use the phrase Behavioural Scripts and describe this work in a feature for *Nursery World* ('My story' 24 March 2005 – accessible on the archive if you are a subscriber, www.nurseryworld.co.uk/news/712636/story/). Both teams reference the ideas of Carol Gray who worked with children and adolescents within autistic spectrum disorder (www.thegraycenter.org). Carol Gray has trademarked the term Social Stories (TM).

Talking within a plan

Regular exchanges with children or adolescents are part of your joint effort to help them achieve agreed behaviour targets in their individual plan. Louisa Leaman (2005) discusses the importance of 'reframing' or redirecting the choices that children or adolescents make.

- This kind of direct help may be within the classroom, as in, 'Gita, I can hear you calling out. I'll be pleased to come across when you are sitting on your chair and have your hand up.' You remind Gita of the behaviour choice for which she is responsible and which has been discussed with her within her personal plan of change.

▪ Perhaps Tyrone has complained bitterly that, 'Everyone always gives me such a hard time!' He has needed guidance to realise, if he made some different choices, then the 'hard time' could not be justified. Tyrone has committed to show that he can be trusted to sit next to his friend, because they will complete their work in this way… Tyrone wants to take his turn with delivering the register to the office and he will show responsibility in these ways…

Problem solving conversations

Sometimes you need to make a timed arrangement to talk – either with an individual or to get together the group of children or adolescents who are at the centre of the current difficulty. When children or adolescents really struggle to make the right choice, these conversations are a regular part of your ongoing relationship with this individual.

Adults usually have to lead this mending fences conversation; you model what you ask of the children or adolescents. The pattern needs to be that:

▪ After a calming down/cooling off time (if necessary), you sit down with the child or adolescent in your class or club. The gap should not be long – ideally later the same day or early the next day after a late afternoon incident.

▪ You explain your perspective on the incident – why you were 'angry' about what happened or similar. Keep it brief and to the point, and very soon…

▪ Invite the child or adolescent to voice their perspective. The atmosphere in this school community or club must be that everyone has 'right of reply', even if what they have done, or not done, is very serious in terms of the code of behaviour here. You have to give them a chance of turn-around.

▪ Listen properly, do not argue or dismiss explanations or feelings. But do be ready to refer back to basic rights and responsibilities in this community, which were disrupted by the behaviour in question.

▪ Do not push for children or adolescents to share their feelings. But, when you know them well, it is right to offer, 'You may be angry about what happened this morning' or, 'You looked very distressed by…'

▪ The aim of this sit-down time is to emerge with how you both – there is a genuine message of 'we' here – could deal with a similar incident 'next time'.

TAKE ANOTHER PERSPECTIVE

Practitioners in school and other settings have become increasingly concerned about their vulnerability to allegations of misconduct of an abusive kind. It is important not to overreact and to consider best practice in the round (see Lindon, 2008a). However, a proportionate response can be to create privacy by talking in a room without listeners and watchers, but to leave the door half open.

The advice for secondary school or sixth form college is often that male teachers talking with a female student should have a female colleague in the room as well. The anxiety is that male practitioners are more vulnerable to malicious allegations of a sexual nature. The problem is then that one student faces two adults and may feel 'outnumbered'. Also, the advice overlooks that allegations can go in the opposite gender direction or be homophobic.

One possible option is to establish a talking place in which it is possible to be seen but not overheard. An alternative is to have as a normal pattern that there are two adults (one of each sex) and that the student has a peer alongside. It should be understood that the adult and student involved in the incident do the main talking. In schools that have developed a thorough mediation approach, the peer would be from that student buddy or negotiation group.

Some strategies, like constructive self-talk depend on practitioners who coach children or adolescents into the links of 'When we think like this… We feel like this… and then we often behave like this…' Bill Rogers stresses that self-talk needs to be optimistic, not the pessimism of 'I'll always be in a mess about…' or 'I'll never…' but on the other hand, not wildly over-optimistic either. There is a close link with a personal plan for changing behaviour and the self-talk can be as simple, 'I can speak in a quiet voice class meetings', 'When I start to get annoyed, I will…' or 'When the work is hard, I will…' Older children and adolescents can begin to understand their personal negative self-talk. It might be, 'When I can't get to play with the other children, I tell them I don't care' (which is not true and does not help), so 'What I can do instead is…'

Bill Rogers also describes a technique of mirroring, as part of helping an older child or adolescent to understand better the behaviour that the adult, or their peers, would much prefer that they change. The aim is to help children recognise what they are currently doing, so they can learn an alternative. The emphasis on learning new behaviours feels more constructive to children and to their parents than focusing a great deal on disruptive current actions, With a, 'Can I show you?' the adult briefly models the child's (unwanted) behaviour) or uses a line drawing (Rogers, 2004 includes a range of visuals to use or adapt). Then you clearly model the alternative, wanted behaviour for that situation and invite the child to practise. Children who are struggling enough to need a personal behaviour plan will need a lot of guidance and friendly reminders.

The behaviour recovery model of Bill Rogers also incorporates the peer support of a child's classmates. His books focus on school, but many ideas are directly applicable to after-school club or youth centres with a strong supportive atmosphere. Any discussion within class or club meetings has to be facilitated carefully by the practitioner. The ideas need to be constructive, no put-downs and no personal attacks. If children or adolescents need to vent a serious backlog of feelings about their peer's unreasonable behaviour, then this release needs to happen in a separate meeting. Children also need to feel confident that the adults are taking appropriate responsibility and not expecting high levels of tolerance from peers to solve this problem.

Peer support can be mobilised to explore how they can best react when another child or adolescent behaves 'like this' or, with care, what will be said to a specific classmate or club member. Peers would usually rather that an unhappy atmosphere improved and are responsive to hearing or generating ideas like, 'We can remind him to…' or 'We will say firmly to her "Stop that"'. Ideas need to be specific and linked with the actual behaviour(s). Children and adolescents may also actively acknowledge when their peer has improved in behaviour.

Using star charts

Sometimes children, and the adults who are trying to help them, find it useful to use the specific focus of a star or tick chart. However, it is important that this approach is tried only when you have genuinely exhausted the simple approaches of saying and showing at the time.

- If you use a star or tick chart, then you focus on a specific behaviour that a child finds hard. Be very clear about the behaviour you want to promote. Is your concern initially phrased as a 'don't' or 'stop'? Then, you need to be clear, and talk over with individual children, what they will do instead when faced with this situation.
- Definitely do not try this approach with children younger than 4 years, they do not understand the abstract nature of the process. In the second half of early childhood, adults have to use their

Peers often watch out for each other in a supportive way

knowledge of individual children and a good dose of common sense. Some four to fives cannot make much sense of the symbolism and you need to address their behaviour simply, at the time, again and again. If children remain puzzled when you talk with them about the plan for a star chart and how it will work, then they are too young, or developmentally immature, for this approach to work.

■ This approach starts with 100 per cent reinforcement. A child gets a star or a tick for each time they manage to eat their meal, complete a task or other specific behaviour. Over time, with the child's full understanding, the star chart shifts to a reward for longer runs of positive behaviour on this specific issue.

■ An agreed number of stars or ticks can then be traded for something that this child would like. In families the reward is sometimes a present of some kind. In a school it would more likely be an experience that is special.

Used carefully, star charts can sometimes help a child to turn around and often, just as important, the shared process can re-cue adults who are struggling to find anything positive to celebrate day by day in this child's behaviour. But...

- Once earned, ticks or stars cannot possibly be unearned. It does not matter how grim a day you have had with a child, the only result is regret, maybe with the child, that he or she has not earned a star or tick today.

- If you support a colleague or a parent, you must make clear that they never cross out ticks or peel off stars. If adults act in this punitive way, then they are forcing the star chart to work as a sanction as well as an incentive. The system collapses because the child experiences adult behaviour as mean and unfair.

- You have to plan an exit route or you are bogged down in charts for ages. Explain to children how pleased you are that you and they no longer have to keep track with the star chart. Ensure that they experience your pleasure at an easy mealtime, or how wonderful it feels that they enjoy story time so much that they are now even able to take the role of storyteller.

- This process is more straightforward when rewards from the star chart are not so impressive that children feel aggrieved by their loss.

- If you use star charts within a group, you need to ensure that children who are well behaved do not feel that their peers who disrupt the day gain considerably more adult attention. Children can be reasonably understanding of a peer who 'needs a lot more help over things that you find easier.'

Adult agreement to change?

Entrenched problems are often a mix of how the child behaves and the way that the adult reacts. It can be very useful to make a commitment of your own. For example, adults are often aware of the need not to shout. But older children, or adolescents, are driven to distraction by annoying adult body language like deep sighs and fed-up shrugs. It may be very important to this child that you commit to, 'Saying and not sighing'. This process becomes more like a give-and-take joint contract. You do not have to award yourself stars. In fact the kind of discussion that leads to a reciprocal agreement often flags up that stars just get in the way.

Physical guidance and intervention

Guidance of behaviour will not always be successful with words and body language. Practitioners would be neglectful if they held back from physically guiding and containing children when that is necessary. You need to keep younger children, or those with serious learning disabilities, safe from actions they do not realise are potentially dangerous. You need to stop actions that are about to hurt or are actually hurting other children. Adults also have the right to be physically safe themselves. Practitioners need to avoid damage to their back caused through action to protect other children from the consequences of behaviour.

Early years provision

It is expected that practitioners will write up incidents with children when it has been necessary to intervene in a squabble that has turned physical or contain children for their own safety or that of their peers. However, you need a proportionate response to this kind of physical contact, or else you will write up every instance of undoing little fingers from someone's hair or the gentle hand-on-hand that catches a hurtful action before it can be completed. Any recording will work best alongside reflection and discussion in the team about what is happening around this child or small group of children.

- Is physical intervention the first response, when clear and firm adult words might do the trick? Never mind the children, what should the adults be doing instead?

- Are practitioners observant of the build-up to a possible incident? Do they get close and use low level intervention at an early stage? Or have bad habits developed in which practitioners watch from a distance until children have flung themselves at each other?

- Are some individual children realistically unable to control themselves because of the stress of their home life or the impact of their disability? Then their key person needs to be given proper training in how to contain and restrain children in a safe way for them and to avoid or minimise injury to the adult.

LOOK, LISTEN, NOTE, LEARN

Discuss in your early years setting how the decision is taken that an incident needs to be recorded as an example of physical intervention or restraint.

Since some potential problems have come from school practice imported down the age range, it is worth noting the advice about recording in the DCSF guidance (2007b). Paragraphs 43 to 45 go into more detail about how to judge 'a significant event in which force has been used'. School practitioners are advised to consider whether the incident caused injury or distress to anyone involved, adults too. Regardless of injury was the incident serious enough that it needed to be written up anyway? Is it necessary to justify the adult's use of force? Did other agencies have to be involved, like the police?

Do your records of incidents meet this criteria of seriousness?

Life in school

Schools have the right to use reasonable force to deal with pupils or students, whose behaviour is genuinely unruly or creates a danger to others. Schools also have the right to search pupils or students for weapons, should they have reason to suspect this problem, because schools have to be safe places for everyone (DCSF, 2007f). However, guidance is clear that physical means should be proportionate to children's behaviour. There is no justification for seizing an adolescent by the arm just because they are slow to respond to an instruction or give you a sulky look. It is unacceptable to use rough physical means to stop or redirect children. There is never a justification for shoving, shaking, dragging or hitting children or adolescents. Nor should the prospect of physical intervention be used as a threat or an actual punishment.

However, school teams need to have the kind of discussions that are necessary in other forms of provision, including conversation around use of words. Some of the minimal levels of 'force' in the DCSF guidance (2007b) are actions like leading a pupil by the hand or ushering a student away with a hand on the centre of their back (neither of these seem like 'force' to me.) In both cases it is expected that the practitioner has exhausted strategies of asking clearly and firmly. This kind of active physical contact, or the passive contact by standing between arguing pupils or blocking a student's path, is on a different level to actual restraint. Jenni Whitehead (2008) offers a concise summary of the issues and confirms that no school team, nor that of any other setting, can possibly meet their responsibilities if they have instituted a 'no-touch' policy. Government guidance on safeguarding (see Lindon, 2008a) is consistent in saying that it is unrealistic to set up rules that teachers never touch pupils or students.

Actual restraint

Techniques of physical restraint need to be learned from reputable trainers and with thorough training which enables practitioners to know what to do, in ways that do not put a child or adolescent at risk of injury. The Scottish Institute of Residential Child Care (2005) describes some of the key issues around using restraint. However, the first options are still to defuse a situation without direct physical intervention if possible.

Louisa Leaman (2005) stresses the importance of sending uninvolved students for help from colleagues and using assertive language to remove the audience, firm words like, 'Step back now. This is not your problem'. Give the students directly involved in a physical confrontation that last chance to respond to very firm, and loud enough, instructions to 'Stop. Back away from each other now'. If there is no response, then direct physical intervention may be the only option. The individuals need to be separated with clear space in between them, and redirected, or actually walked, to a place out of each other's sight line. They need to calm down before there will be any chance of talking about what has happened. The other pupils or students may also need help to regain their composure or settle back after the drama.

However, practitioners still need to make a swift yet considered judgement about whether they will be put unreasonably at risk, even by using proper techniques of restraint. It can be very difficult for one person to separate two fighting individuals, especially when practitioners are working with older and therefore larger children, let alone adolescents. Even if the restraint technique works, the result can be that the practitioner, and the student being held, make an effective double target for the other student to attack.

9 Cooperation between the adults

A considerable number of adults can be professionally involved in the life of children and adolescents. They are all responsible for ensuring that different parts of the experience fit together at any one time and provide a smooth transition at times of change. This chapter considers the importance of team-working within provision and commitment to a problem solving approach. Partnership with families is discussed from the perspective of the relationship between adults and making this communication work well for children and adolescents.

> **The main sections of this chapter are:**
> * **Working together well as professionals**
> * **Problem solving as a team**
> * **Partnership with families**

WORKING TOGETHER WELL AS PROFESSIONALS

Not every practitioner works with a group of colleagues on a daily basis. However, many of the ideas in this section are equally relevant if you mainly work with one or two people, or even as a sole practitioner.

Working as a team

A group of staff employed to work in one setting do not necessarily operate like a team. The sense of working well together, the development of teamwork depends on confidence in each other. With reference to guiding children's behaviour, trust needs to grow from experience that your colleagues are:

- Reliable: that if they promise to contribute to this observation of a child then they keep that commitment. Nobody is perfect – reliable team members speak up if they are uncertain about this observation or if practical issues emerge.
- Consistent: that every member of this team will follow agreed ways to respond to behaviour that could be troublesome or actually challenging. Reactions will not vary according to the adult's mood or their personal feelings about this child or adolescent (or a parent).
- Honest: colleagues will tell you (in a courteous and constructive way) what they feel and what is happening. They do not leave you to guess or to persevere on the basis of a misunderstanding.

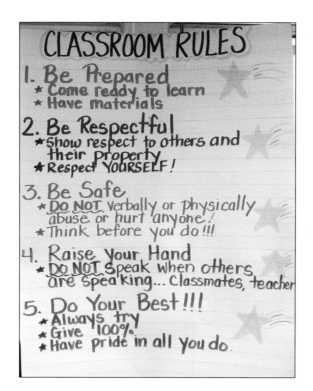

Children and young people need to be part of reaching the ground rules

Teams need time for proper discussion

> ### WHAT DOES IT MEAN?
>
> **Teamwork:** actions and an outlook that enable individuals to work in a way that is consistent and supportive of each other and the values of their setting.
>
> **Interdependence:** that the behaviour of individual practitioners has direct consequences for others in a team situation.

Practitioners need the confidence to deal with children's behaviour at the time and not forever be sending them to the leader of this setting. Behaviour policy and practice is not effective if practitioners feel dependent on a more senior person to deal with anything even mildly difficult. Neither is teamworking promoted if a head or manager refuses to delegate this kind of responsibility to their staff. However, team members are not wholly independent; their actions need to be consistent with key values and approach to behaviour in this provision. Individuals in a team are in a relationship of interdependence.

- One or two practitioners who make little effort to stop shouting at children can undermine the whole approach of setting a good example to children. A colleague who says, 'We say it; we don't shout it' to a child has to deal with a fair reply of 'But Hannah shouts at us all the time'.

- No practitioner can opt out of positive communication with parents about the behaviour of their children or adolescents. Offhand remarks or dismissive body language can reverberate into, 'Staff are so rude in that nursery'. When parents resist this generalisation, the alternative of, 'Neil is so rude, so I avoid him' is not much better for teamworking.

> ### LOOK, LISTEN, NOTE, LEARN
>
> Part of reflective practice is to ensure that practitioners take responsibility for the way that they guide children's behaviour. Daily practice becomes ineffective, if some team members imply that they are under orders to take this option or avoid that possibility. Team leaders in a setting and advisors in a local support team need to pick up on comments like, 'We're not allowed to use the "naughty chair"'. Those practitioners do not sound committed to behaviour policy, neither do they probably understand key reasons for practice.

> ### *Questions*
> - ◆ **Listen in to yourself – do you think in this way sometimes? Do you or your colleagues sometimes say that thought out loud?**
> - ◆ **Do you notice fellow professionals or fellow students shifting the responsibility for thought and choice through, 'We're not allowed to...'?**

Understanding assertiveness

An assertive approach by adults is important for a positive approach to guiding children's behaviour, for example in the classroom (page 173). Much of the guidance you need to give to children and adolescents is to edge them in an assertive direction in their relationship with peers and in how they handle the ordinary problems of interpersonal relationships (page 133). However, assertiveness is equally needed in your working relationship with colleagues, if a group of adults is to operate properly as a team.

MAKE THE CONNECTION WITH.... YOUR OWN PRACTICE

Review the ideas on page 30 with the perspective of adult working relationships. Please reflect on what it means for you. Ideally, discuss the key points with colleagues or fellow students.

- ■ Where can you see yourself in these possibilities? If you are honest, do you incline more towards one style than another?
- ■ What are the advantages of taking an approach that is strongly grounded in assertiveness?
- ■ What are the drawbacks of opting for a style grounded in aggression or passivity?

Team leaders are sometimes more concerned about the impact of practitioners with an aggressive non-assertive style. However, a submissive non-assertive approach often has more layers than is immediately apparent. You have to unpeel these layers if a positive approach to children's behaviour is to work well.

When submissive adults push decisions and choices on to others, their contribution can be lost and that is regrettable. However, they may also, consciously or unconsciously, be keen to hand over responsibility that they should take themselves. They may then blame the other person for wrong advice: 'But I did exactly what you suggested with Aston! Didn't work!'

Advice and support in the team

The point about being a support to team members over behaviour is that you do not take over the problem; you guide them to resolve matters. In some settings the leader/head will be the person who offers this conversation. In other settings it will be a different team member. You need to have an exchange with all the elements of the problem solving approach that runs through this book:

- What has happened so far – what is the child or adolescent doing or not doing, not just a behaviour label?
- What sense does this practitioner make of the situation? Is it all about the child as a problem and little about the situation or the adult's behaviour?
- Does the practitioner feel disheartened, like a 'useless playworker', and are these emotions getting in the way? Does s/he feel criticised by colleagues?
- What strategies have they tried and what happened? Sometimes you need to get beyond a hopeless list of, 'Tried that – didn't work'. In what way did they 'try' it and how come it did not apparently work?
- Have they undertaken any observations – would that be helpful now?

Talk through possible approaches and do not go along with 'I'll do that' from your colleague to the first idea. Quick agreement probably does not indicate commitment. Also you run the risk of taking responsibility for the situation and any changes in the child's behaviour. If 'your' solution works, then colleagues (the same applies when parents ask for advice) have not learned that they can cope. They have learned to ask you for directions. If the solution fails or backfires in some way, then it will be your fault.

Some support needs the more direct involvement of another person.

- Part of the plan to guide a child or adolescent may include the direct involvement of a second practitioner. Some forms of support or serious conversations may typically be offered by the team leader or head.
- The continued professional development of a practitioner may benefit from direct mentoring by a colleague about ways to deal with behaviour. Such a relationship needs to be discussed, including the

aims at each stage, and the mentor colleague needs to be adept at giving honest, constructive feedback about improvement in practice and issues that still need work.

MAKE THE CONNECTION WITH...
TEAM SUPPORT

This direct support may include working side by side. Bill Rogers (2006), writing about schools, describes the need to set up team teaching in a positive way, so that a beleaguered colleague does not appear even less able to cope in the eyes of the children. Teachers need to remain responsible for their class, inviting the senior colleague to join the group and suggesting what s/he might do.

Teams need to discuss appropriate ways to enter a classroom (or other setting) in response to sounds of trouble. A senior colleague should enter in the way that is expected of pupils or students when it is not their room: knocking on the door and saying 'excuse me' – not bursting in like a superhero. Bill Rogers describes how, if a teacher urgently needs time out, then the colleague needs to be empowered to provide a gracious exit, for example that there is an important phone call. If the judgement is that the ringleaders of trouble need to be removed without undue fuss, then the colleague makes a direct request to the teacher to 'spare' the named children or adolescents to help with a task elsewhere.

Louisa Leaman (2005) also discusses a team atmosphere in which class teachers feel confident to call on a senior colleague in an agreed way (but not too often) as part of the strategy for very challenging behaviour. She suggests that trustworthy pupils/students can be used as runners to fetch help, so that a solitary teacher does not leave the classroom. The arrival of the senior colleague is met with a welcome like, 'Pleased to see you, Mr Robertson. Unfortunately you are here because Clement has made some really unhelpful choices about his behaviour today. He is refusing to cooperate over...' Clement is included, by eye contact and other body language, in this explanation. The senior colleague leaves with the child or adolescent in an orderly way.

Questions

■ If you work in a school, then consider in what ways direct colleague support can be valuable – stepping in to help you, not elbowing you out of the way.

■ Similar principles work in nursery, club or youth centre. Think about how these ideas apply to your team and your provision.

What do you want?

Children and adolescents learn about behaviour in a time and place. They learn within their own family home, but also elsewhere. The youngest children may be in a group setting, or with a childminder. Most over-fives will be finding out what is expected of them as a school pupil or member of an after-school club. Older children and adolescents may also attend a youth club or centre.

- A positive adult approach rests on being aware of what you ask of the children or adolescents. What do you want from them in terms of behaviour?
- If you are honest, what do you need from them for your day or session to go reasonably smoothly?

Use the 'Look, listen, note, learn' to explore ideas for your setting, with your colleagues if you work in a team.

LOOK, LISTEN, NOTE, LEARN

It is a useful discipline to limit yourself to a short list of requests (or hopes) for what you want in terms of behaviour from children or adolescents.

If you are reflecting on your own, then limit yourself to five short descriptions of behaviour. If you are working with fellow students or in a team discussion, then limit each small group to three short descriptions, then pool your ideas and look for the common themes. You might agree on one word, like 'courteous' or a short phrase, like 'take care of the school environment'. Any description has to be positive – avoid any 'not...' or 'stop doing...'. Start with a negative, then convert it into a positive – what do you want them to do instead of this unwanted behaviour? How hard is this reflection or discussion to convert?

Now take one description at a time and think, or talk, it through in your group:

- What does it look like when children actually behave in this way. For instance, what does 'kind behaviour' look like – in a 3, 6, 15-year-old?
- Try this approach with at least one more word or phrase. The aim is to generate actual examples that you have observed recently and to support reflection and discussion about types of behaviour that you need to be ready to spot with this age group – realistic expectations.

I have used this group discussion many times in my training days and similar themes usually emerge, despite different choice of words. During one such discussion, an early years practitioner (in Richmond, Surrey)

> read the flip chart list and commented, 'That looks like a job description for adulthood'. This insightful remark links with the next suggestion. Children and adolescents should be able to connect what is wanted from them with how adults behave.
>
> ◆ Take one or two of your words or phrases. Come up with specific, recent examples of how you, possibly with a colleague, have shown this pattern of behaviour within the normal run of your day or session.

When practitioners are clear about what they want, then children feel secure that they know too. Younger children may describe expectations simply but, in middle childhood girls and boys can be clear about how they should behave. In small group discussion with children in primary school, I ask the questions, 'In (name of school) what makes the grown-ups pleased with children?' and then 'What makes the grown-ups disappointed with children?' For instance in Sun Hill Infants the Year 2 children (6 to 7-year-olds) were able to give me specific examples, 'We're a kind school, we look out for other people' and 'We're not rude'. One girl was able to give theoretical examples in actual words, of what it was like to say something bluntly or politely. Other children in the discussion group nodded in agreement. She was further able to explain in words how children could even disagree politely with an adult, saying, 'I think you're wrong about...'

PROBLEM SOLVING AS A TEAM

It is good professional practice to reflect on how you handle situations and react to children or adolescents whom you want to call 'difficult' or 'a problem'. You cannot make anyone directly behave in a particular way – or at least you cannot, unless you are prepared to be intimidating and punitive, in fact a badly behaved adult. However, you can create the circumstances that make it more likely that children will choose one option instead of another. One of those circumstances can be a change in your own behaviour, because this choice is under your direct control. In what is sometimes called a 'dance of behaviour', if you change your own steps, then the pattern is shifted. The same principle applies to family life.

Trouble times and trouble places
A consistent theme through this book is the adult responsibility to step back and observe what is actually happening. Sometimes children and

adolescents are doing their very best and are challenged, perhaps defeated, by the situation in which they find themselves. Supportive adults act with the principles that:

- It is more effective, and appropriate, to address behaviour rather than act as if the child or adolescent has to change their individual characteristics, alter being the person that they are.
- It is often more effective, and considerate, to address the situation, rather than acting as if all problems rest with this child or adolescent's behaviour.

If more than a few children are having difficulty with a particular routine or activity, then the problems almost certainly lie with the situation and not with the children themselves. Responsible adults, with colleagues in a team, problem-solve the situation.

LOOK, LISTEN, NOTE, LEARN

This discussion can follow straight on from the earlier suggestion, or can be a separate reflection and discussion.

- ◆ **What helps the children or adolescents who manage (most of the time) to behave in line with what you want and need?**
- ◆ **What are the times, locations and routines that seem hard to manage for quite a few children or young people?**
- ◆ **Do these trouble times, places and spaces have features in common?**
- ◆ **How can you problem-solve the issues?**

The key questions for you to consider, with your colleagues in a team, are:

- Does this routine or activity have to happen?
- Does every child have to take part, be involved or take their turn?
- Does this routine have to happen right now, or at this time?
- Does this activity or routine have to happen in this exact way?

Take each of these questions in turn and be ready to ask, 'Why?' or 'Why not?' The answer is not allowed to be simply, 'Because we do' or 'We've always done it that way'. You may need to do some unpacking of words like, 'must' 'should' or 'can't'. Recognise that this process is the same kind of problem solving that you want children to learn and use.

Sometimes the honest answer is that a troublesome routine does have to happen much in this way, but there is always some room for manoeuvre. I have spoken with early years practitioners who run their provision in less than ideal spaces. For example, the toilet is located some way from the playroom and it is unrealistic to let independent young children head off entirely on their own.

- If this routine is run as a grudging 'have to do it – get it over quickly' event, then children are far more likely to complain, leave it too late to say they need the toilet, or spice up the trip with escape bids.
- Thoughtful teams have sometimes judged that, in their building, children can be trusted to head for the toilet in pairs. Within a large, rambling building, there may be no option but a toilet trip accompanied by an adult.
- Positive team thinking has led to internal 'outings' in which children enjoy a stroll and chat along the corridors and spotting sights of interest. There are no 'behaviour problems' along the way because a necessary routine has been made interesting. One practitioner explained to me that children sometimes joined the toilet trip solely for the walking conversation.

Is it different for boys?

Feminist theory and practice rightly objected to a deficit model being imposed on girls and women. However, there is now good reason to be concerned about a deficit model being foisted on to boys in early childhood and into primary school (Lindon, 2006b; Neall, 2002).

- Overstructured early years practice is not beneficial for girls but it seems to exert an even stronger impact on little boys, whose greater liveliness risks being labelled as problem behaviour when passivity is required (page 239).
- Practitioners need to offer boys scope to become emotionally literate and respect different ways of safely expressing feelings (page 88).
- All children need generous outdoor time and respect for their imaginative choices in play. Boys have been especially restricted by unreflective bans on 'rough' and superhero play.

The Ofsted (2008) report focused particularly on white boys from low-income backgrounds who are a vulnerable group for school failure. However, the report homed in on the general importance of sustained relationships.

- Boys flourished, and their behaviour was more amenable to friendly guidance, when adults took the trouble to extend from boys' current interests. Examples are the kind of books boys were keener to read or a typical enthusiasm for physical activity and plenty of outdoors Within the school environment, there are plenty of possibilities within the break and lunchtime.

- It was necessary to tackle underachievement before it was too entrenched. But a whole school approach gave full attention to issues around broader behaviour, such as ways of expressing feelings like anger.
- Schools that were effective in supporting the boys had an approach to behaviour in general that aimed to guide, firmly if need be, and which avoided punitive action as the main approach.

Best practice to guide children reflects their current interests

In effective schools, boys were not targeted with special approaches denied to their female peers. It was much more that staff recognised that these boys needed the sustained friendly relationship that was also available for the girls. One example from the Ofsted report (page 10) describes a school (which appeared to be primary) where the head provided a monthly soft drinks and cakes gathering for those children who had achieved well. During the inspection process, the children were asked why there were always more girls in the gathering. One girl explained, 'It's not that boys are not clever. They mostly are but they need quick results. You just have to be showing them the cakes', and the boys present agreed.

Problem solving behaviour and play

Sometimes the adult problem solving over routines and activities needs to encompass an additional step back of reflection. Are avoidable 'behaviour problems' being created by adult practice, including anxiety?

Learning through play

Over the 1990s, the rhetoric around learning through play, applied a great deal to early years practice, increasingly focused on 'play with a purpose', usually very close to what the adults valued as a legitimate purpose. Over the first decade of the twenty-first century, practitioners across the UK became further enmeshed with anxiety about written evidence that children had learned something specific – an outcomes-driven model. The essential uncertainty of play could be seen as a threat; children might learn something that was not on the plan for today. (For further discussion see Lester and Russell, 2008 and Lindon, 2001 and 2008b).

All early years practitioners definitely did not become enmeshed in this unhelpful perspective. I have been privileged to observe excellent practice in many early years settings. Teams like that of Sun Hill have taken concerted action to re-establish early learning led through authentic play experiences. However, support to early years practitioners for 'behaviour problems' frequently has to start with avoidable problems arising from unwise adult practice.

- Young children are not being 'uncooperative' because they object to being moved on from an activity in which they are fully absorbed. This kind of interruption by practitioners usually arises because too much has been packed into the day and adults have come to believe that children only learn the adult planned outcome for an adult-initiated activity.
- Children are not 'defiant' because they do not want to come to the table right now and join the creative conveyer belt of every child making an identical product. Nor do they have 'poor concentration', because they cope with the limitations by taking a daub and dash strategy. Children need time and space to engage with an activity and plenty of scope to make their own choices.
- Young children do not have 'poor social skills' when they struggle to manage or enjoy communication in a large circle in which they have to wait ages for their turn. Nor should they be criticised for being 'fidgety' and 'bothering other children' when the only possible interest in a large group story time is to move about or poke the closest child.

LOOK, LISTEN, NOTE, LEARN

Adults talk so much professionally about difficulties that arise for them from the behaviour of children or young people. Sometimes it is constructive to turn the tables. Think from your own professional and personal experience:

◆ What would children or young people highlight as 'behaviour problems' or 'difficult behaviour' from the adults in their life?

◆ What do they need from you for their day or session to go reasonably smoothly and with contentment?

◆ What are the reasons that adults sometimes do not set a good example in their behaviour? How come we sometimes find it so hard?

Look at the flow

The ABC approach to observation (page 105) is one method to reflect on the pattern around 'problem' behaviour. Wendy Russell (2006) describes a project to support playworkers who were concerned about behaviour that could not be ignored, like aggressive actions and sexually explicit language. However, a focus on behaviour management through sanctions and policing behaviour was not effective, nor did it coexist comfortably with the principles of playwork.

Wendy Russell's aim was to guide reflection on behaviour within the context of play through creating 'play profiles' for some 10 to 12-year-olds. This approach used concepts developed within playwork practice by theorists like Bob Hughes, Perry Else and Gordon Sturrock. The practitioners observed:

▨ What types of play engaged these children – some of the behaviour that concerned practitioners was worked out through role play or in rough and tumble play.

▨ How they used or understood play cues – the verbal or non-verbal invitations to another child to play. Some children had trouble issuing a play invitation to peers and some of their behaviour was not recognised as a play cue by others.

▨ The narrative of the play, also called the play frame – many of the children, whose behaviour concerned the playworkers, had difficulty in holding to a narrative in play. They tended to flit between games and aggravated their peers because they disrupted play they did not really understand.

The team was able to home in on 'critical incidents', events that were significant in the flow of play for what followed. A turning point for practitioners was to see these times as a choice point. It was a time when adults made a decision, even if they were not initially conscious of that choice. A different behaviour choice, sometimes to watch and not intervene, could change the track that children then followed. Once practitioners were more alert to the flow of children's play, it was more possible to guide their behaviour as choices in play rather than as unacceptable behaviour to be corrected.

Wendy Russell also highlights the control issues expressed by other observers (page 159). In these play settings, some behaviour from children, labelled as 'challenging' by the adults, was normal testing of boundaries or could be resolved by low-key adult intervention. Much of children's lively behaviour was not disruptive, so long as the adults no longer felt being a 'good playworker' depended on their ability to manage through direct control, being in charge.

PARTNERSHIP WITH FAMILIES

Families, led by parents, need to be a significant factor in the socialisation of the younger generation. Professionals involved with children and adolescents need to work in partnership with parents and other carers.

A friendly working relationship

Practitioners in any kind of provision need to aim for a friendly relationship with parents and other carers, but it is still a working relationship. Staff and parents have come together over the children, not because they have chosen each other as friends. It is inevitable that you will feel more at ease with some individual parents, and they with you. But the professional role requires you to be even-handed and not to spend more time with some parents, nor to avoid others, dependent on the extent to which you warm towards them.

There is a discussion about children's 'invisible backpack' on page 244, but adults experience something of this nature as well. Parents may be affected by memories of their own schooldays, whether practitioners are teachers or not.

- If the memories are happy then relations may be easier, although parents have to develop an adult-to-adult relationship. They are no longer the child in this situation and may have to balance a wish to be cooperative with the importance of speaking up for their child or adolescent.

Partnership with parents is supported by ordinary conversation

- If the memories are unhappy, then parents are more likely to be suspicious of practitioners, quick to defend themselves and their child against criticism.
- Parents who have continuing difficulties with authority in various guises may view practitioners in their child's setting as yet another example of 'them'. You have to recognise this perspective because parents will take time to make you an exception to their general rule.

There will always be some potential imbalance between practitioners and parents or other family carers. Childminders and practitioners in group settings are responsible for following their agreed behaviour policy and practice. No practitioner can flex on key values, however strongly parents might feel that their child should be exempt from basic ground rules. A lively discussion with a parent might, however, provoke you to reflect on whether you or your colleagues have become too rigid. It is not appropriate for practitioners to tell parents in general how they should run family life. If you are seriously concerned about parents' behaviour then follow safeguarding procedures (see Lindon, 2008a).

MAKE THE CONNECTION WITH...
WHAT IS PARTNERSHIP?

Partnership does not mean agreeing to everything that a parent asks. For example, you should never agree to follow requests that would mean handling a child's behaviour in a way that was emotionally or physically harsh. It does not matter what reason(s) this parent gives, whether personal preference or that this approach is part of the family cultural tradition or faith.

- Partnership means listening to a parent and making sure you understand what they are asking. Sometimes you will be able to say honestly, 'Yes, I/we will be able to be consistent here with how you respond to Lennie at home.'

- When children have disabilities that directly affect behaviour, their parents can have considerable expertise about what works best. Of course, like any hard-pressed parent, they may have got themselves in a serious pickle by following unwise methods.

- Sometimes the answer has to be, 'I need to talk with my manager/colleagues about what we have discussed.' You have that conversation in the very near future and get back to the parent. This holding response can be useful for team members who need to stop themselves saying 'Yes' without thinking.

- Sometimes your answer has to be, 'I understand what you are asking. But I cannot agree to... because...' Your explanation is straightforward, honest and linked with 'what we do here' – not 'I'm/we're not allowed to...' (see page 230).

Questions
- **Have you faced situations like these examples? How did you handle matters?**
- **Looking back, would you make a different choice now?**
- **Are there issues that you judge should be talked through in your own team?**

Shared care in early childhood

Young children need to spend enough time within their own family, so that their emotional attachment is secure and their parents feel confident about dealing with their behaviour. However, a close relationship needs to be nurtured between practitioner and parent(s): a pattern of genuinely shared care and shared affection for a baby or young child. Otherwise, young children are emotionally adrift between two social worlds of day care and family home. Julia Manning-Morton (2006) expresses that 'the personal is professional' in care of young children.

Babies and young children need an affectionate personal relationship with their childminder or named key person in a group setting (Elfer, Goldschmied and Selleck, 2003). The professional contribution to the situation is to ensure that parents are reassured about their babies and children and experience practitioners who make the effort to bridge between home and out-of-home care (Lindon, 2006a). Young children need to see that there is an enduring and friendly relationship between their parent(s) and key person/childminder and that they, the children, are safe within that cradle of understanding and shared commitment.

Young children are active observers and thinkers. They try to make sense of what happens to them and other children. You will hear the results of their thinking when children voice observations like, 'My mummy says I'm bad because...' or 'Why can't I...? My dad lets me.' Adults are sometimes uncomfortable about dealing with the first comment and may prefer to view the second as a cheeky questioning of adult decisions. Good practice across childhood is to show respect for what children are telling you. You can find the careful line between holding to sound principles of guiding behaviour and avoiding blunt criticism of a child's parents.

- In the first example, you could say, 'I can understand why Mummy was cross when you... But I don't think that makes you a bad child.' Depending on the details of the event, it might make sense to continue with, 'I wonder if you and I can think what you could have done instead when...'

- In the second example, the best approach is often along the lines of, 'It is up to your dad how he runs life at home. Here in club we don't...' However, sometimes it is appropriate to say, 'Let me have a chat with your dad. If he thinks you can be trusted to... maybe we can work something out here.'

The invisible backpack

In twenty-first century UK there is a great diversity in family shape and style and there is no good reason to argue that a particular kind of family life is essential or the best. However, children's experiences within their own family exert a significant impact on how they handle the other experiences of life. Like any community, schools need to develop their own values, acknowledging what is brought in by children and adolescents in what I describe as the 'invisible back pack'.

- In some cases, the contents of that backpack will include experiences within the family that support the child to settle into the school environment and to negotiate the adult expectations here.

- For other children their backpack will be brimming with negative views about any type of authority learned from parents who are so disenchanted with their lot that dissatisfaction is sprayed at everyone else.

- Alternatively children may have been so indulged in their early childhood that the prosocial behaviour necessary within a harmonious school community is outside their grasp at the moment.

School teams need to start where the children are at the moment. Some teams need to feel, and many are, appreciative of family experiences that make their job easier. However, the starting point for some school teams is to accept that the contents of the invisible backpack are not on their side. The aim of building strong values in a school about 'what happens here' and 'what we do here when...' is that aspects of an anti-school subculture are left at the gates. In the same way schools, just like after school clubs, sometimes need to acknowledge that yes, out on the street or in this child's family, that swear word or this racist term can be heard on a daily basis. Practitioners make the point that those words are not acceptable language in this community.

MAKE THE CONNECTION WITH...
SCHOOL AS A COMMUNITY

The strong philosophy underpinning practice at Thongsley Fields Nursery and Primary is that a school should not be isolated from the local community: children's own families but also the neighbourhood as a whole. Rachel Myer, the head, expressed this approach as, 'What is outside your school is also in it'. In order to support children with their behaviour, and their general learning, a school team has to acknowledge what travels on to school grounds (or any setting) with the children or adolescents.

Some school teams prefer to ring-fence their teaching task and imply that family pressures on children are an intrusion into the educational process that should be resisted. The Thongsley Fields' head and staff, like other teams who take a holistic (and a realistic) view of their task, do not expect troubles to be left at the school gate. They recognise how much the stresses of home life affects how children behave. Boys and girls cannot learn to regulate their own behaviour if their teachers insist on ignoring the experiences that make self-regulation so difficult for some children.

Agreements and expectations

The Schools Standards and Framework Act 1998 required that all schools across the UK should have a home–school agreement, developed by the governing body in consultation with parents. The exact format of the agreement is left to the setting and behaviour is part of the whole context of partnership. These agreements are not legally binding contracts and, although parents and older children are encouraged to commit to the agreement by their signature, reluctance or refusal to sign cannot be used to penalise the family in any way.

A written agreement, used constructively, is one way of making explicit fair commitments and realistic expectations on both sides of the partnership. Practitioners need to be willing to explain key aspects of practice again and in more detail when parents are unclear. Useful agreements are often part of a more general setting-home information pack (not too enormous) that further creates the feel of working together for the well-being of the children, and is definitely not a one-way relationship, telling parents what they have to do.

LOOK, LISTEN, NOTE, LEARN

Revisit the agreement in your own setting, with particular attention to what it says about behaviour:

◆ How even-handed are the commitments? Is it clear what parents can expect of practitioners in a positive approach to behaviour? Or is the agreement weighting towards parents' agreement to support your behaviour policy?

◆ Does the school team (or any other setting) commit to regular communication with parents, as well as asking parents to be willing to talk with staff about their child's behaviour?

Look at the agreements of other settings – pool them in a network or student discussion group or do an Internet search. For instance, the agreement of Bar Hill Community Primary.
www.barhillschool.co.uk/home-school-agreement

Look also at the general information about agreements on
www.standards.dfes.gov.uk/parentalinvolvement/hsa/?version=1

More detailed agreements are part of close partnership with parents when their child or adolescent needs more support than usual for their behaviour. More structured approaches to guiding behaviour (from page 215) are far more likely to work when the family is part of the enterprise. Firmer agreements, which might be called contracts, can be part of very focused work with a child or adolescent who has serious problems in managing in school. The working group chaired by Alan Steer (2005) recommended that schools be ready to call the meeting to create a parenting contract before a pupil or student has been excluded. This kind of focused discussion will need to involve the child or adolescent, as well as other professionals who are involved.

Courtesy and open communication

A wise guideline is to treat parents with the same level of adult-to-adult respect that you would like in return. They are in no sense 'just parents', any more than you are 'just an early years practitioner' or 'just a teacher'.

- Explain your own, or your team's, reasons for taking this approach for guiding behaviour and be ready to talk through the 'Ah, buts' that matter to this parent. He or she may well ask questions or express a confusion that is shared by other parents who have not said anything.

- If a parent is bamboozled by the workings of your system of rewards and sanctions, perhaps it is not transparent nor up to the task of effectively guiding behaviour. Perhaps children are also perplexed but felt they had no choice but to continue to negotiate the maze.

TAKE ANOTHER PERSPECTIVE

Practitioners need sometimes to let off steam within the limits of their staff group.

- However, everyone – especially the team leader – needs to ensure that venting feelings does not slide into revisiting the behaviour of children or their parents as dramatic staff room gossip.

- Genuine problems with one or two parents must not be spread to a negative view of 'the parents!' in general. Nor is it professional to label parents as 'difficult', 'over-protective' or 'always anxious'. You would experience this reaction as rude, if you received it.

- Using the good practice that you need to apply to time with children, rework labels to a more constructive view, such as 'Stefan's mother finds it hard when we raise problems about his behaviour. How can we open the conversation and still be honest?'

Balance and description

Parents need to hear just as much about their child's positive behaviour as the times when there are problems that need to be discussed and resolved.

- Make sure there is regular conversation about the highlights of a child's day and that examples of positive behaviour are not communicated solely by stickers (page 189).

- If problems develop around how a child behaves, it is better to talk sooner rather than later. The conversation, and invitation for any ideas, can start at a low key level. You also avoid the fair question after a delay of, 'Why on earth didn't you talk with me before it got this bad?'

- Make sure there are positives from the day of children who need special attention for their behaviour. An approach like 'say three good things' (page 187) can support a balanced conversation with parents. Keep a clear sense of 'and' and not 'but': 'Sandy managed well with... and he managed to calm down with help when...' The word 'but' can bring a sting in the tail and parents may feel that positives are just to soften the blow.

- Parents do not need to hear about every minor scuffle that was resolved at the time. If practitioners have developed habits of always delivering bad news, then a team leader needs to create pause for thought. A practitioner notebook, with short descriptions of incidents, can provide the basis for a brief discussion with the team leader, before parents arrive, about what should be shared.

- The more serious incidents will need to be explained, if only because other children are likely to chat with their parents and the event will travel the local grapevine. Part of this conversation needs to be how the child had made amends and that you really do not want this parent to impose a sanction of their own. Once you get to know individual parents, you will realise that anger or embarrassment may tempt some to this action.

Conversations with parents should be as discreet as you can make them. Longer and more sensitive conversations have to be managed by asking a parent to come in for a private meeting. Ideally you want children and adolescents to be part of the conversation – the delight about, 'How well Teja is working as a playground buddy' as well as, 'Teja and I need to chat with you about what happened today in assembly'. You should already have discussed with Teja that, 'You know we'll have to tell your mum about...' and come to an agreement about how much Teja will say or whether she would rather you did all the talking.

Concern, disagreement and potential conflict

The discussion about assertiveness on page 93 also applies to adults as parents. One mother's 'honest outspoken approach' can feel to a practitioner like 'aggressive in-your-face' – and vice versa.

- Some parents will be fairly confident to describe what worries them and why. But it is crucial that no team member immediately assumes that any parent is about to argue or be 'awkward'. The most easy-going and articulate of parents can be driven to less friendly ways of expressing themselves.

- Some parents may find it hard to express a concern without cranking up the volume or using gestures that may feel aggressive. Your calm voice and obvious listening behaviour will shift the conversation with those parents whose bluster is out of habit, or comes from a real conviction that professionals will not listen unless they shout or demand immediate action.

- Some parents will have trouble coming to the point. For personal or cultural reasons, they may be very concerned that they do not appear rude or unappreciative. They still have concerns that should be heard. You need to look and listen beyond comments like, 'I don't want you to feel I am making a fuss...' Hear the 'but...' and invite the parent to say more.

The best approach will always be to listen to what a parent wishes to say.

- Focus on the listening and hold back from leaping in with explanations, justifications or advice. Useful open-ended questions start with 'what?' or 'how?' or the request to, 'Please tell me more about what Peter said to you.'

- Parents should be focused on the well-being of their own son or daughter; you should worry if they do not seem to care. Of course parents would prefer to believe another child or adolescent is most at fault.

- Good practice in partnership is to recognise the parent's commitment and to describe the to-and-fro of this particular scuffle, including the reason that you spoke firmly to their child or adolescent.

Once you have listened, you can make a more appropriate response.

- Sometimes you will need to say, 'Thank you for telling me about this. I will talk with the other children about what happened yesterday. Can I see you again at the end of the day/session?'

- Do not agree to haul out the named 'culprits' and impose sanctions, apologies or anything else. You need to hear the other side(s) of this story.

- On some issues it can make sense to ask, 'What would you like to happen now?' or 'In your opinion, what would help now?' But take care that you do not make promises you may not be able to keep.

Sometimes parents will be angry. There is no magical solution to dealing with anger from other adults but some approaches are more effective for salvaging a working relationship. The professional role is to defuse and not escalate a confrontation, to avoid meeting anger with yet more anger.

- Some adults have learned to use anger even over minor issues. There is no point trying to offer rational explanations or information; let them run out of steam. Look calm and patient (no matter how you feel inside) and, if they take breath, invite them to sit down. Bill Rogers (2006) points out that it is less easy to be very angry in a sitting position.

- As the parent (or any other angry adult) calms somewhat or gives you a pause, then acknowledge the strong feelings, 'Mrs Dunbar, I can see you're very angry about…' or 'I know how much you care about Maria. So do we.'

- Recognise that whatever you say will be filtered through the anger until the other person calms. So, keep it simple, wait to explain your perspective or what you are sure actually happened. When adults are angry, they are poor listeners, unresponsive to logical argument and generally do not welcome questions, certainly 'Why?' questions that can sound confrontational.

- If there is a quick and appropriate solution, then offer it. If apologies are due, then say 'Sorry' without lots of self-justification and find out how to avoid this mistake or oversight in the future. However, it is unwise to use an apology just to stop the conversation.

There is a good chance that most parents will calm down and problem solving conversation can follow. You do not hark back to the anger; you show commitment to talking through the problem now. Depending on the details, you may need to schedule another meeting.

Your professional role demands self-restraint but practitioners are not required to be a verbal or physical punch bag. It is appropriate to set limits and these can be communicated assertively by words and body language. You might say, 'Mrs Dunbar, I realise that you're angry on Maria's behalf. I'm willing to talk with you right now. I'm not shouting and swearing at you. I expect you not to swear at me.' You might give one more of these comments and then continual yelling and bad language leads to, 'Mrs Dunbar, this meeting is over', with the follow up if necessary of, 'I've tried to discuss your concerns calmly. You continue to use language which is unacceptable in this school (club, nursery). Please leave now.'

In any setting, it is important that practitioners know colleagues will respond to raised voices. Provision that serves a volatile parent body needs a system of panic buttons. More often, the protection is that other team members will appear. A parent who has been told to leave has to be invited to return for a proper conversation as soon as possible because the problem needs to be resolved.

Advice to parents

Within partnership, you can talk around ideas for guiding behaviour when parents ask for suggestions. You may explain how you handle this kind of situation when their child is within your care. A clear message within your advice will be that you consider your own behaviour and not simply that of this child or adolescent. Some parents may need the reassurance that this kind of behaviour is very usual for this age. However, it is not psychologically healthy for children if early years or other practitioners are seen by parents as experts who will guide their children's behaviour instead of family members. There are many years of family life and parents need to feel skilled and to be their child's continuity through middle childhood and adolescence.

You may offer advice about behaviour through conversations or within parenting programmes offered within your setting (for more information see Barrett, 2003 and Scott et al., 2006). Advice to parents has much in common with colleague support (page 232) and needs to be underpinned with key messages that:

- There is rarely a quick fix; most issues around normal behaviour from children or adolescents take time and emotional energy to guide in a positive way. Even good ideas do not necessarily work straight away. It is tough for parents to see through sensible strategies at the end of a long working day.
- Guiding behaviour works within a relationship: it is not an abstract ten-point plan to a better child or adolescent. It is crucial to build up the enjoyable backdrop of experiences – chat, play, shared mealtimes, doing ordinary things together – that mean life does not feel like one long struggle.

You need to create time for a reasonable length conversation. Otherwise you offer ideas without knowing what this parent is facing and what they have already tried. Even more than with a colleague, you will not be able to guide how any idea is put into practice. Children's choices over behaviour are responsive to the details of the social situation – hence why they may 'behave better' for some adults than others. Their positive strategies from time with you will not necessarily generalise to home life, unless their parents take a similar approach.

FURTHER RESOURCES

Further resources – books and articles

- **Armitage, Marc** (2001) 'The ins and outs of school playground play' in Bishop, Julia and Curtis, Mavis (eds) *Play today in the primary school playground*. Buckingham: Open University Press.

- **Baginsky, William** (2004) *Peer mediation in the UK: a guide for schools*. London: NSPCC. www.nspcc.org.uk/inform

- **Bailey, Shaun** (2005) *No man's land: how Britain's inner city youth are being failed*. London: Centre for Young Policy Studies. www.cps.org.uk

- **Bain, Alastair** and **Barnett, Lyn** (1986) *The design of a day care system in a nursery setting for children under five*. Occasional Paper No. 8. London: The Tavistock Institute of Human Relations.

- **Ball, Sue** (2005) *Bystanders and bullying: a summary of research for Anti-Bullying Week*. www.anti-bullyingalliance.org.uk/downloads/pdf/bystanders_and_bullying.pdf

- **Baron-Cohen, Simon; Golan, Ofer; Chapman, Emma** and **Granader, Yael** (2007) 'Transported to a world of emotion'. *The Psychologist*, February, vol 20, no 2. www.thepsychologist.org.uk/archive/archive_home.cfm?volumeID=20&editionID=154&ArticleID=1140

- **Barrett, Helen** (2003) *Parenting programmes for families at risk: a source book*. London: National Parenting and Family Institute.

- **Barratt, Penny; Joy, Helen; Potter, Mo; Thomas, George** and **Whitaker, Philip** (undated, about 2003) *Circle of Friends: a peer based approach to supporting children with autistic spectrum disorders in school*. www.leics.gov.uk/index.htm (Go in through Home Page and Search 'Circle of Friends booklet')

- **Batmanghelidjh, Camila** (2006) *Shattered lives: children who live with courage and dignity*. London: Jessica Kingsley.

- **Baumrind, Diana** – her ideas are reported in journal articles and not easy for readers to access. You can follow up her ideas in a child development textbook, like Bee and Boyd (below). Alternatively, I found a good summary on www.athealth.com/Practitioner/ceduc/parentingstyles.html

- **Bee, Helen** and **Boyd, Denise** (2004, tenth edition) *The developing child*. London: Pearson Education.

- **Belsky, Jay** and **Steinberg, Laurence** (1978) 'The effects of day care – a critical review'. *Child Development*, vol 49, pages 929–49.

- **Belsky, Jay** (2001) 'Emanuel Miller Lecture – Developmental risks (still) associated with early child care'. *Journal of Child Psychology and Psychiatry*, vol 42, no 7, pages 845–59. Download from http://cep.lse.ac.uk/seminarpapers/23-02-07-BEL.pdf

FURTHER RESOURCES

✷ **Benton, David** (2008) 'A fishy tale? What impact does diet have on behaviour and intelligence?'. *The Psychologist*, vol 21, no 10, October 2008, pages 850–3. www.thepsychologist.org.uk/archive/archive_home.cfm?volumeID=21&editionID=165&ArticleID=1409

✷ **Beyer, Jannik** and **Gammeltoft, Lone** (2000) *Autism and play.* London: Jessica Kingsley.

✷ **Biddulph, Steve** (2005) *Raising babies: should under threes go to nursery?* London: HarperThorsons.

✷ **Bilton, Helen** (2002) *Outdoor play in the early years: management and innovation.* London: David Fulton.

✷ **Blatchford, Peter** and **Sharp, Sonia** (eds) (1994) *Breaktime and the school: understanding and changing playground behaviour* . London: Routledge.

✷ **Blatchford, Peter** and **Pellegrini, Anthony** (2000) *The child at school: interactions with peers and teachers.* London: Hodder Arnold.

✷ **Blythe, Sally Goddard** (2004) *The well balanced child: movement and early learning.* Stroud: Hawthorn Press.

✷ **Blythe, Sally Goddard** (2008) *What babies and children really need: how mothers and fathers can nurture children's growth for health and well being.* Stroud: Hawthorn Press. (See also www.inpp.org.uk)

✷ **Bowlby, John** (1965) *Child care and the growth of love.* London: Penguin.

✷ **Boxall, Marjorie** (2002) *Nurture groups in school: principles and practice* London: Paul Chapman Publishing.

✷ **Bronfenbrenner, Urie** (1979) *The ecology of human development.* Cambridge, MA: Harvard University Press.

✷ **Brooks, Robert** and **Goldstein, Sam** (2007) *Raising a self-disciplined child – help your child to become more responsible, confident and resilient.* Maidenhead: McGraw Hill.

✷ **Brown, David** (1994) 'Play, the playground and the culture of childhood' in Moyles, Janet (ed.) (1994) *The excellence of play.* Buckingham: Open University Press.

✷ **Byron, Tanya** (2005) *The house of tiny tearaways.* London: BBC Worldwide Limited.

✷ **Byron, Tanya** (2007) *Your child your way: create a positive parenting pattern for life.* London: Michael Joseph.

✷ **Cairns, Warwick** (2008) *How to live dangerously: why we should all stop worrying and start living.* Basingstoke: Macmillan.

✷ **Campbell, Susan** (2006) *Behaviour problems in preschool children: clinical and developmental issues.* London: The Guildford Press.

✳ **Casey, Theresa** (2005) *Inclusive play: practical strategies for working with children ages 3–8.* London: Paul Chapman Publishing.

✳ **Casey, Theresa** with **Harper, Ivan** and **MacIntyre, Susan** (2004) *Play Inclusive Handbook: a practical guide to supporting inclusive play for children of primary school age.* Edinburgh: Scotland Yard Adventure (tel: 0131 476 4506).

✳ **Caspi, Avshalom; Harrington, HonaLee; Milne, Barry; Amell, James; Theodore, Reremoana** and **Moffitt, Terrie** (2003) 'Children's behavioural styles at age 3 are linked to their adult personality traits at age 26'. *Journal of Personality*, vol 71, issue 4, pages 495–513, summary on www.education-consumers.org/briefpdfs/4.7-childrens_behavior_age_3.pdf

✳ **Centre for Educational Research and Innovation** (2007) *Understanding the brain: the birth of a learning science* – a substantial report, with two separate articles: one on brain development over early childhood and another on adolescence. www.dcsf.gov.uk/research/data/uploadfiles/DCSF-RW030.pdf

✳ **Children's Play Council** (2002) *Making the case for play: building policies and strategies for school-aged children.* London: National Children's Bureau. www.playengland.org.uk/Page.asp and go into Resources

✳ **Children's Project, The** (2005) *The social toddler: understanding toddlers and why they do the things they do* (DVD). Richmond: The Children's Project.

✳ **Clark, Eric** (2007) *The real toy story: inside the ruthless battle for Britain's youngest consumers.* London: Black Swan.

✳ **Clarke, Ann** and **Clarke, Alan** (1998) 'Early experience and the life path'. *The Psychologist*, September 1998, pages 433–6, www.thepsychologist.org.uk/archive (from this page go to the correct year and month and download this paper).

✳ **Clifford-Poston, Andrea** (2007) *When Harry hit Sally: understanding your child's behaviour.* London: Simon and Schuster.

✳ **Clifford-Poston, Andrea** (2008) *A playworker's guide to understanding children's behaviour – working with the 8–12 age range.* London: Karnac.

✳ **Collins, Margaret** (2005) *Young buddies: teaching peer support skills to children aged 6 to 11.* London: Sage/Lucky Duck Publishing.

✳ **Coloroso, Barbara** (2005) *The bully, the bullied and the bystander.* London: Picadilly Press.

✳ **Costabile, Angela** (1999) *An observational approach to study social and aggressive behaviour of children.* http://old.gold.ac.uk/tmr/reports/aim2_calabria1.html

✶ **Cousins, Jacqui** (2003) *Listening to four year olds: how they can help us plan their education and care.* London: National Children's Bureau.

✶ **Cremin, Hilary** (2000) *Learning how to mediate.* Bristol: Lucky Duck Publishing.

✶ **Cremin, Hilary** (2002) 'Circle time – why it doesn't always work'. *Primary Practice,* Spring, vol 30.

✶ **Cremin, Hilary** (2003) *Pupils resolving disputes.* Research paper, Second International Conference on Violence in School, Quebec. www.brookes.ac.uk/schools/education/rescon/Violence%20in%20Schools%20Quebec%20conf.%20paper%20May%2003.pdf!

✶ **Department for Children, Schools and Families** (2006) *Bullying around racism, religion and culture.* www.teachernet.gov.uk/wholeschool/behaviour/tacklingbullying

✶ **Department for Children, Schools and Families** (2007a) *Confident, capable and creative: supporting boys' achievements.* http://nationalstrategies.standards.dcsf.gov.uk/primary/publications/foundation_stage/supporting_achievements

✶ **Department for Children, Schools and Families** (2007b) *The use of force to control or restrain pupils: non-statutory guidance for schools in England.* www.teachernet.gov.uk/_doc/12187/ACFD89B.pdf

✶ **Department for Children, Schools and Families** (2007c) *Safe to learn: embedding anti-bullying work in schools.* Also related guidance documents on different kinds of bullying; access all through www.teachernet.gov.uk/wholeschool/behaviour/tacklingbullying

✶ **Department for Children, Schools and Families** (second edition, 2007d) *Social and emotional aspects of learning (SEAL).* www.standards.dfes.gov.uk/primary/publications/banda/seal

✶ **Department for Children, Schools and Families** (2007e) *Social and emotional aspects of learning for secondary schools.* www.bandapilot.org.uk/secondary

✶ **Department for Children, Schools and Families** (2007f) *Screening and searching of pupils for weapons: guidance for school staff.* www.teachernet.gov.uk/docbank/index.cfm?id=11454

✶ **Department for Children, Schools and Families** (second edition 2008) *The Early Years Foundation Stage – Setting the Standards for Learning, Development and Care for children from birth to five.* London: DCSF. www.teachernet.gov.uk/teachingandlearning/EYFS

✶ **Department for Education and Skills** (2003) *Behaviour management: introductory training for school support staff.* www.teachernet.gov.uk/_doc/4970/Unit%202_Behaviour.pdf

FURTHER RESOURCES

✱ **Dinkmeyer, Don Sr; McKay, Gary** and **Dinkmeyer, Don Jr** (1997) *The parent's handbook.* Bowling Green, KY: Step Publishers.

✱ **Dinkmeyer, Don Sr; McKay, Gary; Dinkmeyer, James** and **McKay, Joyce** (2008) *Parenting young children – systematic training for effective parenting of children under six.* Bowling Green, KY: Step Publishers. www.steppublishers.com

✱ **Dorman, Helen** and **Dorman, Clive** (2002) *The social toddler: promoting positive behaviour.* Richmond: The Children's Project. www.childrensproject.co.uk

✱ **Dreikurs, Rudolf** and **Soltz, Vicki** (1995) *Happy children: a challenge to parents.* Melbourne: Australian Council for Educational Research.

✱ **Dreikurs, Rudolf; Grunwald, Bernice** and **Pepper, Floy** (1998, second edition) *Maintaining sanity in the classroom: classroom management techniques.* Hove: Taylor and Francis Group.

✱ **Duncan, Neil** (1999) *Sexual bullying: gender conflict and pupil culture in secondary schools.* London: Routledge.

✱ **Dunn, Judy** (1993) *Young children's close relationships beyond attachment.* London: Sage.

✱ **Eisenberg, Nancy** (1992) *The caring child.* Cambridge, MA: Harvard University Press.

✱ **Elfer, Peter** (2006) 'Exploring children's expressions of attachment in nursery'. *European Early Childhood Education Journal*, vol 14, no 2, pages 81–95.

✱ **Elfer, Peter** (2007) 'Babies and young children in nursery: using psychoanalytic ideas to explore tasks and interaction'. *Children in Society*, vol 21, no 2, pages 111–22.

✱ **Elfer, Peter; Goldschmied, Elinor** and **Selleck, Dorothy** (2003) *Key persons in the nursery: building relationships for quality provision.* London: David Fulton.

✱ **Elliott, Michele** (ed.) (2002) *Bullying: a practical guide to coping in schools.* London: Pearson.

✱ **Evans, Betsy** (2002) *You can't come to my birthday party: conflict resolution with young children.* Ypsilanti: High Scope Press.

✱ **Evans, Karen** (2007) 'The brain and learning in adolescence' in Centre for Educational Research and Innovation, *Understanding the brain: the birth of a learning science*, Part II, pages 185–210. www.dcsf.gov.uk/research/data/uploadfiles/DCSF-RW030.pdf

✱ **Finch, Sue** (2003) *'An eye for an eye leaves everyone blind': teaching young children to settle conflicts without violence.* London: Save the Children.

FURTHER RESOURCES

★ **Fowler, Beth** and **Taylor, Chris** (2006) *The benefits of play and playwork: best evidence-based research demonstrating the impact and benefits of play and playwork.* London: SkillsActive. www.skillsactive.com

★ **Fowler, Sandra** (2004) *Making schools safer using effective anti-bullying strategies.* Spotlight Briefing. London: National Children's Bureau. www.ncb.org.uk

★ **Free Play Network** (2005) *Places for Play*; also *Places of woe, places of possibility* and (2008) *Design for Play*; see also *No risk. No Play?* and *Give us a cuddle: child protection and adult anxiety* online discussion forum highlights. www.freeplaynetwork.org.uk

★ **Gerhardt, Sue** (2004) *Why love matters: how affection shapes a baby's brain.* Hove: Routledge.

★ **Glasser, William** (second edition 1998) *Choice theory in the classroom.* New York: Harper Collins. See also www.wglasser.com and www.choicetheory.com

★ **Glasser, William** and **Glasser, Carleen** (1999) *The language of choice theory.* New York: Harper Collins.

★ **Gill, Tim** (2007) *No fear: growing up in a risk-averse society.* London: Calouste Gulbenkian. Summary and full book on www.gulbenkian .org.uk

★ **Gilligan, Carol** (1982) *In a different voice: psychological theory and women's development.* Cambridge, MA: Harvard University Press.

★ **Gleave, Josie** (2008) *Risk and play: a literature review.* London: Play England. www.playday.org.uk/PDF/Risk-and-play-a-literature-review.pdf

★ **Goleman, Daniel** (1996) *Emotional intelligence – why it can matter more than IQ.* London: Bloomsbury.

★ **Gottman, John** and **Declaire, Joan** (1997) *The heart of parenting: how to raise an emotionally intelligent child.* London: Bloomsbury.

★ **Healy, Jane** (2004) *Your child's growing mind: brain development and learning from birth to adolescence.* New York: Broadway Books.

★ **Hewlett, Sylvia Ann** (1993) *Child neglect in rich nations.* New York: UNICEF.

★ **High/Scope UK** Video/DVDs: Under threes: (2003) *It's mine! Responding to problems and conflicts*, the Social Conflict section in (1999) *The High/Scope approach to under threes.* Over threes: (1988) *Supporting children in resolving conflicts.* www.high-scope.org.uk/publications/42.asp

★ **Honore, Carl** (2008) *Under pressure: rescuing our children from the culture of hyper-parenting.* London: Orion Books.

FURTHER RESOURCES

* **Hopkins, Belinda** (2008) *Restorative approaches in residential care.* Highlight no 242. London: National Children's Bureau.

* **Hosking, George** and **Walsh, Ita** (2005) *Violence and what to do about it.* Croydon: WAVE Trust. www.actiononviolence.co.uk/aov/files/ WAVE_Report_2005.pdf

* **Jarrett, Christian** (2008) 'Foundations of sand?'. *The Psychologist*, vol 21, no 9, September. www.thepsychologist.org.uk/archive/archive_ home.cfm?volumeID=21&editionID=164&ArticleID=1394

* **Kindlon, Dan** and **Thompson, Michael** (1999) *Raising Cain: Protecting the Emotional Life of Boys.* New York: Ballantine Books.

* **Laishley, Jennie** (1984) *Taking responsibility for young children: Who? Where? When? – a consideration of issue, evidence and implications.* Discussion Paper 1 for the National Nursery Examination Board. London: NNEB.

* **Leaman, Louisa** (2005) *Managing very challenging behaviour.* London: Continuum.

* **Learning and Teaching Scotland** (2005) *Birth to Three: supporting our youngest children.* Glasgow: Learning and Teaching Scotland. www.ltscotland.org.uk/earlyyears/about/birthtothree/guidance.asp

* **Lester, Stuart** and **Russell, Wendy** (2008) *Play for a change. Play, policy and practice: a review of contemporary perspectives.* Summary and full report www.playengland.org.uk/resources

* **Lindenfield, Gael** (1994) *Confident teens: how to raise a positive, confident and happy teenager, helping build self-esteem and social skills.* London: Thorsons.

* **Lines, Dennis** (2008) *The bullies: understanding bullies and bullying.* London: Jessica Kingsley.

* **Lindon, Jennie** (2001) *Understanding children's play.* Cheltenham: Nelson Thornes.

* **Lindon, Jennie** (2003) *Too safe for their own good? Helping children learn about risk and lifeskills.* London: National Children's Bureau.

* **Lindon, Jennie** (2005) *Understanding child development – linking theory and practice.* London: Hodder Arnold.

* **Lindon, Jennie** (2006a) *Care and caring matter: young children learning through care.* London: Early Education.

* **Lindon, Jennie** (2006b) *Equality in early childhood: linking theory and practice.* London: Hodder Arnold.

* **Lindon, Jennie** (2006c) *Helping babies and toddlers learn: a guide to good practice with under threes.* London: National Children's Bureau.

★ **Lindon, Jennie** (2007) *Understanding children and young people: development from 5–18 years*. London: Hodder Arnold.

★ **Lindon, Jennie** (2008a) *Safeguarding children and young people: child protection 0–18 years*. London: Hodder Arnold.

★ **Lindon, Jennie** (2008b) 'Child initiated learning: what does it mean, where does it fit and why is it important for young children? Key messages from the Early Years Foundation Stage' in Featherstone, Sally and Featherstone, Phill (eds) *Like bees, not butterflies – child-initiated learning in the early years*. London: A&C Black.

★ **Lindon, Jennie** and **Lindon, Lance** (second edition, 2008) *Mastering counselling skills*. Basingstoke: Palgrave Macmillan.

★ **Lloyd, Gwynedd; McCluskey, Gillean; Riddell, Sheila; Stead, Joan** and **Weedon, Elisabet** (2007) *Restorative Practices in Three Scottish Councils: Final Report of the Evaluation of the First Two Years of the Pilot Projects 2004–6*. Edinburgh: Scottish Executive. www.scotland.gov.uk/Publications/2007/08/24093135

★ **London Play** (2008) *London Play Briefing*. www.londonplay.org.uk/file/584.pdf

★ **Luxmoore, Nick** (2006) *Working with Anger and Young People*. London: Jessica Kingsley.

★ **Maccoby, Eleanor** and **Martin, John** (1983) 'Socialization in the context of the family: parent-child interaction' in Hetherington, E.M. (ed.) *Handbook of child psychology: socialization, personality and social development*, Vol 4, pages 1–102. New York: Wiley.

★ **Madge, Nicola** and **Barker, John** (2007) *Risk and childhood*. London: Royal Society for the Arts. www.rsariskcommission.org.uk/uploads/documents/Risk%20and%20Childhood%20Final%20Report_139.pdf

★ **Maines, Barbara** and **Robinson, George** (1991) *Punishment, the milder the better*. Bristol: Lucky Duck Publishing.

★ **Mamen, Maggie** (2006) *The pampered child syndrome: how to recognise it, how to manage it and how to avoid it. A guide for parents and professionals*. London: Jessica Kingsley.

★ **Manning-Morton, Julia** (2006) 'The personal is professional: professionalism and the birth to three practitioner'. *Contemporary Issues in Early Childhood*, vol 7, no 1.

★ **Maslow, Abraham** (1943) 'A theory of human motivation' *Psychological Review*, 50, pages 370–96; download from http://psychclassics.yorku.ca/Maslow/motivation.htm; also try these online sources, www.teacherstoolbox.co.uk/T_maslow.html and www.businessballs.com/maslow.htm

FURTHER RESOURCES

⭐ **Mayall, Berry** (1994) *Children's childhoods: observed and experienced.* London: Falmer Press.

⭐ **Mayall, Berry** (2002) *Towards a sociology of childhood: thinking from children's lives.* Buckingham: Open University Press.

⭐ **Mental Health Foundation, The** (2001) *I want to be your friend but I don't know how.* www.mentalhealth.org.uk

⭐ **Millie, Andrew; Jacobson, Jessica; McDonald, Eraina** and **Hough, Mike** (2005) *Anti-social behaviour strategies: finding a balance.* Bristol: The Policy Press. Access on www.jrf.org.uk/knowledge/findings/housing/0305.asp

⭐ **Miller, Judy** (2003) *Never too young: how young children can take responsibility and make decisions.* London: Save the Children.

⭐ **Mosley, Jenny** (1996) *Quality circle time in the primary classroom – your essential guide to enhancing self-esteem, self-discipline and positive relationships.* Cambridge: LDA.

⭐ **Mosley, Jenny** and **Sonnet, Helen** (2005) *Better behaviour through Golden Time: practical ideas for a calm school ethos.* Cambridge: LDA.

⭐ **Mosley, Jenny** and **Sonnet, Helen** (2006) *Using rewards wisely.* Cambridge: LDA.

⭐ **Murray, Lynne** and **Andrews, Liz** (2000) *The social baby: understanding babies' communication from birth* (Book and DVD). Richmond: The Children's Project.

⭐ **Mynard, Steve** (2008) *Making provision for how boys learn best.* www.teachingexpertise.com/articles/making-provision-for-how-boys-learn-best-3130

⭐ **Neall, Lucinda** (2002) *Bringing out the best in boys: communication strategies for teachers.* Stroud: Hawthorn Press.

⭐ **Oates, John** (ed.) (2007) *Attachment relationships – quality of care for young children* in the *Early Childhood in Focus* series. Bernard Van Leer Foundation and Open University. www.bernardvanleer.org

⭐ **OFSTED** (2007) *Developing social, emotional and behavioural skills in secondary schools.* www.ofsted.gov.uk/Ofsted-home/Publications-and-research From this Home Page search by the title; reference number 070048.

⭐ **OFSTED** (2008) *White boys from low-income backgrounds: good practice in schools.* www.ofsted.gov.uk Search under Publications and Research; reference 070220.

⭐ **Paley, Vivian Gussin** (1998) *Bad guys don't have birthdays: fantasy play at four.* Chicago: Chicago University Press.

FURTHER RESOURCES

★ **Paley, Vivian Gussin** (2004) *A child's work: the importance of fantasy play*. Chicago: University of Chicago Press.

★ **Pellegrini, Anthony** and **Blatchford, Peter** (2002) 'Time for a break'. *The Psychologist*, February, vol 15, no 2. www.thepsychologist.org.uk/archive/archive_home.cfm?volumeID=15&editionID=77&ArticleID=360

★ **Piper, Heather** and **Stronach, Ian** (2008) *Don't touch: the educational story of a panic*. Abingdon: Routledge.

★ **Play Safety Forum** (2002) *Managing risk in play provision*. www.playengland.org.uk/Page.asp?originx_4178si_56947549249695b31j_20079193740c

★ **PLAYLINK** (1999) *Play at school*. www.playlink.org.uk

★ **Rawlings, Anne** (1996) *Ways and means: conflict resolution, training, resources*. Kingston: Kingston Friends Workshop Group.

★ **Ripley, Kate** and **Simpson, Elspeth** (2007) *First steps to emotional literacy: a programme for children in the FS and KS1 and for older children who have language and/or social difficulties*. London: David Fulton.

★ **Rodd, Jillian** (1997) *Understanding young children's behaviour: a guide for early childhood professionals*. London: Allen and Unwin.

★ **Roffey, Sue** (2007) 'Taking account of emotions in student-teacher relationships'. *Raising Achievement Update*, March. www.teachingexpertise.com/articles (search using the article title).

★ **Rogers, Bill** (1997) *The language of discipline: a practical approach to effective classroom management*. Plymouth: Northcote House Publishers.

★ **Rogers, Bill** (2004) *Behaviour recovery*. London: Paul Chapman Publishing.

★ **Rogers, Bill** (2006) *Classroom behaviour: a practical guide to effective teaching, behaviour management and colleague support*. London: Paul Chapman Publishing.

★ **Rowe, Geraldine** (2008) 'Replacing punishment with education'. *Raising Achievement Update*, March. www.teachingexpertise.com/articles

★ **Russell, Wendy** (2006) *Reframing playwork: reframing challenging behaviour*. Nottingham: Nottingham City Play Service.

★ **Russell, Wendy** (2008) 'Reframing behaviour and playwork' (a summary of the above project). *Playwords*, issue 29, Summer. www.commonthreads.org.uk

★ **Rutter, Michael** (1972) *Maternal deprivation reassessed*. London: Penguin.

FURTHER RESOURCES

⭐ **Santer, Joan** and **Griffiths, Carol** with **Goodall, Deborah** (2007) *Free play in early childhood: a literature review*. London: Play England. www.playengland.org.uk/resources/free-play-in-early-childhood.pdf

⭐ **Scott, Stephen; O'Connor, Thomas** and **Futh, Annabel** (2006) *What makes parenting programmes work in disadvantaged areas? The PALS trial*. York: Joseph Rowntree Foundation. Summary and report on www.jrf.org.uk/knowledge/findings/socialpolicy/0386.asp

⭐ **Scottish Institute for Residential Child Care** (2005) *The practice of restraining children* and other relevant papers on www.sircc.org.uk (Use search facility.)

⭐ **Seaman, Peter; Turner, Katrina; Hill, Malcolm; Stafford, Anne** and **Walker, Moira** (2006) *Parenting and children's resilience in disadvantaged communities*. London: National Children's Bureau. Summary on www.jrf.org.uk/knowledge/findings/socialpolicy/0096.asp

⭐ **Shariff, Shaheen** (2008) *Cyber-bullying: issues and situations for the school, the classroom and the home*. London: Routledge.

⭐ **Shore, Rima** (1997) *Rethinking the brain: new insights into early development*. New York: Families and Work Institute.

⭐ **Skiba, Russell; Reynolds, Cecil; Graham, Sandra; Sheras, Peter; Conoley, Jane Close** and **Garcia-Vazquez, Enedina** (2006) *Are zero tolerance policies effective in the schools? An evidentiary review and recommendations*. Washington: American Psychological Association. (This is a long report but it has a 15 page executive summary.) www.apa.org/releases/ZTTFReportBODRevisions5-15.pdf

⭐ **Siren Films Ltd** (2008) *The wonder year: 1st year development and shaping the brain* (DVD). Newcastle-upon-Tyne: Siren Films Ltd.

⭐ **Slaby, Ronald; Roedell, Wendy; Arezzo, Diana** and **Hendrix, Kate** (1995) *Early violence prevention: tools for teachers of young children*. Washington: National Association for the Education of Young Children.

⭐ **Smith, Peter** (1994) 'Play and the uses of play' in Moyles, Janet (ed.) *The excellence of play*. Buckingham: Open University Press.

⭐ **Smith, Peter** (2005) *An investigation into cyberbullying*. www.anti-bullyingalliance.org.uk/downloads/pdf/cyberbullyingreport final230106_000.pdf

⭐ **Spiegal, Bernard** (2008) 'Play in school: the challenge' and 'Play in school: releasing the strangle-hold'. *Playwords*, issue 35, Summer and issue 36, Autumn. www.commonthreads.org.uk

✴ **Social and Emotional Aspects of Learning (SEAL)** (accessed on 30 January 2009) posters found in Attachments and resources section: http://nationalstrategies.standards.dcsf.gov.uk/primary/publications/banda/seal

✴ **Stacey, Hilary** and **Robinson, Pat** (1997) *Let's mediate: a teachers' guide to peer support and conflict resolution skills for all ages.* Bristol: Lucky Duck Publishing.

✴ **Steer, Alan** (2005) *Learning behaviour: the report of the practitioners' group on school behaviour and discipline.* www.dcsf.gov.uk/behaviourand attendance/about/learning_behaviour.cfm

✴ **Stein, Nan** (1999) *Classrooms and courtrooms: facing sexual harassment in K-12 schools.* New York: Teachers College Press.

✴ **Stothard, Val** (1998) 'The gradual development of intensive interaction in a school setting' in Hewett, Dave and Nind, Melanie (eds) *Interaction in action: reflections on the use of intensive interaction.* London: David Fulton.

✴ **Sullivan, Keith** (2000) *The anti-bullying handbook.* South Melbourne: Oxford University Press.

✴ **Sutton, Carole; Utting, David** and **Farrington, David** (2006) 'Nipping criminality in the bud'. *The Psychologist*, vol 19, no 8. www.thepsychologist.org.uk/archive/archive_home.cfm?volumeID=19

✴ **Sutton, Jon** (2001) 'Bullies: thugs or thinkers'. *The Psychologist.* October, vol 14, no 10. www.thepsychologist.org.uk/archive/archive_home.cfm?volumeID=14

✴ **Tayler, Collette** (2007) 'The brain, development and learning in early childhood' in Centre for Educational Research and Innovation, *Understanding the brain: the birth of a learning science*, Part II, pages 161–83. www.dcsf.gov.uk/research/data/uploadfiles/DCSF-RW030.pdf

✴ **Taylor, Gill** (1996) 'Creating a circle of friends: a case study' in Cowie, Helen and Sharp, Sonia (eds) *Peer counselling in schools: a time to listen.* London: David Fulton.

✴ **Teaching Expertise** *Behaviour management.* A resource of articles online www.teachingexpertise.com/articles/behaviour-management

✴ **Titman, Wendy** (1992) *Play, playtime and playgrounds.* Winchester: Learning Through Landscapes/WWF UK.

✴ **Titman, Wendy** (1994) *Special places; special people: the hidden curriculum of school grounds.* Winchester: Learning Through Landscapes/WWF UK.

FURTHER RESOURCES

★ **Tizard, Barbara** (1986) *The care of young children: implications of recent research*. Thomas Coram Research Unit Occasional Papers. www.ioe.ac.uk/tcru/pdfs/The%20care%20of%20young%20children.pdf

★ **Trevarthen, Colwyn** et al. (2003) *Meeting the needs of children from birth to three*. Summary on www.scotland.gov.uk/Publications/2003/06/17458/22696

★ **UK Children's Commissioners** (2008) *Report to the UN Committee on the Rights of the Child*. www.11million.org.uk (Go into 'adult info' from the home page and search publications.)

★ **Wallis, Pete** and **Tudor, Barbara** (2008) *The pocket guide to restorative justice*. London: Jessica Kingsley.

★ **Waylen, Andrea** and **Stewart-Brown, Sarah** (2008) *Parenting in ordinary families: diversity, complexity and change*. York: York Publishing Services Ltd. Download from www.jrf.org.uk/knowledge/findings/socialpolicy/2247.asp

★ **Whitehead, Jenni** (2008) *Restraining pupils: guidance on the use of force*. www.teachingexpertise.com/articles (and use the search facility).

★ **Whiting, Mary** (2005) 'Diets and their effects on children's behaviour'. *Early Years Update*, October. www.teachingexpertise.com (Behaviour Management section)

★ **Woolley, Helen** with **Armitage, Marc; Bishop, Julia; Curtis, Mavis** and **Ginsborg, Jane** (2005) *Inclusion of disabled children in primary school playgrounds*. London: National Children's Bureau. Summary on www.jrf.org.uk/knowledge/findings/socialpolicy/0016.asp

Further resources – organisations

All addresses for organisations are in the UK. Guidance for good practice on any of the sites is always of general interest. But you need to be alert for information linked closely with the legal or educational framework of one country within the UK.

★ *Adlerian Workshops and Publications* www.adlerian.com 216 Tring Road, Aylesbury, Buckinghamshire HP20 1JS. Tel: 01296 482148. Information about the ideas of Alfred Adler, Rudolf Dreikurs and others within this tradition.

★ *Anti-Bullying Alliance* www.anti-bullyingalliance.org.uk National Children's Bureau, 8 Wakley Street, London EC1V 7QE. Brings together about 50 other organisations with the aim of reducing bullying and creating safer environments for children and young people.

★ *Anti-Bullying Network* www.antibullying.net Simpson House, 52 Queen Street, Edinburgh EH2 3NS. Aims to support anti-bullying work in schools and provide an information service. Materials to download from the site.

FURTHER RESOURCES

* *Betterbehaviourscotland* www.betterbehaviourscotland.gov.uk Range of online resources for primary and secondary schools, case studies, papers, leaflets.

* *Children and Young People Now* also includes *Youth Work Now* – update of events and developments across services for children and families. Free to members of the National Children's Bureau or by subscription www.cypnow.co.uk

* *Children's Legal Centre* www.childrenslegalcentre.com University of Essex, Wivenhoe Park, Colchester, Essex CO4 3SQ. Tel: 01206 877 910. Advice and information about the law in England and Wales.

* *Children's Play Information Service* www.ncb.org.uk/library/cpis 8 Wakley Street, London EC1V 7QE. Tel: 020 7843 6303. Information about children's play, factsheets and issues of *Play Today*.

* *Children's Project, The* www.socialbaby.com PO Box 2, Richmond TW10 7FL. Tel: 0845 094 5494. Books and DVDs about many aspects of child development and behaviour.

* *Freeplay Network* www.freeplaynetwork.org.uk 129 Lancaster Road, New Barnet, Herts EN4 8AJ. Tel: 020 8440 9276. Website offers many images of play, briefing papers and links to other useful sites.

* *JABADAO National Centre for Movement, Learning and Health* www.jabadao.org The Yard, Viaduct Street, Stanningley, Leeds LS28 6AU. Tel: 0113 236 3311. Offers training to promote children's free flow spontaneous movement and specific activities that help to develop body and brain.

* *Joseph Rowntree Foundation* www.jrf.org.uk The Homestead, 40 Water End, York, North Yorkshire YO30 6WP. Tel: 01904 629241. Research, useful research reports and summaries on www.jrf.org.uk/publications

* *Kidscape* www.kidscape.org.uk 2 Grosvenor Gardens, London SW1W 0DH. Tel: 020 7730 3300; helpline 08451 205 204 for parents and other concerned adults. Information and advice on child protection, personal safety and bullying.

* *Learning and Teaching Scotland* www.ltscotland.org.uk The Optima, 58 Robertson Street, Glasgow G2 8DU. Tel: 08700 100 297. Information about the curriculum in Scotland, useful resources for practitioners across the UK.

* *Learning Through Landscapes* www.ltl.org.uk 3rd Floor, Southside Offices, The Law Courts, Winchester SO23 9DL. Tel: 01962 845811. Consultation and development work about school grounds, examples on the website.

FURTHER RESOURCES

★ *National Centre for Excellence in Residential Child Care* www.ncb.org.uk/ncercc 8 Wakley Street, London EC1V 7QE. Tel: 020 7843 1168. Collaborative initiative to improve practice for children and young people in residential care.

★ *Northern Ireland Anti-Bullying Forum* www.niabf.org.uk Resources that focus on work in schools in Northern Ireland.

★ *Play England* www.playengland.org.uk Play England, 8 Wakley Street, London EC1V 7QE. Tel: 020 7843 6300. Useful reports and summaries.

★ *Psychologist, The* Monthly journal from the British Psychological Society. Articles can be accessed online, except the most recent six issues. www.thepsychologist.org.uk

★ *Scottish Child Law Centre* www.sclc.org.uk 54 East Crosscauseway, Edinburgh EH8 9HD. Tel: 0131 667 6333; freephone for under 18s 0800 328 8970. Advice and information about the law in Scotland.

★ *Siren Films Ltd* www.sirenfilms.co.uk 5 Charlotte Square, Newcastle-upon-Tyne NE1 4XF. Tel: 0191 232 7900. A wide range of DVDs about child development and behaviour.

★ *Teachernet* www.teachernet.gov.uk. Information and guidance for practice in schools (England) but relevant more generally.

★ *Transforming Conflict* www.transformingconflict.org Mortimer Hill, Mortimer, Berkshire RG7 3PW. Tel: 0118 933 1520. Materials about the approach of restorative justice with children and adolescents in different settings.

★ *Trust for the Study of Adolescence* www.studyofadolescence.org.uk TSA Ltd, 23 New Road, Brighton, East Sussex BN1 1WZ. Tel: 01273 693311. Aims to address lack of knowledge and understanding about adolescents and young people through research, publications and training.

★ *Womankind* www.womankind.org.uk An organisation working with UK schools to deal with sexual bullying – resources and links.

★ *Young Minds* www.youngminds.org.uk 48–50 St John Street, London EC1M 4DG. Tel: 020 7336 8445. Focus on improving the mental health of children and young people, helpline for anyone concerned about a child or young person.

★ *Young Voice* www.young-voice.org 25a Creek Road, East Molesey, Surrey KT8 9BE. Tel: 020 8979 4991. Aims to make the views of young people count by inviting and publishing their views on important issues.

INDEX

INDEX

INDEX

INDEX

INDEX